Latinos in Dixie

Latinos in Dixie

Class and Assimilation in Richmond, Virginia

Debra J. Schleef and H. B. Cavalcanti

SUNY PRESS

Published by State University of New York Press, Albany

For information, contact State University of New York Press, Albany, NY
www.sunypress.edu

Production by Ryan Morris
Marketing by Anne M. Valentine

Library of Congress Cataloging-in-Publication Data

Schleef, Debra J.
  Latinos in Dixie : class and assimilation in Richmond, Virginia / Debra J. Schleef and H. B. Cavalcanti.
    p. cm.
  Includes bibliographical references.
  ISBN 978-1-4384-2879-6 (hardcover : alk. paper)
  1. Hispanic Americans—Virginia—Richmond—Social conditions. 2. Hispanic Americans—Cultural assimilation—Virginia—Richmond. 3. Social classes—Virginia—Richmond.
  4. Community life—Virginia—Richmond. 5. Richmond (Va.)—Ethnic relations.
  6. Richmond (Va.)—Social conditions. I. Cavalcanti, H. B., 1956– II. Title.
  F234.R59S756 2009
  305.868'075523—dc22

                                                        2009000583

10 9 8 7 6 5 4 3 2 1

To Gui, my son,
Who fuels my immigrant hope.

H. B. Cavalcanti

To Eric and Abigail,
With strength for what lies ahead.

Debra Schleef

Contents

Illustrations

Tables

Figures

Foreword

This work is truly a labor of love, patience, and many passionate caffeine-fueled debates. We came into this research for reasons of our own and for shared interests as well. For one of us, the research came out of his experience of becoming a U.S. citizen in 1999 and immediately finding out his "hyphenated-American" condition (Hispanic American), one that he shared with a large number of Latinos in Richmond from many countries, backgrounds, and varied career paths. For the other author, teaching courses in race and ethnicity led to her interest in examining for herself the experience of one particular ethnic group in the community where she worked (it also led to her later on to taking Spanish classes and developing a broader interest in the world of Latino cultures).

Obviously, for both of us there was always the overarching sociological interest in understanding the mechanisms by which new immigrant groups arrive in a particular location in the United States and negotiate their insertion into everyday life. There were issues related to the job market, to participation in the local schools, clubs, churches, and political organizations. Over and over, a foremost question in our minds was how groups become part of a distinctive region of the United States, and a traditional Southern city.

For five years we mapped out, surveyed, and analyzed the experience of Latinos in the greater Richmond area. The greater Richmond area is comprised of nine counties and four cities, and those multiple jurisdictions had to come to grips with the growth of the Latino population within their boundaries. As our survey of individual Latinos unfolded, we also contacted and worked with a variety of Latino business groups, churches, cultural associations, and service agencies. Our preliminary results were shared with the Latino community through workshops, adult evening classes, and private presentations for the boards of Latino organizations.

We also shared our results with the larger Richmond community. We made a number of presentations to Richmond political and business leaders (including the city mayor), we talked with the editors of Richmond's local newspaper (the *Richmond Times Dispatch*) about Latino coverage, we discussed the needs of the Latino community with the members of local school systems, the staffs of police departments, and health care practitioners. We worked with organizations such as the Richmond Red Cross, who welcomed us with open arms, and who worked steadfastly to integrate the newcomers into the larger Richmond community.

We are grateful to the Latino community of Richmond, who provided us with many memorable opportunities. We were fortunate that our research began at a point in the life of the Richmond Latino community when Latinos were finally becoming a visible and vocal population. At that point Latino leaders were struggling with ways to explain the gifts and talents they brought to the city, while Richmond city officials were searching for means to integrate this growing population into the hustle and bustle of a culturally unique city.

Watching the efforts of the Latino community to educate local Richmonders of its presence added a rich layer of ethnographic material to our research. And it also helped us understand how newcomer groups can become *intentional* participants in the local life; how they can approach the settling down of roots in a given location in ways that help the locals understand the newcomers' reasons for being there and their interest in pursuing rather similar dreams side by side.

Along those five years, we were honored to witness the process in a number of different arenas. For instance, we accompanied the first stirring of Latino political organizing in Richmond (both Democrats and Republicans) as state and national elections approached. We were invited to fundraisers and political work sponsored by the Latino community. We followed the evolution of community efforts to create chambers of commerce that would represent the interests of Latino professionals and business owners. Business leaders from both sides worked to find common ground and to create space for Latino business interests in the city (the Virginia Hispanic Chamber of Commerce, for instance, holds close relations to the Richmond Chamber of Commerce).

We were also enchanted by the efforts of Latino to introduce the locals to the cultures they represented. We watched citywide performances staged by Latino Ballet of Virginia whose Richmond origins gave us ample opportunity to witness the preservation of Latino culture firsthand. We followed the travails of local Latino radio stations, newspapers, and musical bands. We also enjoyed the annual programs staged in Richmond's city parks by Latino cultural organizations—events filled with pan-ethnic displays from multiple Latin American countries.

Debra Schleef and H. B. Cavalcanti
Harrisonburg/Fredericksburg, VA, May 2008

Acknowledgments

The work could not have been done without the eager interest and energy of our students at the University of Richmond (data collection) and at the University of Mary Washington (data entry and preliminary analysis). Their diligent work and their concern with the quality of the product inspired and encouraged us. At one point in the project we had six student-schedulers and thirty-eight student interviewers, and that was just on the data collection side. We are especially grateful to Christina (Stina) McLamore, Holly Gordon, and Coleman Rose, who worked tirelessly as project coordinators and helped us with the management of interviews and interviewers (and conducted interviews themselves) as the project matured. At UMW, we acknowledge the efforts of Seth Kennard, Erin Murphy, Jessica Johnson, and especially Christine Rose, who spent a hot Virginia summer coding and entering data.

Coleman Rose and Jo Tyler read and commented on drafts of the material. Audiences at two presentations at UMW, one for Latino Identities Month and the other to students in the Teaching English as a Second Language masters' program, provided helpful feedback on the research. The project was funded in part by several faculty development grants from UR and UMW, as well as a UMW Jepson Fellowship. Finally, we must say we finished this book despite the best efforts of our errant friends, loved ones, and baristas, who plied us with sugar, caffeine, and tempting extracurricular activities in a vain attempt to prevent us ever writing anything (though we acknowledge that could have been our own procrastination).

The research was an immersion in the ways and processes by which people come to the United States—individually and as a group. It provided us with the privilege to watch firsthand what happens early on when those efforts take place in a city such as Richmond. We are grateful for the opportunity to study that process, document it, and now share it with our readers. We hope that the lessons we found along the way can contribute to a better understanding of the immigration and assimilation processes experienced by Latinos, and the transformation that is taking place throughout the U.S. South.

An earlier version of chapter 7 appears in the *Journal for the Scientific Study of Religion* 44 (4):473–83.

Chapter 1

Why Study Latinos in Richmond?

When I was a kid there were only five "Reyes" in the [Richmond]
phone book (and my family accounted for two of them). My, how the
number has grown!
                                        —Thirty-year-old Dominican

The turn of the twenty-first century finds our nation at its most pluralistic stage, with an immigration surge that parallels the large immigrant wave of the early twentieth century. This second wave is far more diverse, cutting across religion, social class, ethnic identity, and country of origin. For the first time in its history, the United States has more Muslims than Presbyterians, more citizens of Mexican than Irish descent (Eck 2001). The new immigration brings ethnic groups to regions of the country that traditionally have had little exposure to diverse cultures, challenging the face of Anglo conformity as never before. Witness the presence of Hmong Vietnamese in St. Paul, Minnesota; Chinese Americans in the Mississippi delta; or Ethiopians in Dallas, Texas.

Our book focuses on the experience of one ethnic group, Latinos, in Richmond, Virginia, a midsize Southern city with no history of Latino settlement. Whereas Latinos are now the largest minority in the country—approximately forty-one million people (Cohn 2005), their presence in the South is a relatively recent phenomenon. In many ways, what is happening in Richmond today is emblematic of a larger trend for Latinos in the United States. During the last decade, they have moved away from traditional places of settlement in the United States to regions of the country with little presence of Latinos (Durand, Massey, and Charvet 2000; Hernández-León and Zuñiga 2000). In this book, we examine the experiences of the middle-class Latinos who move to such places, and the relationships they have with the working-class Latinos who come after them. In doing so, we illustrate the relationship between geographic mobility, social class, and diverse forms of acculturation, using segmented assimilation theory.

According to the Census Bureau, the South now has the fastest growing Latino population in the United States. Latinos grew 46 percent in the South between 1990 and 2000, from 7.9 to 11.6 million. Some Southern states have experienced even higher Latino growth rates—more than 100 percent increases in North Carolina and Georgia, for example. The Virginia Latino population increased 56 percent between 1990 and 2000, from approximately 155,000 to 240,000 Latinos (Pressley 2000). Estimates from the American Community Survey for 2008 now set that number at almost double that of 2000—471,000 Latinos, about 6 percent of Virginia's population.

This surge in the Latino population is rapidly changing the face the South. Half of the foreign-born population in the United States today was born in Latin American countries (Schmidley 2001:1), and one-third of that population now fills Southern neighborhoods, schools, factories, and churches (Pressley 2000). Their presence is felt in places as varied as the chicken-processing plants of rural North Carolina to the large urban areas of Richmond, Atlanta, Nashville, and Birmingham. Latinos are the new faces working in fast food places, department stores, local banks, and construction companies. Latino restaurants and *bodegas* are becoming part and parcel of many Southern cities.

Academics are just beginning to pay attention to this demographic shift (see, for instance, Atiles and Bohon 2002; Hernández-León and Zuñiga 2000; Murphy, Blanchard, and Hill 2001; Neal and Bohon 2002; Saenz et al. 2003; Schmid 2002; Smith and Furuseth 2006), but journalists have written extensively about the Latino influx into the region. Unfortunately, without careful empirical evidence to convey the diverse experiences of the Latino community, this often anecdotal coverage almost invariably focuses on the extent to which cities and localities have been strained by the new arrivals. Media highlight particularly the issues faced by working-class Latinos, some unknown number of whom are undocumented immigrants (see, e.g., Bradley 1999; Carter 2003; Klein 1999; Moreno 2000; Pressley 2000; Scott 2004).

Schools are viewed as particularly ill equipped to handle large numbers of Latino children. In Dalton, Georgia, where the population went from 1 to 42 percent Latino in twelve years, schools were hard pressed to find enough Spanish-speaking staff, and lacked sufficient bilingual and English as a Second Language programs (Hernández-León and Zuñiga 2000; Klein 1999). While the long-term effect of these changes across Southern cities is still unknown, the lack of sufficient language resources or Latino mentors will have a profound impact on the educational opportunity of Latino children across the country, who are more likely to drop out of high school and have lower graduation rates (Valez and Saenz 2001).

Media accounts draw attention to the difficulties cities have managing the new arrivals in other areas as well, citing rising public costs. Cities report strains on police resources due to greater incidences of drunk driving and driving without a license by Latinos, as well as inadequate crime reporting because of language barriers (Chapman 2004). Other problematic arenas include housing, emergency management, and social services; with new arrivals creating a greater need for food stamps, welfare, and unemployment insurance (Clock 2004). Moreover, many immigrants lack proper immunizations and have no health insurance (Poole 2004). A number of factories and plants have experienced INS raids, including arrests of hundreds of immigrant workers with phony documents (Mohl 2000).

Given the negative media coverage, it is not surprising to find long-term residents of Southern municipalities viewing any new arrivals as a threat, despite the fact that the immigrants often fill a demand for low-wage labor not met by existing populations. Relationships between the new immigrants and natives have sometimes become quite strained. A new nativism has emerged in certain areas, supported by English-only movements and increased anti-immigration sentiment. In several cities, for example, there have been stirrings of activities by the Ku Klux Klan and other white supremacist groups (Mohl 2000; Pressley 2000). Anti-immigration sentiment continues to grow across the state of Virginia, where denial of social services to illegal immigrants has grown steadily in the last two years. In Richmond, dozens of workers were arrested on immigration violations in 2008 (Bowes 2008).

Lack of understanding, however, contributes to an overstatement of the degree to which Latinos strain local resources. Accounts simultaneously suggest that Latinos are both *overtaxing* social services *and* unable fully to utilize them. In many cases, Latino immigrants do not use resources, even when legally entitled to them. Undocumented immigrant laborers who "work off the books," of course, do not receive social security benefits (Hogan, Kim, and Perrucci 1997). At the same time, recent Latino immigrants in some jurisdictions have done significantly better than local townspeople, tapping into regional needs for Latino police officers, teachers, and sales people (Hull 2000).

Although the implicit assumptions of many media accounts is that the Latino migrants are unskilled laborers whose families will deplete public education resources and social services, many of the new Latino arrivals to the South are middle-class professionals. Research that sheds light on the economic well-being and social integration of Latino communities is important because it modifies the artificially uniform picture we have now, one that often reduces the diverse experiences of all Latinos to a monolithic group of undocumented workers. In Richmond we find Latino groups that are well off and others who are struggling. This book is an effort to understand the unique intersection of spatial mobility, Latinos segmented by different assimilation experiences, and Southern traditions. These themes exacerbate divisions in social class leading to a lack of unity and community among Latinos.

Richmond is an ideal locale for exploring these issues. Its Latino population is small, but relatively diverse in terms of country of origin, economic opportunity, and other variables. Latinos have varying trajectories of economic, political, and cultural integration into U.S. society. Groups that have very little in common in terms of culture, nativity, racial makeup, history, self-identity, and economic situation have been consolidated for bureaucratic convenience. For some scholars it is unclear that the category of "Hispanic," created by the U.S. statisticians, really signifies anything at all. Tienda and Mitchell (2006), for instance, argue that no unique national identity has emerged that embraces the entire community. On the other hand, other writers argue for the meaningfulness of a pan-ethnic identity among Latinos (as well as Asians), who share a similar "racialization" by U.S. society as well as similar transnational settlement patterns (see Suárez-Orozco and Páez 2002). This setting provides an opportunity to see the effects of intermingling ethnic groups and social classes among Latinos. We observe here what happens when such divergent groups are treated as one—does a Latino identity materialize even in one community?

Social Class, Assimilation, and the Latino Experience

For a variety of reasons, there is little research on the experiences of either middle-class Latinos or those who live outside of large urban areas. Studies of post-1965 waves of immigrants focus on poor or working-class, low-skilled Latinos residing in urban or inner city landscapes (Bobo et al. 2000; Logan, Alba, and Zhang 2002; Tienda 1995; Waldinger 2001). Many of them scrutinize leading immigrant centers—Mexicans in Los Angeles, for example, or Cubans in Miami. Since these metropolitan areas have historically served as ports of entry, they have large, permanent Latino communities that aid transition into a new country and continue to attract many new immigrants. In addition, researchers still highlight the economic disparity of Latinos in comparison to whites and even blacks, for example, in terms of high rates of poverty, unemployment, and high school dropouts (Rodriguez 2000:23).

So far, the research on Latinos living in the South has followed a similar preoccupation, except that scholars have predominantly looked at economically disadvantaged Latinos living in *nonurban* areas. Hernández-León and Zuñiga, for example, examine how working-class Mexican immigrants move to "Carpet City," an industrial region of northwest Georgia, rapidly becoming more than 40 percent of the local population (2000). Atiles and Bohon show the adjustment difficulties of recent Latino immigrants in Georgia (2002). McDaniel and Casanova describe migrant laborers working in the forests of Alabama (2003). Smith and Furuseth note the rise in the demand for rental housing in the suburbs and the growth in the disproportionately male Latino population settling outside of Charlotte, North Carolina (2004). An entire issue of *Southern Rural Sociology* was devoted to Latinos in the South in 2003 (Saenz et al. 2003).

We find interest in these trends understandable, and naturally would not urge researchers to suspend examining the experiences of working-class and poor Latinos. On the other hand, we feel that the adaptation and assimilation processes of middle-class Latinos, as well as their relationships with working-class Latinos, have gone underexamined. Pedraza, for example, argues for a better understanding of middle-class Latinos and those with economic mobility (1998).

The relationship between assimilation and social class is a tangled one, in part because social class or economic status is often treated as both a *predictor* of assimilation, and as a unit of *measurement* of it. Yet, assimilation research has seldom looked specifically at social class. The variable is always assumed to be relevant, but kept at the margins. Gordon, for example, does not include a measure of socioeconomic assimilation in his seven types of assimilation (Alba and Nee 1997:835). Thus, although socioeconomic assimilation is a very common assumption of the literature—Waldinger, for example, states, "Sociologists now agree that economic progress is the linchpin of assimilation, driving all other shifts in the social structure of ethnicity" (2001:15)—it is often implied in other measures of social assimilation, rather than measured directly (see also Nee and Sanders 2001).

Recently, spatial assimilation theory has demonstrated how assimilation incorporates both geographic mobility and social class: Latinos with educational credentials and employment opportunities are more likely to leave their ethnic communities, moving to areas with fewer Latinos (Rodrigues 1992). The argument approximates similar findings for middle-class African Americans—who migrate from central cities to predominantly white suburbs. Wilson argues in *The Declining Significance of Race* (1978) that as middle-class African Americans moved from black neighborhoods, the African American community was split in two: middle-class blacks could make some economic gains relative to the white population, while the condition for poor blacks deteriorated. As a result, research on non-poor African Americans virtually disappeared for a time (Patillo-McCoy 1999).

Latinos, like other immigrant groups, often settle in large ethnic enclaves—Miami, New York, Los Angeles—where they retain language and culture.[1] Enclaves shelter members of the ethnic group from external discrimination and hostility, and provide them with the needed economic support and means for eventual upward mobility. Because enclaves employ skilled or semi-skilled workers, they create markets for unique products, generate opportunities for the economic advancement of group members, provide access to credit, and support the formation of small enterprises (Cobas 1984; Pessar 1995; Portes and Bach 1985; Portes and Jensen 1989). In doing so, they undoubtedly enhance the life chances for many in the second generation by allowing them to obtain higher education and enter the primary labor market.

At the same time, critics of ethnic enclaves argue that enclaves provide benefits to a small entrepreneurial group, but can also block the economic mobility of many immigrants laboring in those systems. Concentrated in the low-wage enclave economy, these workers retain their home cultures longer than earlier waves of immigrants, making the transition into the host culture more problematic. Continued limited exposure to English, as can happen in enclaves, keeps these immigrants from learning the language sooner. Enclaves also prevent the successful integration of most immigrants into the primary labor market (Bonacich 1973; Bonacich and Modell 1980; Waldinger 1993).

Furthermore, although the Cuban ethnic enclave in Miami is touted as one of the more successful Latino immigrant enclaves, Cubans earn more in areas with the lowest Cuban populations (Davis 2004). In fact, many immigrants living outside ethnic enclaves earn higher incomes than those inside (Mar 1991). On the other hand, Logan, Alba, and Zhang argue that even high-status immigrants sometimes prefer to live in *suburban* immigrant enclaves as an "alternative to assimilation" (2002).

Regardless of which argument prevails, what does emerge from this research is that people are leaving ethnic enclaves more than ever, and the moves are connected to social class: those who are better off economically are more likely to move. Because researchers focus on ethnic enclaves in large cities, we know less about Latinos who migrate to other areas of the nation. From our previous research, we know that Latinos living in cities with a small Latino population have a different profile than those living in similarly sized cities with larger Latino population. Using 1990 census data, we looked at Latinos in one hundred midsized U.S. cities with varying sizes of Latino populations. Latinos in cities where they are less than 2 percent of the population have higher incomes (both absolutely and in ratio to the Anglo community) and higher rates of employment and high school graduation, sometimes better than those of local non-Latinos. Furthermore, the percentage of Latina-headed households and of Latinos in poverty grows as the size of the Latino population increases (Cavalcanti and Schleef 2000).

Literature on racial inequality suggests that population size does play a role in the integration of minority groups. Studies on African Americans, for instance, provide evidence that the smaller the size of the nonwhite population in a community, the lower the level of racial inequality experienced by the group. The larger the group, the greater the perceived threat for the dominant group (Becker 1971; Burr, Galle, and Fosset 1991; Fosset and Kiecolt 1989; Frisbie and Niedert 1977; Martin and Poston 1976; Taylor 1998; Wilcox and Roof 1978). Small Latino populations might provide Latinos with less visibility, less danger of being perceived as a threat, and possibly with more educational and economic opportunities.

In fact, Yinger includes small population size in a list of twenty variables that facilitate the process of incorporation of ethnic groups (1994). More than a decade ago, Alba and Nee predicted that the rapid growth of immigrant populations in the twentieth century would create new areas of immigrant concentration that would be culturally and ethnically diverse outside the traditional ports of entry. Immigrant segregation in these new centers would also be less extreme (Alba and Nee 1997:858–59). In search of data to address these speculations about spatial mobility, population size, and diverse acculturation experiences, we turned to Richmond, Virginia.

Richmond as a Case Study

As the former capital of the Confederacy, Richmond preserves the most traditional aspects of Southern culture (Dabney 1990; Hoffman 2004). It embodies, in many ways, the values and traditions that made the South such a unique region, one previously characterized by a patrician system based on plantation life. More importantly for our purposes, Richmond is the part of the South that has been least effective in expanding its local elite across racial lines (Randolph 2003; Rouse 1996). Unlike other metropolitan areas in the region, the city has not experienced much economic or social transformation (Silver 1984; Silver and Moeser 1995).[2] Studying Richmond Latinos allows us understand how a Latino community manages in such a traditional Southern setting. It is a place where the diversity among Latinos is framed by other cultural and racial differences specific to the South.

Richmond is still very much defined by the usual Southern racial fault lines (Moeser and Dennis 1982). For example, in 1996, many Richmonders balked at having a statue of the African American tennis legend Arthur Ashe erected on the city's Monument Avenue, alongside Robert E. Lee, Stonewall Jackson, and other Confederate heroes. More recently, a statue of Abraham Lincoln and his son Tad commemorating their postwar visit to Richmond sparked controversy (even though the statue was built outside the city proper). Detractors referred to Lincoln as "this country's most notorious war criminal" (Fisher 2003).

Richmond demographics demonstrate an economic disparity most evident along its racial axis. Comparisons between Richmond's African American and white populations are predictable—the ratio of black to white median household income is 0.67. For college education the ratio is 0.55; for professional occupations, 0.68; and in home ownership, 0.78 (if there were no disparities, all ratios would be 1.0). The percentage of unemployed blacks is 2.4 times that of whites, and the percentage of blacks below the poverty level is 2.6 times that of whites (Lewis Mumford Center 2002). On several of these measures, Richmond's African Americans—about 30 percent of its population—are worse off than their counterparts in a number of other midsize Southern cities with large black populations (see Table 1.1).

However, the city's racial dynamics are becoming more complex. Between 1990 and 2000, the city population increased by 130,000; with its Latino population increasing by fourteen thousand. Latinos comprised roughly 11 percent of Richmond's growth (Rose 2002). They may not easily straddle the city's racial divide, but Latinos fare better statistically than Richmond's local black population. For instance, the ratio of Latino to white in median household income is 0.80. For college education, the ratio is 0.77; for professional occupations, 0.81; and for home ownership, 0.80. The percentage of unemployed Latinos is only one and one-half times that of whites, and the percentage of Latinos below poverty level is 1.7 that of whites (Lewis Mumford Center 2002).

Although we focus on Richmond in this book, it is important to note that these factors do not make Richmond unique among Southern cities of its size, particularly those with few Latinos. In addition to Richmond, we selected eight Southern cities ranging in population from 600,000 to 1,200,000, and with Latino populations between 1 and 5 percent (see Table 1.1). On most variables, Richmond Latinos fall within the center of the distribution. For example, the median household income for Richmond Latinos in comparison to whites is .80, as noted above; it ranges from .77 to .93 in these other cities (the overall U.S. ratio of Latino to white income is .72). Richmond Latinos rank near the bottom in the ratios of Latino/white education levels and percentage in professional occupations compared to other cities, but these ratios still remain higher than they do in other areas of the country.

Table 1.1. Selected Demographic Data for Mid-Size Southern Cities, 2000
(Metropolitan Areas with 1–5% Hispanic Population)

	Total Population	% Min.	Median Household Income*	% Below Poverty*	% Unem-ployed*	% Profes-sional*	% College Educated*	% Home-owners*
Black Statistics								
Richmond,VA	996,512	30.0	0.67	2.59	2.4	0.68	0.55	0.78
Baton Rouge, LA	602,894	31.6	0.66	2.15	2.04	0.72	0.67	0.81
Birmingham, AL	921,106	30.0	0.59	2.78	2.80	0.65	0.54	0.77
Greensboro, NC	1,251,509	20.1	0.75	2.07	1.96	0.76	0.76	0.73
Greenville, SC	962,441	17.5	0.80	1.66	1.60	0.80	0.74	0.82
Knoxville, TN	687,249	5.8	0.66	2.28	2.09	0.83	0.75	0.71
Little Rock, AR	583,845	21.9	0.71	2.13	2.03	0.79	0.70	0.81
Memphis, TN	1,135,614	43.2	0.61	2.63	2.48	0.64	0.49	0.79
Latino Statistics								
Nashville, TN	1,231,311	15.6	0.68	2.34	1.93	0.77	0.70	0.73
Richmond, VA	996,512	2.3	0.80	1.66	1.45	0.81	0.77	0.80
Baton Rouge, LA	602,894	1.8	0.89	1.48	1.27	0.99	1.12	0.84
Birmingham, AL	921,106	1.8	0.83	1.56	1.47	0.92	0.94	0.80
Greensboro, NC	1,251,509	5.0	0.80	1.76	1.59	0.79	0.78	0.79
Greenville, SC	962,441	2.6	0.91	1.24	1.17	0.90	0.88	0.87
Knoxville, TN	687,249	1.1	0.93	1.26	1.11	1.01	1.06	0.88
Little Rock, AR	583,845	2.1	0.88	1.34	1.28	0.91	0.88	0.87
Memphis, TN	1,135,614	2.3	0.77	1.65	1.48	0.78	0.72	0.80
Nashville, TN	1,231,311	3.2	0.82	1.47	1.29	0.85	0.84	0.78

*Ratio of Minority Group to White Values.

Source: Lewis Mumford Center for Comparative Urban and Regional Research, 2002.

Thus, the presence of Latinos in Richmond is comparable to other Southern cities with small, relatively well-off, geographically mobile Latino populations; particularly in contrast to more rural areas of the South. Yet, there has not been much media attention to this type of migration. Until recently the Latino community in Richmond remained largely invisible.3 Census data from 1990 indicate that no census tract in the greater Richmond area was more than 5 percent Latino. During the last decade, however, the Latino community shed its quiet presence, growing from less than 1 percent of the population into a community that has a significant presence in the area. However, no one has mapped Latino growth in Richmond or monitored its impact on the central

Virginia region. The appearance of Latinos in traditional areas of the South represents a new dynamic in terms of race relations—a small patch of brown in a sea of black and white.

The Richmond Latino Profile

We use census data to provide an initial profile of the Richmond Latino population and demonstrate recent changes in population demographics. The most obvious trend is the growth of Latinos during the last decade (Table 1.2). The Latino population in Virginia grew by 56 percent from 1990 to 2000. In Richmond, by comparison, the Latino population grew by 165 percent during that time period: from 8,788 in 1990 to 23,283 in 2000 (and the actual number may be larger—we were told by the Catholic archdiocese and others who worked closely with Latinos that the 2000 census undercounted the Latino population, especially the undocumented). In 2000, Latinos made up 5 percent of the Virginia population, and just over 2 percent of the population of greater Richmond. By 2008, the census bureau estimated the Latino population in the Richmond area had surpassed forty thousand.

Table 1.2. Latinos in Greater Richmond by City and County
(Counts and Percentage)

Counties	1990	%	2000	%
Charles City	38	0.6	45	0.6
Chesterfield	2,099	1.0	7,617	2.9
Dinwiddie	197	0.9	237	0.9
Goochland	43	0.3	144	0.9
Hanover	330	0.5	847	1.0
Henrico	2,220	1.0	5,946	2.3
New Kent	91	0.9	176	1.3
Powhatan	37	0.2	184	0.8
Prince George	982	3.5	1,625	4.9
Cities				
Colonial Heights	199	1.0	274	1.6
Hopewell	435	2.0	651	2.9
Petersburg	373	0.9	463	1.4
Richmond	1,744	0.8	5,074	2.6
Total	8,788	1.1	23,283	2.3

Source: Bureau of the Census, 1990 and 2000.

Latino growth touched nearly all of four cities and nine counties in the Richmond metropolitan area. The fastest growth occurred in Richmond city itself, and in Henrico, Chesterfield, and Hanover counties. The core areas of Richmond doubled in their Latino population, and in some case tripled. But the growth was not limited to central cities; outlying and rural areas of greater Richmond experienced Latino expansion as well.

Richmond Latinos come from a variety of countries that represent most regions of Latin America. In many other urban areas, especially in the South,

Table 1.3. Countries of Origin for Richmond Latinos
(Counts and Percentages, 1990, 2000)

Countries	1990		2000	
	N	%	N	%
Mexican	2,282	26.8	7,153	30.7
Central American	826	9.4	3,618	15.5
Costa Rican			187	0.8
Guatemalan	48	0.6	973	4.2
Honduran	92	1.1	260	1.1
Nicaraguan	20	2.3	60	0.3
Panamanian	325	3.7	358	1.5
Salvadoran	324	3.7	1,624	6.9
Other	17	0.2	156	0.7
Caribbean	3,020	34.4	5,992	25.7
Cuban	556	6.3	1,010	4.3
Dominican	215	2.5	335	1.4
Puerto Rican	2,249	25.6	4,647	19.9
South American	627	7.1	1,285	5.5
Argentinean			132	0.6
Bolivian			71	0.3
Chilean			41	0.2
Colombian	132	1.5	485	2.1
Ecuadorean	50	0.6	102	0.4
Paraguayan			47	0.2
Peruvian	128	1.5	192	0.8
Uruguayan			16	0.1
Venezuelan			144	0.6
Other	317	3.6	55	0.2
Other Hispanic	2,033	23.1	5,235	22.5
Total	8,788	1.1*	23,283	2.3*

*As a percentage of overall population

Source: Bureau of the Census, 1990, 2000.

Mexicans make up the majority of Latinos. Although Mexicans comprise the largest group here (almost one-third of Richmond Latinos in 2000), no country of origin overwhelmingly predominates. Puerto Ricans form another large group in Richmond, about 20 percent of the population. In 2000, the Latino population was even more diverse than in 1990, with almost twice as many Central Americans, specifically Guatemalans and Salvadorans, as before. There was also some growth in Latinos from South American countries, several of which were represented in 2000 that were not there at all in 1990.

We use census comparisons to show how Richmond Latinos differed from non-Latinos, as well as from Latino populations elsewhere in the United States. Figure 1.1 compares census data on age cohorts for Latinos and for non-Latinos in 2000. The Richmond Latino population is younger than the rest of Richmond. In general, Richmond residents follow the national trend toward a graying population; 15 percent fall in the sixty-plus cohort (compared to only 4 percent of Latinos). Latinos are much younger—34 percent of Latinos in Richmond are younger than twenty. Forty-four percent are between the ages of twenty and thirty-nine, swelling and potentially replenishing an aging work force. The Latino age distribution changed little from 1990 to 2000, indicating that Richmond continues to attract a group of relatively young Latinos.

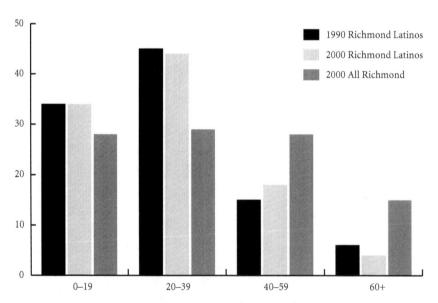

Figure 1.1. Ages of Richmond Latinos and All Richmond Residents (in Percentages)
Source: Bureau of the Census, 1990, 2000.

Given this youthful makeup, it is not unexpected to find that family composition differs between Latinos and other Richmonders. Richmond Latinos have more married-couple families with children than the local residents (Figure 1.2). Some 45 percent of Latino families have children under eighteen, compared to 40 percent for other locals. Also, there are more Latino-headed single households than in the overall population. Male-headed households comprise 13 percent of Latino families, compared to 6 percent for Richmond overall. Conversely, there are fewer *Latina*-headed single households than female-headed households for the Richmond area.

On a number of socioeconomic variables, Richmond Latinos compare favorably to Latinos in other parts of the country. The educational attainment of Richmond Latinos is striking in contrast to national trends, at rates that are almost comparable to non-Latino in Richmond (Figure 1.3). Richmond Latinos have high school and college graduation rates that are much higher than those of Latinos nationwide. According to the 2000 Census, only 52 percent of Latinos in the United States have at least a high school diploma, and only 11 percent have a bachelor's degree or higher. Sixty-eight percent of Latinos in Richmond have at least a high school diploma (compared to 82 percent of the city population). Some 20 percent of Latinos in the area have at

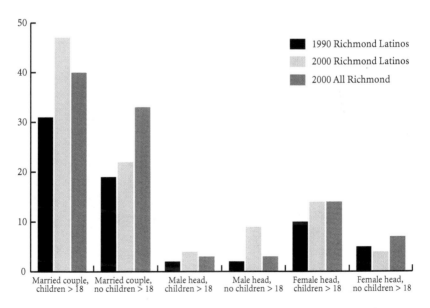

Figure 1.2. Household Type for Richmond Latinos and All Richmond Residents (in Percentages)
Source: U.S. Bureau of the Census, 1990, 2000.

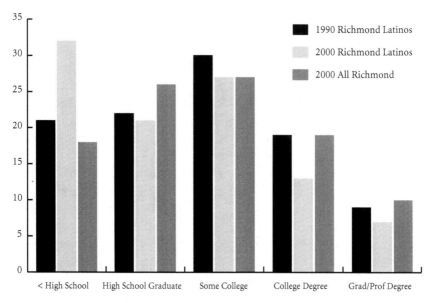

Figure 1.3. Education for Richmond Latinos and All Richmond Residents over 25
         (in Percentages)
Source: Bureau of the Census, 1990, 2000

least a college degree (compared to 29 percent of the city population). Rates of education were higher in 1990 than 2000, however, suggesting a trend of lower educational attainment among more recent arrivals.

Richmond Latinos also experience the benefit of levels of income more similar to those of all residents of the region, than of Latinos elsewhere in the United States. Approximately 16 percent of Latinos in Richmond lived below the poverty level in 1999, less than the rate for Latinos nationwide, which is almost 23 percent (Census 2000). Moreover, from 1990 to 2000, the wealth of the Latino population in Richmond increased, while its poor decreased. Despite their levels of educational attainment, however, Latinos in Richmond do lag behind other Richmonders in terms of income. Some 38 percent of Latinos had household incomes above $50,000 in 1999, compared to 46 percent of all Richmond residents (nationally, 30 percent of Latinos had incomes over $50,000). Nine percent of Latinos have incomes of $100,000 and above, compared to 13 percent of the overall population of Richmond.

Richmond Latinos, both men and women, have rates of employment comparable to others in Richmond. Latino men actually fare a little better than all male residents in terms of percentage in the labor force, although this disparity decreased from 1990 to 2000. Also, Latinos in Richmond share unemployment

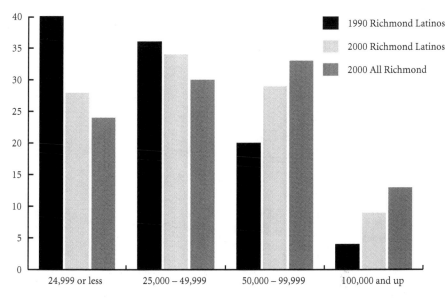

Figure 1.4. Household Income for Richmond Latinos and All Richmond Residents
            (in Percentages)
Source: Bureau of the Census, 1990, 2000.

rates similar to the general population of Richmond, rates that are considerably lower than the national averages (approximately 9 percent nationwide for Latinos, compared to 4 percent for Richmond Latinos). Women are less likely to be employed than men (73 percent versus 58 percent) but *are* employed at the same levels as all other women in Richmond.

The percentage of Richmond Latino homeowners is much lower than that of overall Richmond inhabitants (respectively 40 to 68 percent), and that percentage fell between 1990 and 2000. This is a puzzling aspect of our profile, given their high rates of education, employment, and income. Richmond Latinos are even less likely to own their own homes than Latinos in other areas of the United States. According to the 2000 Census, 46 percent of all U.S. Latinos are homeowners, compared to just 40 percent of Richmond Latinos, although this factor may be an indicator of the recent arrival of Latinos in the city. The amount of renting among Latinos in Richmond *is* considerably lower than in some other areas of the South, where rental rates reach as high as 80 percent of the population. In some of the new settlement areas, Latinos who are recent arrivals are more likely to be single male workers, possibly temporary, who are renters (Kochhar, Suro, and Tafoya 2005; Smith and Furuseth 2004).

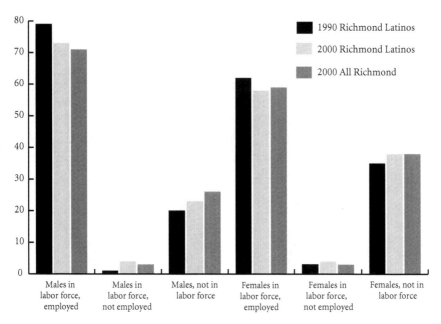

Figure 1.5. Employment Status for Richmond Latinos and All Richmond Residents (in Percentages)
Source: Bureau of the Census, 1990, 2000

The data reviewed so far portrays a distinctive Latino community in Virginia's capital. Richmond Latinos represent a small but ethnically diverse community that is growing at a steady pace, though Richmond is not experiencing the "hyper growth" of some areas of the South (Suro and Singer 2002). There is no long-term community of Latinos in Richmond, no ethnically identified neighborhoods. Latinos are younger than the overall population, with more married families with young children. They are also well educated and fully employed, but with a lower median income than Richmonders in general. However, they enjoy higher rates of income, education, and employment than Latinos throughout the United States. Given such a profile, it is clear that the Richmond Latino community is unlike many Latino communities in traditional Latino enclaves.

Explaining Assimilation in Areas with Low Latino Population

The aggregate data we examined in previous research are causally indistinct in terms of the relationship between internal migration and the observed

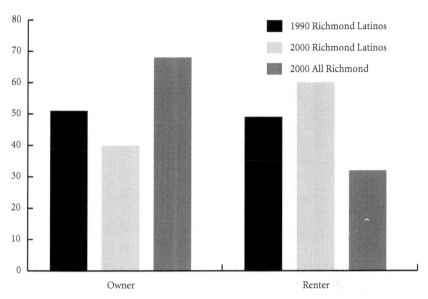

Figure 1.6. Homeownership Status for Richmond Latinos and All Richmond Residents
(in Percentages)
Source: Bureau of the Census, 1990, 2000.

economic and educational achievement. Several questions remain to be answered in this book. Are Latinos with educational credentials and employment opportunities leaving ethnic communities behind to move to areas like Richmond? How do middle-class Latinos—broadly conceived here by us as those respondents with white-collar occupations—fare after they move? When small pockets of Latinos migrate to areas with little or no Latino settlement, do they experience less discrimination, thus facilitating economic integration? The price of such success then would be potential isolation and cultural invisibility (see, e.g., Aranda 2006 on the dislocation and emotional experiences of middle-class Puerto Ricans). What types of relationships do they have with the working-class Latinos who move into the area?

For many current scholars of ethnicity and migration, the traditional concepts of assimilation no longer fit very well the post-1965 wave. Instead, it is understood that there are multiple possibilities for ethnic incorporation. For a small patch of brown coming to rest in black and white central Virginia, assimilation could follow one of several "segmented" pathways described in assimilation literature. The first could be adopting the values of the dominant white middle class in an effort to fit into the culture and values of its new environment. The second would be to acculturate into Richmond's urban underclass, with a culture of resistance that responds to the dominant group's exclusion of the minority group. The third is a "selective acculturation" pathway, whereby the immigrant community can preserve its culture and values of origin (differentiating itself from local minorities) while becoming economically integrated into the U.S. system (Portes and Zhou 1993; Portes and Rumbaut 1996, 2001; Waters 1999).

We will argue that the major factor that determines the quality of experiences among these paths of adaptation within the Latino community is social class. Richmond Latinos are a segmented community—an initial elite group of business and professional individuals followed by other white-collar workers and an even more recent population of less-well-off immigrants. These social divisions affect everything else about life in Richmond. To the extent that Latinos are becoming visible in the area, it is through the participation of the Latino elite in city life, through its ability to create organizations that represent its interests. The success of the elite groups, along with the overall invisibility of the less-well-off group, means that the impact of Latino presence in Richmond is not yet that of a united Latino community with a set of common goals. Thus, social policies developed by different localities may not adequately address the needs of the entire Latino population.

Researching the Richmond Latino Population

We collected data on Richmond Latinos in several ways. Our initial forays into the Latino community occurred after we had compiled information about Richmond Latinos using 1990 census data, beginning in 1999. We were invited to present the census data to community groups and at meetings of two fledgling Latino organizations, the Virginia Hispanic Chamber of Commerce and the American Hispanics of Richmond Association (AHORA). We also attended events such as business mixers, political fundraisers, and a local Latino job fair. Eventually, we made contact with Latino individuals from a number of political, religious, nonprofit, and business organizations.

Each time we presented our information, we made more contacts in the community. In each case, we took ethnographic notes on the events and people involved. This period of initial contact yielded a considerable amount of information about the Latino community, especially a sense of what it was like to move among the more institutionally integrated segment of Richmond's Latino population. These experiences informed the creation of our questionnaire, and provided us with names for our qualitative sampling frame. When word got around that we were distributing a survey, this in turn made us more in demand to speak to community groups. We discuss aspects of this initial ethnographic research throughout the book, although the bulk of our research consists of a cross-sectional survey of more than three hundred local Latinos.

In an attempt to reach a representative sample of the Latino community, we designed a probability sample for the greater Richmond Latino population. For a sampling frame, we purchased a listed household sample of names, addresses, and phone records for 1,100 individuals, adults eighteen years and older with Hispanic surnames.[4]

There were numerous advantages to such a sample. It gave us a large pool of names, rather than filtering through thousands of non-Latinos to find enough Latinos to create a reasonably sized sample. The cost of the screening required to reach a sufficient number of Latino households would have been prohibitive. Creating a sample this way allowed us to reach Latino households in predominantly non-Latino neighborhoods, which was especially useful in a low-Latino-density city. Using a sample compiled from additional data sources meant that we reached a larger number of unlisted households as well.

Sampling frames based on surnames, however, involve some significant compromises in coverage. By using a surname sample, we missed those Latinos without Hispanic-sounding last names of both genders, but especially Latinas who married Anglos and legally changed their names. Moreover, because we relied on a sampling frame based on telephone accounts, motor vehicle records, and the like, males outnumbered females two to one in the sampling frame, since they are more likely to have such accounts drawn in their names. We thus contacted and interviewed a larger number of male respondents (32 percent of those interviewed were women), because Latinas were actually less likely to refuse an interview. However, disproportionate samples of male respondents are not uncommon in studies of Latino populations. All in all, we feel that our technique provided a useful random probability sample for the subset of the Richmond Latino population with Hispanic surnames. In the end, it proved to be an adequate compromise between coverage and efficiency.

An initial screening weeded out individuals in the sampling frame who did not have Latino ancestry. As our schedulers contacted potential respondents, they asked about Latino background. We identified as *Latino* persons of Mexican, Puerto Rican, Cuban, or other Latin American culture or origin. If the respondent was hesitant to use a Latino or Hispanic label, we asked whether any of the respondent's parents or grandparents were Hispanic or Latino. If the respondent had at least one grandparent from South or Central America, she or he was included. In casting this broader net, we were able to reach respondents who might not commonly define themselves as Hispanic/Latino, even though the views of such respondents are very relevant to understanding Latino acculturation. That allowed us to compare the experiences of highly assimilated Latinos with others.

In the fall of 2000, we conducted a pretest using a subsample of one hundred individuals from the representative sampling frame. Twenty-two respondents were interviewed. Their input allowed us to identify the items requiring further refinement or deletion, but this data is not part of our analysis. We also corrected problems with our Spanish translation. We began administering the final version of the questionnaire in January 2001 and conducted interviews through the spring of 2002.

Ultimately, we interviewed 174 individuals from our sampling frame of one thousand (not including the pretest sample). The purchased list had many names that were rendered ineligible (see Table 1.4). A considerable number of phone numbers were inoperative. We tracked down as many of these individuals as we could using phone directories and mail forwarding services, but in the end almost one-third of the sample was lost in this fashion. Second, many of those on the list with "Hispanic" surnames were not, in fact, Latino. Approximately 16 percent of these were non-Latino women who were married to Latinos. Twenty-six percent of these individuals were of Italian origin, 14 percent were Filipino, and 10 percent were of European Spanish origin.

Our response rate of the usable names was 50 percent. Of those who gave a reason for their refusal, 56 percent said that they were "too busy" or had "no time" to be interviewed. Twenty-two percent said they were not interested. Two percent were hang-ups. Only 2 percent refused because they did not feel Latino despite Latin American origins (our sample *does* incorporate a number of individuals who did not really see themselves as Latino, but agreed because of their ancestry to be included anyway). We note that a number of our refusals initially seemed interested or even agreed to an interview, though we were unable to schedule these interviews. Unfortunately, it is impossible to tell how often people untruthfully used the "not Hispanic" statement as an escape from

Table 1.4. Latinos in Richmond Survey Response Rates

| Sample | Usable Names | Not Latino | Unable to Arrange* | Eligible for Interview | | Response Rate |
				Agreed	Refused	
994+	662	201	114	174	173	50%

+ The original sample without the pretest sample, minus six duplicate names.

* Never responded to phone calls or other contact, or agreed but was never interviewed.

doing the interview. This was probably true in at least a few of the cases. From the limited amount of information available, however, it does not seem that our response rate is subject to any systematic bias based on the types of individuals who did agree to do the interview.

To capture a number of groups missed by the probability sample, we created a second sample. Using lists and contacts from public agencies, businesses, and organizations in the community, we compiled a master list of more than one hundred area Latinos who did not have Hispanic surnames (primarily women) and other individuals who were difficult to locate using the probability sample (for example, undocumented immigrants). Interviewers also contacted Latinos at churches, Latino groceries and restaurants, and the relatives, friends, and acquaintances of those interviewed in the probability sample. More than 90 percent of these respondents were interviewed. The individuals from agencies and organizations were disproportionately middle-class; those from groceries and churches, working-class and recent migrants.

The same questionnaire was administered to this snowball sample of individuals, and the results compared to the probability sample based on Hispanic surnames. The second sample provided us with additional data from Latino individuals who were difficult to locate. However, the two samples differed only on three major variables—gender (expected, since the qualitative sample was an effort to reach more women), occupation, and country of origin. We feel confident that the two samples complement one another in capturing the segments of the Richmond Latino population we most wanted to study.

A comparison to census data shows that the two samples combined still do not reflect the entire Latino population of Richmond (see Appendix C). For example, it is clear that we oversampled those with higher incomes and educations and undersampled the very poor. Despite our attempts to find the latter, they were more likely to be transitory and difficult to find. The census may have its own problems accurately measuring the local Latino population, but it is safe to say that it probably does not undercount more privileged Latinos in Richmond to the degree that it does undocumented or poor Latinos. Therefore, we cannot argue that our sample is fully representative of the Latino population. However, since we wished to focus on the differences between middle-class and working-class Latinos, the slight overemphasis on the middle class in our sample is justifiable. In this book, we will continue to use Census data to make general statements about Richmond Latinos, and our data to explain *why* different social and ethnic groups behave differently.

Our questionnaire was a primarily closed-ended instrument, with English, Spanish, and Portuguese versions (see Appendix B for a copy of the questionnaire in English). The Spanish version was translated by a professional translator and reviewed and revised by the principal investigators and a professor of Spanish. The Portuguese version was translated by one of the principal investigators, a native Brazilian. Our questions were modeled after questions in the U.S. Census, the General Social Survey, and several questionnaire instruments focusing on Latinos or immigrants (Cuellar, Arnold, and Maldonado 1995; Hurh, Kim, and Kim 1978; Keefe and Padilla 1987; Portes and Bach 1985). Out of one hundred questions, approximately 10 percent were open-ended or provided an "other" category with a written response. In order to incorporate more reflexivity in our analysis, the questions were analyzed both quantitatively *and* qualitatively, a process we discuss at greater length in Appendix A.

We provided question-by-question instruction on conducting the interviews, and practiced interviewing sessions in English and Spanish. Trainees were taught to protect the confidentiality of the subjects, as well as to be sensitive to the potential cultural differences involved between interviewers and respondents. One-third of the interviews were conducted in Spanish, the other two-thirds in English. Although most interviewers were white (see Appendix A for a discussion of race and gender issues related to matching interviewers and respondents), those conducting the interviews in Spanish were fluent, and many had lived in Latin America or Spain and been immersed in Latino culture. Two student volunteers spoke Portuguese, and interviewed the two Brazilians in their native language.

We administered the face-to-face interviews primarily in respondents' homes, although a few interviews were conducted in places of business or restaurants. In rare cases the interviews were given over the phone or mailed to the respondent, and a handful of the nonprobability surveys were self-administered (though supervised by an interviewer). Interviews averaged forty-five minutes in length, although some sessions lasted more than two hours. At the conclusion of the interview, interviewers checked the questionnaire for accuracy and completeness, and after leaving the respondent's home, wrote a short set of notes about the interview. Interviewers also wrote notes in the margins of the survey form, which we analyzed qualitatively.

Looking at Class and Latino Assimilation in a Southern City

We share the results of our in-depth look into the Richmond Latino experience in the following chapters. Chapter 2 reviews the classical and contemporary theories on assimilation, framing the experience of Richmond Latinos within the context of geographic propinquity and segmented assimilation theory. We conclude with three vignettes that represent the differences in social class and migration for Richmond Latinos: a third-generation Latino born in Richmond; an older, highly assimilated immigrant who made several stops in the United States on his way to Richmond; and a very recent arrival that came directly from his home country to the area.

Chapter 3 describes the migratory patterns of Richmond Latinos—what types of Latinos are attracted to Richmond, where they come from, and why they chose Richmond. We show that the Richmond Latino migration has so far consisted of two waves of migrants, whose experiences are strongly correlated with social class. Living in Richmond, moreover, requires processing new information about the South and Latino identity. Relationships with Anglos, with African Americans, and even with other Latinos illustrate socioeconomic divisions in the community, albeit ones based on structural differences rather than overt class antagonism.

Chapter 4 examines patterns of assimilation among Richmond Latinos. Although Latinos in Richmond demonstrate fairly high rates of English usage and the incorporation of U.S. customs, there is no clear pattern connecting social class with more traditional acculturation. Indeed, we document evidence for "selective acculturation"—demonstrated by considerable use of Spanish as well as English, continued Latino contact, retention of customs from the country of origin, and identification with a "pan-ethnic" identity as Hispanic despite economic assimilation.

In chapter 5 we review family life for Latinos in Richmond. Immigrant status, ethnicity, and social class predict family composition, the likelihood of living in an extended family, and perceptions of the effects of Anglo culture on child rearing. Almost universally, however, Richmond Latinos indicate the importance of raising their children in their culture and the value of education. Their concern with preserving cultural heritage extends to the school system, and support for Spanish education is strong among both middle- and working-class Latinos. Parental concerns about maintaining the culture of origin as a way of protecting children demonstrate first-generation efforts to steer children toward certain segments of the ethnic community and away from others.

Work opportunities are the main reason that Richmond Latinos migrate to the area, which we turn to in chapter 6. We show how the white- and blue-collar segments experience the labor market in Richmond in different ways. White-collar workers who migrate to Richmond find more traditional occupational integration with little discrimination, and they perceive success as based on one's own merits. Some white-collar workers, however, are quite successful *as Latino* rather than because they are fully culturally integrated. Blue-collar workers, especially those in the urban underclass, are more likely to see occupational discrimination, although they still experience economic success in Richmond relative to other markets in which they had worked previously.

Turning to institutional practices, chapter 7 examines the religious participation of Richmond Latinos. The diversity of religious forms introduced into U.S. society creates new options for immigrants. Here we examine the absence of religion as one of those options. The secular path chosen by Latinos in Richmond has implications for the way they integrate into the community, especially in comparison to those Latinos who remain members of their religion of origin or who convert upon immigration to the United States.

In chapter 8 we document Latino participation in civic life. Our findings show that with this new wave of immigration it can no longer be assumed that Latinos will have low rates of political participation or that they will identify themselves monolithically with a single political party. We document the rise of Latino community associations dedicated to the cultural enhancement, economic growth, and political presence of middle-class Latinos in Richmond. This presence is paradoxical, however, as it does not bring solidarity and cohesion to the Latino community, but rather exacerbates class divisions.

Finally, in chapter 9 we summarize our findings about Latinos in the greater Richmond metropolitan area as a case study for segmented assimilation and selective acculturation. We explore how this particular wave of immigrants is challenging old assumptions about immigrant assimilation and geographic and social mobility. We find evidence of a smooth, more traditional linear assimilation for some, a more nuanced selective acculturation process for others, and parental actions and choices that represent a fear of adaptation into the urban underclass.

Latinos in "Dixie" consist of elite, well-educated Latino professionals who dominate the cultural and political landscape, and newer, less-well-off immigrants who remain marginal, sometimes lacking essential experiences and facing discrimination based on ethnicity, language, and social status. While these two communities interact with one another, they live in separate circles and have rather different goals and aspirations even as they express the need to affirm their ethnicity within those circles.

Chapter 2

Segmented Paths to Richmond

Richmond is not [as] initially accepting of other cultural backgrounds,
but once they get to know you they can come to accept you.

—Forty-eight-year-old Costa Rican

Two large immigration waves bookended the twentieth century. The first took place right at the turn of the century as the United States industrialized. Job opportunities, fast-paced urbanization, and modernization attracted masses of largely white, European immigrants to our shores. Much of what we assume about immigrants today is based on that earlier experience, including the expectation that assimilation follows a smooth linear trajectory, and means the wholesale adoption of U.S. culture (including language use and middle-class values). Indeed, the idea of the "melting pot" arises from our imperfect understanding of how Irish, Italian, German, Swedish, Polish and Jewish immigrants quickly shed their Old World identities and adopted a new, uniquely American sense of self and society.

The second great wave in the United States occurred just as the world began to feel most acutely the effects of deindustrialization and globalization. Starting in 1965, but increasing in volume and diversity as the century waned, Asian, African, and Latin American immigrants arrived at a time of massive structural readjustment and economic transition. The industrial surge of the early decades had by now given way to a bipolar informational economy marked by high-end professional jobs and a large low-end service industry.

Unlike the first wave, this second wave of immigrants did not share a common European culture or origin. These ethnic groups have strong, in some case millenarian, ways of life. They speak a greater variety of languages (sometimes non-Indo-European) and worship faiths other than Christianity. Fitting this new wave into the old immigration model is proving to be a frustrating exercise for academics used to a more straight-line model.

The traditional immigration model posits a one-way process of assimilation, with immigrants adopting the cultural ways and social institutions of the dominant host culture. Park and Burgess defined assimilation as a process in which "persons and groups acquire the memories, the sentiments, and attitudes

.r persons and groups, and by sharing their experience and history, are porated with them in a common cultural life" (1921:735). According to this model, the process unfolds in intergenerational stages: immigrants are partially assimilated, while their children are more fully so (Gans 1973; Warner and Srole 1945). By the third or fourth generation, assimilation is complete. A corollary of the first assumption is that along with assimilation comes social mobility: each subsequent generation achieves further economic success, until the whole ethnic group is fully absorbed into the Anglo middle-class majority (Gordon 1964; Park 1950).

Although the traditional immigration model fell out of favor during the last few decades, variants on the assimilationist process have experienced recent resurgence. Researchers now argue that the experience of most immigrants still fits that model even if some unusual examples exist on the margins (see Alba and Nee 2003; Perlmann and Waldinger 1997). As of late, even the popular press has adopted this argument, assuming an eventual traditional assimilation model for Latinos by claiming them as "The New Irish." Much like the earlier European immigrant group, once viewed as intractable ethnic outsiders, Latinos, too, will be "stripped of their foreignness and [achieve] mainstream acceptance" in a couple of generations, suggests editorialist Gregory Rodriguez (2005:35). Given the racial and cultural diversity of the Latino population, however, that assumption seems highly unlikely (it also appears to focus on the middle-class rung of the ladder). Recently, authors have argued that linear mobility models are not particularly applicable to Mexican Americans, for instance (Livingston and Kahn 2002).

Unlike the assimilationist model, a class model proposes that in a split labor market (such as the one that developed in the United States after World War II), native groups dominate the stable, unionized, high-paying jobs while immigrants are concentrated at the bottom of the market. Also known as the internal colonialism perspective (see, e.g., Bailey and Flores 1973; Blauner 1972; Carmichael and Hamilton 1967), this approach makes social class a more overt part of the process (Bonacich 1972), focusing on the degree to which the majority dominates, discriminates, and otherwise controls the minority groups within its borders.

To some extent, a class model does describe Latino assimilation throughout the twentieth century, beginning with the widespread discrimination and even segregation of Chicanos in the Southwest, and it is still applicable to many waves of recent immigrants (Bendick et al. 1992; Bernal and Knight 1993; Cobas 1984; Jones-Correa 1998; Negy and Woods 1992). At the same time, one finds considerable social mobility for some Latinos, and even acceptance by the dominant population, despite overall economic subordination.

The segmented assimilation model addresses more directly the unique characteristics of the second wave of immigrants in the twentieth century. Theorists recognize a diverse and multicultural population, and acknowledge the inherent tensions that come with incorporating a large number of immigrants. The model takes into account the already racially, ethnically, and economically segmented conditions present in U.S. society, allowing researchers to ask questions such as, "Do West Indian middle-class immigrants have the option of being anything other than Black Americans? Are recent Chinese arrivals automatically granted the same perception attached to successful Chinese Americans? Are well-educated Argentines able to move beyond negative labeling attached to native Latino populations?"

Theorists of segmented assimilation argue that acculturation for the current immigration wave may follow three segmented pathways (Bankston and Zhou 1997; Portes, Ferndandez-Kelly, and Haller 2005; Portes and Rumbaut 2001b; Portes and Zhou 1993; Waters 1999). The first pathway looks very similar to the traditional assimilation model: immigrants assume the mainstream values of the dominant white middle class in an effort to adapt to the culture of their adopted country (however, acceptance by the host society may not happen). The second pathway leads to adoption of the values of a minority culture in the United States. Labeled and treated as marginal by the dominant white culture, recent arrivals may experience blocked mobility, and thus incorporate the ethos of resistance of a minority population (see especially Waters 1999). The third pathway leads to a "selective acculturation," whereby the immigrant community preserves the integrity of its original culture while becoming economically integrated into the U.S. system. In this case, class mobility occurs without Americanization. Indeed, some may use a continued attachment to the ethnic community to distance themselves from other members of their ethnic group (e.g., the Caribbean blacks Mary Waters studied use West Indian identity to disassociate themselves from U.S.-born blacks).

The focus of segmented assimilation is primarily the relationship between first-generation parents and their second-generation children, especially in large urban areas. Not much of the segmented assimilation literature focuses specifically on *Latinos* (for one exception, see McKeever and Kleinberg 1999). Nor is segmented assimilation a unified theory, easily operationalized through specific variables. It is descriptive rather than predictive.

milation allows us to organize into recognizable patterns the
ichmond Latino experience. While the traditional assimila-
)ove can explain some of the Richmond Latino experience,
not address a series of important issues. Some Latinos have
lived in the United States for a long time without necessarily assimilating. Even
when making an effort to assimilate, many Latinos experience a high degree of
discrimination that prohibits them from fully participating in U.S. institutions.
Racial barriers may contribute to a different process of interaction between
immigrants and locals. Finally, traditional assimilation underestimates the
efforts of Latinos to maintain cultural and ethnic integrity. Technology that
provides real-time access to their homelands makes the choice to discard their
cultural ways less of a requirement in this case.

Here we wish to use the assumptions of segmented assimilation theory to
examine what might happen in a variety of day-to-day facets of life in Richmond: leaving ethnic enclaves or other traditional ports of entry; experiencing
discrimination; workplace aspects; and in family, religious, and political life.
We will not be comparing discrete groups so much looking at how the lives of
migrants to Richmond are affected by struggles between traditional assimilation, selective acculturation, and minority assimilation.

The recent changes in the forms taken by assimilation have had profound
effects on where immigrants settle in the United States. Until fairly recently, the
location of many immigrants could be described by geographic propinquity.
As immigrants came to this country, they settled in or near the port of entry
closest to home. Theirs was a calculated choice: settling close to home reduced
the cost of the journey to the United States and the possible price of an eventual return (Portes and Rumbaut 2006). Thus, one was more likely to find Irish
along the Northeastern seaboard, Latin American immigrants in the Sun Belt,
and Asian immigrants settling on the West Coast.

As more waves of immigrants followed the early ones, the ethnic communities grew in those areas, facilitating the creation of networks between
newcomers and communities of origin (Pessar 1995; Portes and Jensen 1989;
Portes and Manning 1986). Networks automatically directed newcomers into
ethnic enclaves. As Portes and Rumbaut argue, "[T]he operation of kin and
friendship ties is nowhere more effective than in guiding new arrivals toward
pre-established ethnic communities" (1996:32).

Some of the earlier immigrants who settled nearer their countries of origin
saw their stay in the United States as temporary. Often the goal was to work
hard, do well economically, and then go back home to enjoy the fruits of their
success. Taking advantage of job markets in other regions of the United States,

however, meant settling deeper roots in the host country. The offer of better job opportunities, especially for the middle class, would push immigrants farther inland and away from a valued connection to their earlier cultures (Chavez 1996; Fox 1996). The possibilities of economic mobility had to be weighed against the costs of leaving local ethnic communities that provided them with economic and cultural support.

A high concentration of ethnic presence provides future immigrants with an array of resources. Connections with earlier immigrants already settled in those ethnic communities offer newcomers the means to withstand the difficulties of a drastic life change. The established ethnic community serves as a buffer between them and the larger host society, affording new immigrants important local contacts and possible job offers (Greenwell, DaVanzo, and Valdez 1993). Ethnic enclaves allow immigrants to enjoy a wealth of cultural activities: newspapers in their language of origin, ethnic restaurants, and grocery stores with homeland staples, ethnic music bands, and similarly related businesses. A cohesive ethnic community gives newcomers the comfort of cultural familiarity in a foreign landscape while shielding them against possible native prejudice and discrimination (Fosset and Kiecolt 1989; Yang 2000).

This combination of geographic propinquity and ethnic enclave settlement was prevalent in the United States for most of the twentieth century and it is still helpful in explaining the disproportionate number of immigrants who reside in traditionally immigrant-dense regions of the country. Once ethnic communities created roots in a location, they continued to draw members from the group's homeland in multiple waves of immigration. And as more immigrants were attracted to the area, a thriving local immigrant economy developed with its own job market and new settlement opportunities (Lieberson and Waters 1987; Portes and Rumbaut 1996). As long as these communities are able to provide immigrants with the needed resources to rebuild their lives in the host country, those immigrants and their families are more likely to remain in a given geographical area. Even now, as continued waves of ethnic successors from Latin American and Asia enter the United States, ethnic enclaves grow even if earlier immigrants move away.

Historical research indicates that only as ethnic populations became more assimilated, typically not until the second or third generation, did they move out of ethnic enclaves (Alba et al. 1999; Sowell 1981; Steinberg 1981). As we begin the twenty-first century, however, we find more and more immigrants moving to areas in the United States where few immigrants have been before. Many are no longer bound to their traditional entry ports or to ethnic enclaves as they seek out better living conditions. While individual variables such as time in the United States, educational achievement, and occupational skills still predict such ethnic resettlement, now even some recently arrived, low-skilled immigrants migrate immediately to non-enclave areas seeking better opportunities (Portes and Rumbaut 2001b; Rodriguez 1992).

Spatial assimilation—the movement of immigrants away from ethnic enclaves—is also determined by a number of structural factors. One is the region's business cycle—whether its labor market is expanding or contracting (Borjas 1990; Farley 1987). The availability of significant entry-level jobs in a given industry (poultry processing in North Carolina, for example) and the availability of those jobs to newcomers is also important (Bonacich 1984; Cabezas and Kawaguchi 1990; Palm 1985). A third factor is the amount of governmental attention given to immigrants in a given area (Reisler 1996; Rumbaut 1989). For instance, Portes and Rumbaut report that Salvadorans choose to settle in Washington, D.C., because they face less harassment by INS personnel there than they did on the West Coast (1996:304). Finally, another aspect immigrants may take into account is the level of local hostility toward an incoming ethnic group (Cruz 1995; Taylor 1998).

Whether drawn to new economic opportunities farther inland, or following extended family to other areas of the country, immigrants calculate the pros and cons of settling permanently in more remote interior areas of the United States. Immigrant farm hands move to remote rural areas of the United States such as Idaho, Minnesota, or North Dakota, far away from borders. Mexican groups who used to move to California or Arizona now settle in places such as North Carolina, Georgia, or Tennessee (Hernández-León and Zuñiga 2003); recruiters even post job notices in Mexico or elsewhere in Central America to attract workers to manufacturing work in those states. Labor contractors in the forestry industry in rural Alabama recruit temporary workers with no U.S. experience on seasonal work visas (McDaniel and Casanova 2003).

In reformulating theories of assimilation to describe the case of Latinos in Richmond, we must acknowledge the larger point that there is no one narrative of immigration in the United States (Hollinger 1995). We use both segmented assimilation and spatial assimilation to explain the presence and experiences of Latinos in Richmond. For instance, recent Latino migration to the South illustrates that certain immigrants no longer follow the geographic propinquity model. In describing the relationships among different Latino ethnic groups in Richmond, and their relationships with white Anglos and African Americans, we recognize that as these groups interact they create innovative spaces for their ways of life. We do not yet fully understand what form these relationships will ultimately take—will Latinos settle comfortably into a middle-man minority status (Bonacich 1973)? Adopt a minority perspective? Or experience economic and other forms of assimilation? Surely some of all three.

Three Tales of Migration

The trajectories that Latinos travel to get to Richmond are quite multifaceted. To explaining the factors that determine segmented assimilation outcomes, we focus specifically on social class, but also acknowledge the importance of gender, family structure, social capital, and ethno-racial identity (Farley and Alba 2002; Hirschman 2001; Portes and Rumbaut 2001b; Waters 1999). In this section we offer vignettes of three respondents who represent in miniature the migration experience of Latinos in Richmond—a Latina who was born near Richmond, a Mexican American who found his way to the city as a young man, and a recent arrival from Guatemala who is still carefully navigating his way in the United States. The first two illuminate the lives of Richmond's middle-class Latino community, while the latter is typical of the experiences of recent, working-class migrants. All three vignettes illustrate issues we address in the rest of the book.

Marianne Gomez

Marianne Gomez[1] was born in a small town about fifteen miles south of Richmond. She has lived in or near Richmond all her life. A middle-aged dental hygienist with a college degree, Marianne is married but has no children. Her mother was born in the United States, of Eastern European immigrants; her father came from Puerto Rico. Marianne grew up in a middle-class family, with all the educational and social opportunities that kind of family membership affords. A blonde-haired, blue-eyed Latina, Marianne identifies herself as "Hispanic," but also says she typically "chooses not to think of" her race.

As someone with deep ties to Richmond, Marianne is very involved in the local community. An active Democrat, she votes in presidential and local elections, contributes money to liberal political causes, and feels that she has a strong say in what her government does. She is also engaged in her religious community, attending an Episcopal church several times a week, serving in the altar guild and as a lay reader for worship. Other signs of assimilation are clear: her co-workers, fellow churchgoers, and neighbors are mostly Anglos, although her friends are a bit more diverse—"Jewish, international, et cetera," she elaborates.

Though she speaks very little Spanish, Marianne says that being Latino is very important to her. Her family still cooks Puerto Rican meals on a regular basis, but more importantly, she is very aware of the cultural barriers faced by Latinos in the region. As an example, she cites how difficult it was for her father to join a service club such as Kiwanis or Rotary, despite the fact that he was a health care professional. She also thinks that it is still difficult for a Latino to get a job or to buy a house in Richmond, mentioning the problems faced by Latinos today such as real estate red-lining. To her, a person's appearance and accent play an important role in whether or not that person experiences discrimination. Nevertheless, Marianne's personal experience, as a long-term Richmonder, has not been one of racial discrimination. Instead, she emphasizes what it was like to be a woman growing up in the South in the seventies.

Marianne is a perfect example of what Mary Waters terms symbolic ethnicity, "a personal choice of whether to be ethnic at all . . . something that does not affect much in everyday life . . . [but] matters in voluntary ways" (1990:147). Although her ethnicity is important to her, she can choose the aspects of her heritage she wants to celebrate, rather than having them thrust upon her. She emphasizes positive ethnic traits, such as the importance of touching for Puerto Ricans, and how warm relations and tight bonds govern their families. She is aware of ethnic discrimination, and can give examples of it from her background, but is not personally affected by it. Like the European Americans interviewed by Waters, Marianne is able to enjoy all the benefits of being a Latina while not experiencing any negative aspects.

Tony Gallegos

Tony Gallegos, a second-generation Chicano, was born in the United States of a Mexican-born father and a Texan Latino mother. Unlike Marianne, Tony grew up in a working-class family, migrating to nearby Fort Lee, Virginia, in his early twenties, while serving in the army. Once he left the military, he settled in Richmond. For a working-class man, Tony achieved an unusual level of social mobility, starting his own car rental company after getting a college degree in business administration. Now in his sixties, Gallegos makes more than a hundred thousand dollars a year. He is married and has three adult children.

The experience of growing up in a Mexican home was foundational for Gallegos. Tony says that being Chicano is very important to him. He relishes his cultural ties on an everyday basis: he still cooks Mexican food, and speaks Spanish at home during family gatherings and with his friends. He enjoys reading newspapers and listening to music in Spanish. Tony feels strongly about the importance of preserving his ethnic culture and raising children in that culture. Spanish-speaking children should be taught Spanish in U.S. schools and should then have bilingual classes for several years (in fact, he believes *everyone* should speak two languages).

A devout Roman Catholic, Tony attends mass every week and is an active participant in other church activities. He serves as a reader in church, he is a member of a folk singing group, and he is a religious education teacher. Tony is also very politically active. As a moderate Republican, he votes regularly in presidential and local elections, gives money to political causes, and attends political rallies. He feels very politically empowered; believing, like Marianne, that he has an input in what his government does.

Although he feels that he is rarely the target of racial or ethnic discrimination these days, he was treated unfairly when applying for jobs in his youth. Such experiences, however, have not tainted his perception of the larger Richmond community. He does not believe, for instance, that it is difficult nowadays for other Latinos in Richmond to get a loan, find a job, or buy a house. He does think, nevertheless, that Latinos have to work a lot harder than Anglos in order to get ahead in Richmond.

Tony is a part of the large subgroup of professional and entrepreneurial Richmond Latinos who are well-educated and successful. These Latinos do not experience a lot of personal discrimination, and are eager to create a more visible Latino cultural presence in the city. They are the ones who create cultural and business organizations representing their ethnicity, organizations such as a Hispanic Chamber of Commerce (actually, Richmond has two), the Latino ballet, citywide *Cinco de Mayo* celebrations, and other Latino community organizations. Such residents worry about the work, housing, and schooling needs of recent Latino arrivals, but are also keenly interested in promoting the concerns and pursuits of middle-class Latinos. Above all, however, though economically and politically integrated, they remain *Latinos* rather than (merely) fully assimilated "Americans"; consciously and faithfully preserving ethnic ties through language, cultural activities, and self-identification.

Eduardo Montes

Eduardo Montes was interviewed in Spanish, since he knows very little English. A Guatemalan native, he arrived in the United States only four years ago. Montes is thirty-eight years old and has a grade school education. His parents were both peasants and still live in his village in Guatemala. Eduardo is not a citizen of the United States and does not know whether he will choose to become one. He came to this country looking for better work opportunities and the financial means to support his parents in their old age. Finding no work in New York, he relocated to Richmond.

In Richmond, Eduardo lives in a working-class neighborhood, sharing his household with two other Latino friends. He works in a construction company, installing pipes and electrical wiring. His long work hours leave little time for social activities, especially those involving the larger Richmond community. As far as we could ascertain, his only community involvement is through his church. As a Catholic, he attends mass two to three times a month, and says that while most of his co-workers are Latinos, his friends, neighbors, and church acquaintances are of mixed ancestry and race.

Despite the fact that he has been in the United States for several years, Eduardo is still deeply immersed in his native culture and language. He cooks Guatemalan meals at home on a regular basis. He is surrounded by family, since one brother and several nephews live in Richmond. And he speaks Spanish almost exclusively, although he enjoys entertainment activities in both English and Spanish. Perhaps it is this immersion in his culture that keeps Eduardo from being more aware of the obstacles recent immigrants to Richmond, especially laborers, face. While he is not completely satisfied with his job, he thinks that he is being paid a fair wage relative to his level of education or in comparison to the wages of his co-workers. He says that Latinos may face discrimination from some companies in the area, but he is certain that he would have the ability to switch jobs or choose other employers if that were to happen to him. He identifies himself as a brown-skinned Guatelmateco ("It is hard to deny your identity," he says, "when you are *from* there"), which probably makes him more visible in a city marked by an inflexible racial system.

Eduardo is still untouched by the larger local institutions that made cultural immersion easier for Marianne and Tony. His lack of citizenship precludes participation in political activities, especially membership in a political party or participation in local and national elections. Not surprisingly, he does not have the same sense of political empowerment experienced by middle-class Latinos. Eduardo is surrounded by the weight and presence of his native country's culture, both in his tastes and personal interactions.

Our three tales of migration illustrate elements of the theoretical connections we will highlight throughout the rest of the book. Marianne is an example of the native or long-term Richmonder whose ethnicity is mostly symbolic— her middle-class life is both highly assimilated and deeply embedded in the Anglo world of the city. Tony migrated some thirty years ago from the Southwest to Virginia. He has become a successful entrepreneur, and in that way he is representative of a group of former outsiders who are well-educated and fully conversant with Richmond's Anglo world, but who retain strong ties to their Latino roots, "selectively acculturating" elements of the dominant culture.

Freshly arrived, Eduardo came to Richmond only a few months after immigrating to New York, looking for better job opportunities. He represents those Latino Richmonders who are still most thoroughly insulated in their home culture and least anchored in the local institutions the city has to offer. It is unclear at the moment whether the city's cultural and economic institutions support a straightforward transition to life in the United States and in Richmond for such individuals.

The reasons Latinos move to Richmond, explained in more detail in the next chapter, make clear the relationship between various forms of segmented assimilation, spatial assimilation, and social class mobility. While we do not find many manifestations of the minority model described by Waters, is it clear that many Richmond Latinos moved to Richmond in order to escape exactly such an experience for their families. Moves to Richmond, and perhaps to other non-enclave cities, signal if nothing else the threat to the first generation posed by assimilation into U.S. minority cultures, especially given the discrimination barriers found in ports of entry.

At the same time, these moves do not indicate an embrace of dominant white culture as the only, or even the main, method of achieving success. Especially for middle-class Latinos in Richmond, traditional assimilation involves a cost in terms of what makes them distinctive citizens of the local community. Some actively avoid it, others alternate between embracing dominant values and norms and honoring their culture of origin. Some even find economic advantage in emphasizing a Latino identity, as we discuss in the next chapters.

Chapter 3

Many Roads to Richmond

I stopped for gas, started looking for work and ended up staying.
—Thirty-four-year-old Guatemalan carpenter

I played professional soccer and saw Richmond on tour. I liked it.
—Fifty-two-year-old retired Paraguayan immigrant

As the former capital of the Confederacy, Richmond is certainly not the first city that comes to mind when thinking of places to study Latino migration. A midsize city steeped in Southern history and racial antagonism, the city has never had many (or really, any) Latino immigrants. We find no reference to any Latino settlement in central Virginia prior to 1970. The city is far from traditional Latino ports of entry into the United States. Neither the greater Richmond metropolitan area nor the state of Virginia has made many efforts to recruit foreign professional workers or laborers for industries as in other regions of the South. That the area is experiencing a surge of immigration, especially of Latinos, is somewhat baffling.

Given the crucial role that geographical propinquity had played in previous immigrant settlement in the United States, we sought to explain whether the settlement of Latinos in the South indicates a new path for migration. We wanted to know what was driving immigrants in general, and Latinos in particular, to move away from traditional areas of settlement. Why would people trade the safety of their own ethnic communities for unknown regions with no history of hosting their group? More specifically, we wondered what appeal cities such as Richmond held for Latinos. Given the invisibility that must accompany such a move, we set out to discover how Latinos justify the decision to start over in a place where they are relatively unknown.

While these recent patterns of settlement signal a new geographic mobility, they also ably illustrate scenarios predicted by segmented assimilation theory. Latinos who share the mainstream values of the dominant white middle class have greater choices and therefore are no longer singularly bound by ethnic ties and obligations to remain in ports of entry. Having human capital and economic resources, they are free to move for any reason, especially for economic or professional opportunities. Those plagued by discrimination based on minority status might move to other areas of the country to avoid the harsh effects of majority prejudice, or to prevent their children from incorporating an ethos of minority resistance. Finally, immigrants who engage in "selective acculturation" may be interested in moving to areas that afford a degree of economic integration without exacting a strict demand for cultural uniformity.

We argue here that these patterns are becoming prevalent in Richmond and other cities all over the South, but are potentially true of other non-Latino regions of the United States as well. New forms of spatial and segmented assimilation are less driven by the actual ease of assimilation, including linguistic assimilation, than by economic adaptation (see Alba et al. 1999). What is significant about Southern relocation is not only the level of individual mobility, but also that immigrants are settling new communities in regions with no previous Latino presence.

An Immigrant Community

Richmond Latinos are first and foremost a group of immigrants. While there are a few third- or fourth-generation Latinos in our sample, the majority are still vitally connected to the memories and culture of their homelands. Sounds, food, and stories from a home country are deeply ingrained in their experience, and form an important part of their identities (we discuss culture and identity further in chapter 4). As Figure 3.1 indicates, almost 70 percent of the Latinos in our sample are first-generation immigrants. Approximately 20 percent have at least one parent born outside the United States, while 9 percent are third-generation. Only 1 percent of those studied have families who have lived in the United States for at least three generations (both parents and grandparents born in the United States). The perspectives of these Latinos, little studied until now, are potentially very illuminating of the experiences of fully assimilated Latinos.

In terms of ancestry, our sample mirrors approximately the census information we provided in chapter 1. One-quarter of our respondents are Mexican in origin and 20 percent are Puerto Rican. We have a greater Cuban representation (about 9 percent versus 4 percent in the census), as well as more South Americans, particularly Colombians. Our contacts in Richmond indicate that census officials, though very conscientious about undercounts in 2000, still managed to miss much of Richmond's undocumented immigrant population.[1] Guatemalans and Salvadorans are more likely to fall into this category,

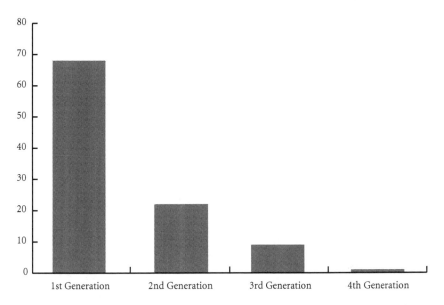

Figure 3.1. Immigrant Status of Richmond Latino Respondents

especially recent arrivals to this country as a result of strife in those countries. Indeed, our survey located more Salvadorans and Guatemalans than the census did for the Richmond area (11 and 10 percent in each case, respectively, versus 7 and 4 percent in the census). Immigrant status does not vary significantly by gender, but ancestry does: Mexicans and Salvadorans are more likely to be female than male, while males are overrepresented among Guatemalans.

Among foreign-born Latinos specifically, we expected a high representation of Mexicans in our sample, but were surprised by the numbers of respondents from El Salvador and Guatemala (see Figure 3.3). Perhaps this is an indication of how much these Central American groups characterize the immigrants who have moved into the area since 1990 (see chapter 1). Also, although U.S. citizens, the Puerto Rican–born comprise 10 percent of the non-mainland-born sample.[2] Outside of the U.S. mainland, the bulk of our respondents (43 percent) were born in those four places.

Although Richmond Latinos are largely immigrants, a number of them have been long-term residents of this country. The average length of time lived in the United States for the 203 immigrant respondents is twenty-one years. However, as Figure 3.4 indicates, there is a good deal of variation in tenure of residency. Almost one-quarter of the immigrant Latinos have lived in the United States for thirty years or more, but a similar number have lived here ten years or less.

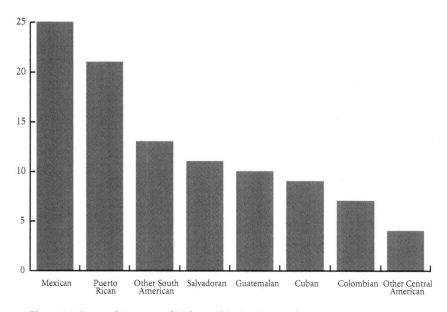

Figure 3.2. Parental Ancestry of Richmond Latino Respondents

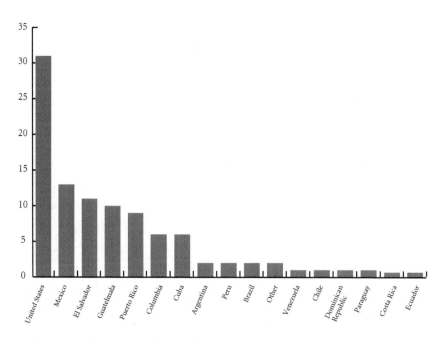

Figure 3.3. Country of Birth for Richmond Latino Respondents

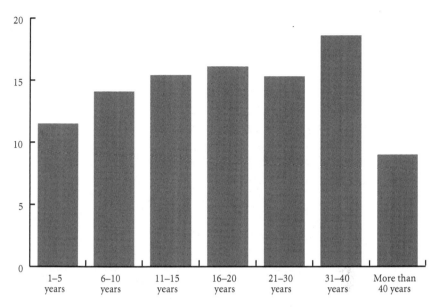

Figure 3.4. Years in the United States, Immigrants Respondents Only (N = 203)

This indicates that the immigrant Latino population in Richmond brings to the city a range of familiarity with U.S. ways of life. Some respondents have been adapting over a long period of time—first to the United States, and then again to Richmond—and are far more knowledgeable of U.S. mores and institutions, while others are just beginning to understand the intricacies of a new culture.

Respondents also differ in their age of entry into the United States. Twenty-four percent of the Richmond immigrants came to this country as children, comprising that "1.5" immigrant generation, not quite first-generation, as their lifetime experiences have mostly been in the host country, but not born in the United States either (Portes and Rumbaut 2001a). Still, a similar number of immigrants in our sample migrated in their forties and fifties. They are thus more likely to be culturally connected to their home countries, perhaps facing a greater difficulty in navigating between two cultures late in life.

The reasons respondents gave for coming to the United States vary as well. A little over one-third said that they came to this country for family-related reasons, coming to the United States with parents or with a spouse, or to reunite with their family. Another 42 percent chose the United States for better education (8 percent), better wages (29 percent), or both. Finally, 11 percent of the immigrant group in our sample chose to relocate to the United States to escape war or persecution in their native land (Table 3.1); and 10 percent cited other reasons. Outside of those whose decisions to come to the United States were made for them (by their parents), then, the majority of Richmond Latinos came to the United States seeking better economic opportunities broadly construed (of course, parental decisions, too, can be motivated by economic choices).[3]

Ancestry is significantly related to motivations for coming to the mainland United States. For Mexicans, Puerto Ricans, and the majority of South and Central Americans, wages or educational opportunities were the main reason for migration. For Cubans and Salvadorans, other reasons (primarily persecution or war) prevailed. For Colombians and Guatemalans the reasons are more evenly spread between family, wages and educational opportunities, and other factors.[4]

Social class, measured by occupational status, also affects migration choice. White-collar workers were twice as likely to say that they moved to the United States for family reasons (coming with spouse, parents, or family). Blue-collar workers, on the other hand, were far more likely to say they moved to this country for better wages (43 percent of them, compared to 20 percent of white-collar individuals). Both groups were as likely to say they came for other reasons, although blue-collar workers were more likely to have migrated due to war or persecution (15 percent versus 8 percent for white-collar workers).

Table 3.1. Reasons for Coming to the U.S. (Immigrants Only)

Family Reasons	N	%
Came with Parents	48	23
Reunite with Family	17	8
Came with Spouse	12	6
Work/Study Reasons		
Better Wages	60	29
Better Education	17	8
Both	9	5
Other Reasons		
Escape War/Persecution	23	11
Other	21	10
*Total**	207	100

*One case is missing data.
Source: Latinos in Richmond Survey.

Where Do They Come From?

For our respondents, the process of settling in Richmond involved a series of stops and starts in different regions of the United States, either in leaving ethnic enclaves or bypassing traditional ports of entry altogether. We asked all respondents to list the last three cities they had lived in the United States before coming to Richmond. The big surprise is that almost 20 percent of the respondents (N = 58) came directly to Richmond from their home countries (most notably Mexico and El Salvador). This is astonishing, considering that Richmond has no history as a port of entry for any immigrant population, harbors such a small percentage of Latinos, and does no advertising in Central America, as some other Southern cities have done. In Dalton, Georgia, as well, Hernández-León and Zuñiga document that more than 40 percent of Mexicans arrive directly from Mexico, especially women, the most recent entrants, but this is the result of recruiting (2000:60–61). In Richmond, this group is also disproportionately female (45 percent) compared to the rest of the sample. They are more likely to be working-class, less well educated, and not citizens of the United States, although not necessarily recent arrivals. Their reasons for coming to the United States and to Richmond are quite varied—they are not

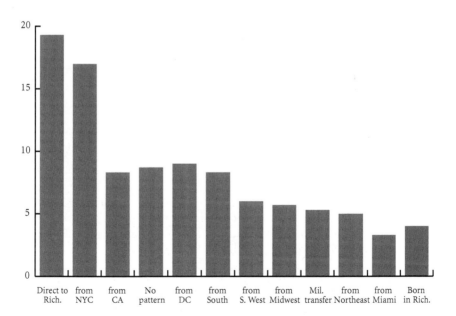

Figure 3.5. Patterns of U.S. Migration of Richmond Latinos Respondents

merely labor migrants. This group challenges the geographical propinquity model, since they are traveling much farther from their homelands than ever before in order to resettle.

A good many Richmond Latinos do come from traditional ports of entry: Los Angeles, New York City, Miami, and cities in the Southwest. Since we wanted to understand why Latinos might be moving from ethnic enclaves in large cities to places like Richmond, we were particularly interested in this group of individuals. Were they able to draw on the knowledge and networks established in ethnic enclaves to get to Richmond? The three largest Hispanic groups in the country—Mexicans, Puerto Ricans, and Cubans—have traditionally migrated to distinct areas in the mainland United States (Waldinger 2001). Mexican immigrants tend to settle near the Texas border, other parts of Texas, and in Los Angeles. And indeed, about 6 percent of our sample, largely Mexican, came from the Southwest (excluding California), mostly from the Dallas-Forth Worth metropolitan area. Another 8 percent hailed most recently from Los Angeles or San Francisco (a group largely comprised of Mexicans, Salvadorans, and Guatemalans).

New York City has traditionally hosted most of the Puerto Rican exodus, and is also home to Latinos of other origins. Not surprisingly, many of our respondents arrived from New York and its environs. After the group who came directly to Richmond from their homelands, the New York group is the second largest, 17 percent of the survey. Half of that group is Puerto Rican, with South and Central Americans also represented. A small group of respondents moved from New York to Washington, D.C., and then to Richmond.

Washington is quite a common, albeit typically brief, stopping place before moving to Richmond. About 9 percent of our respondents made their way to Richmond from the national capital. Like the Latinos who came from New York, many of the Latinos who came via Washington indicated that they moved to Richmond because they felt Washington was not a healthy or safe environment for their families.

Miami has been home to many Cuban and Nicaraguan Americans, and about 3 percent of our respondents arrived from that area, in most cases Cuban. Six percent of the Latinos in our sample came from the Midwest, not a common geographic region for Latinos. Eight percent migrated from other parts of the South, including Virginia. Another 5 percent of the Richmond Latinos in our sample came from the Northeast.

Of the remainder, 5 percent moved around the country, and the globe, due to military transfers. Being in the military is a relatively common occurrence for Latinos in our study. According to census data for Richmond, Latinos are twice as likely to be in the military as other ethnic groups. The travels of our respondents took them to such diverse locations as Germany, Korea, and well-known army bases in the United States (Fort Bragg, Fort Lee outside Richmond), so that we find no typical migration patterns in their moving. There were also a number of nonmilitary individuals (9 percent) whose internal migration fits no discernible pattern—that is, prior to Richmond they lived in such diverse locations in the United States that their paths do not lend themselves to a separate story about migration (we feel this finding is quite out of the ordinary, because it fits with no known models of internal migration; however, the numbers are too small to provide any statistically meaningful characteristics of this group). Finally, twelve respondents in our study (4 percent) were actually born in Richmond, to parents who were among the first of the Latino arrivals to the area.

Despite their travels until now, our survey respondents do not envision much further migration within the United States. Most of the Latino migrants who make Richmond their home do not see their living there as a temporary phenomenon (after all, the average number of years lived in Richmond is thirteen). Most indicated that they are in Richmond to stay—more than three-quarters of our sample said they had no plans to move to another area.

Why Do They Come to Richmond?

Until recently, most Latino immigrants settled in ethnic enclaves regardless of their levels of education and occupational status. They were more geographically concentrated than the native-born and more likely to be urban, living in the largest cities in the United States. Latinos exhibited a greater unwillingness to relocate than other groups, especially when the new areas do not have high concentrations of Latinos (Edwards et al. 1993). Unlike other ethnic groups, it was not until the second generation that Latinos would leave ethnic enclaves in large urban areas (Bartel 1989; Portes and Rumbaut 1996; Rodrigues 1992). Education and social class are crucial. Reviewing the evidence, Portes and Rumbaut (1996) argue that professional and entrepreneurial immigrants, more than laborers and refugees, have greater geographical mobility—professionals tend to go where the jobs are, and entrepreneurs have the business expertise and economic means to resettle in other areas. Those who were not economically integrated were less likely to move, although this is now changing.

What this suggests for the new trend of settlement into non-Latino areas, then, is that upper- and middle-class immigrants might pave the way for later groups. Successful white-collar or business-owner immigrants depend on a number of ethnic services to sustain their connections with the culture of origin (although they are leaving ethnic enclaves, they now may be seeking selective, rather than full, acculturation). In that sense, the cultural needs of middle-class Latinos can determine the socioeconomic levels of the next immigrant waves. Opening ethnic restaurants require ethnic staff. Ethnic grocery stores depend on effective migrant networks established between the country of origin and the host country for their survival. Ethnic bands depend on ethnic musicians who are familiar with the musical repertoires of the country of origin. The professionals and business owners often move individually as they receive better job offers, but the laborers who came later often move in clusters, either groups of single men or extended families. Of course, as more Latinos settle into a region, their newly created communities provide even more newcomers with job opportunities, and serve as a buffer between them and the larger metropolitan area.[5]

In Richmond, as well, the Latino community relocated to the city in two distinct waves. Early arrivals were typically Latino professionals or business owners. This wave was very small and completely invisible to the larger population—a respondent who is now the director of a not-for-profit organization recounted that when he was recruited to Richmond in the early nineties, an executive at the corporation where he interviewed told him that there were no Latinos in Richmond at all.

The settlement of professionals and entrepreneurs provided an opening for less skilled laborers, now leaving ethnic enclaves without first achieving economic integration, but taking advantage of occupational opportunities in the South. Geographic mobility does not create social mobility for all, however. One important by-product of this segmented migration process is the replication of class differences from ethnic enclave to nontraditional settlement area. Social hierarchies that preceded Richmond become the pattern for the local Richmond hierarchy. This wave, though less well off economically, is much larger and more visible.

This two-step migration pattern for Richmond Latinos is demonstrated by comparing long-term Latino residents of Richmond with more recent arrivals. Those who have lived in Richmond more than ten years (N = 136) have higher personal and household incomes. They also have higher levels of education. This first group was not merely succeeding as a result of the economic strength of the region or a lack of discrimination once they arrived in Richmond. They were different types of people before they arrived. The earliest arrivals were mostly Mexican and Cuban. As predicted, earlier migrants are more likely to be professionals and business owners, and overall occupational prestige is higher for them than for successive arrivals (this pattern is not unique to Richmond: see also Borjas 1985).

We asked respondents to explain their reasons for moving to Richmond, and their responses tell us much about the impetus behind the migration of different groups to the area. Table 3.2 lists the first stated reason provided by each respondent for coming to Richmond. Half of them chose the city for either occupational or educational reasons. One-third of them reported that they came to the area for family reasons (either with their parents or spouse or to reunite with their family). Five percent primarily relocated to Richmond because they liked the city or its quality of life. Finally, 3 percent came to Richmond because they wanted a change of pace or to leave another location.

The bulk of those who made occupational choices moved because of better jobs or wages specifically. More than 40 percent of the overall total offered these answers as the main reason for moving to the area. That number is even higher if we take into account those who said they moved to Richmond for "economic reasons," a catchall category wherein, for example, people referred

Table 3.2. Main Reason for Coming to Richmond (in Percentages)

Family Reasons	%	
Came with Parents	8	
Reunite with Family	13	
Came with Spouse	11	
For Family/Children	2	
Work/Study Reasons		
Job or Wages	41	
Better Education	6	
Economic Reasons	3	
Other Reasons		
Quality of Life, Peaceful	4	
Liked Richmond	1	
Change of Pace	2	
To Leave a Location	1	
Other	8	
*Total**	100	

*N = 286. Five cases are missing data; twelve cases were born in Richmond.
Source: Latinos in Richmond Survey.

in qualitative asides to Richmond's lower cost of living, or to a poor economy in their previous location.

Of the one-third that came to Richmond for family reasons, the largest number (13 percent) came to reunite with family already here. Although many of them came following previous relatives who migrated to the area, some came to tend to elderly parents or to reunite with their grown children. One-third of those moving for family reasons came to the area with their spouses, including those who moved due to a spouse's job relocation. Finally, one-quarter of this group had come to Richmond with their parents.

Latinos who gave other reasons for moving to Richmond cited the city's quality of life, including their perception that life in Richmond was peaceful. Others came to the area seeking either a change of pace or to leave a previous location. People in the "other" category (8 percent of the total) also gave reasons such as having a friend residing in the area, for medical services, for safety reasons, or because they were seeking political asylum. That category provided some of our favorite responses to this question, emphasizing equal elements of uncertainty, fate, or serendipity; for instance, the man we quote at the beginning of the chapter who was just looking for gas when he happened upon Richmond, or another person whose response was simply a shrug and, "*No se. Por suerte* [I don't know. By chance]."

Some respondents had both primary and secondary rationales for moving to Richmond. A review of all responses given for coming to Richmond (results not shown) indicates that the secondary patterns are not dissimilar to the primary motivations. However, when noting their secondary motivations for moving to the area, people were much more likely to add (usually to an economic reason) that they also wanted to reunite with family members, to leave a specific location, or because of the quality of life in Richmond. We note this emphasis on quality of life because it becomes even more important later in the chapter, when we report respondents' descriptions of what they like about Richmond.

While the literature, discussed in chapter 2, predicts that entrepreneurial and professional immigrants may have more mobility than blue-collar workers, we find that they were not more likely to come to Richmond for occupational or educational opportunities. In fact, laborers and professionals were equally as likely to state that they came for occupational reasons (63 percent for laborers compared to 62 percent for professionals and 42 percent for entrepreneurs). The chief difference is that laborers were more likely to say that they came because wages were better or because of the poor economic situation (high unemployment rate, cost of living, etc.) in their previous area of residence, while professionals and entrepreneurs were more likely to cite job transfers, opening a new business, or educational opportunities. So, both groups are leaving ethnic enclaves for economic opportunities, but for different reasons.

Even controlling for ancestry, jobs and educational opportunity remain the primary motivation for moving to Richmond, although there are some significant differences across groups (see Table 3.3). Mexicans are the most likely to say that jobs and educational opportunity were the reason (at 63 percent) for moving to the area. Puerto Ricans, on the other hand, rank factors other than family or job opportunities very highly compared to other nationalities (with close to 30 percent choosing from the "other" category).

When we control for both social class and ancestry, the picture becomes even more nuanced. For instance, white-collar Cubans and Mexicans are more likely to cite family reasons for moving to Richmond, whereas blue-collar Cubans and Mexicans tend to talk about jobs. White-collar Puerto Ricans are more likely to state other reasons for their resettlement, whereas blue-collar Puerto Ricans even more strongly emphasize the economic factors than Puerto Ricans overall. South and Central Americans do not demonstrate any class-based differences. Social class status (through occupation) does have an effect on internal migration decisions, but it is one that is mitigated by some ancestries.

Table 3.3. Main Reason for Coming to Richmond, Controlling for Class and Ancestry (in Percentages)

Class Both Groups	Ancestry				
	Mexican	P. Rican	Cuban	South American	Central American
Family	35	29	32	37	39
Work/Education	63	42	56	51	48
Other	2	29	12	12	13
$\chi 2 = 21.2, p < .01, N = 286$					
Blue Collar					
Family	27	28	18	37	41
Work/Education	73	55	65	56	52
Other	0	17	17	07	07
$\chi 2 = 10.9,$ not sig., $N = 98$					
White Collar					
Family	43	26	63	33	33
Work/Education	54	33	37	50	47
Other	03	41	0	17	20
$\chi 2 = 16.3, p < .05, N = 123$					

Source: Latinos in Richmond Survey.

The Peaceful City

As the second quote introducing the chapter indicates, Latinos often view Richmond as an attractive place to live. Some respondents chose Richmond because they found it a peaceful place and were impressed with the quality of life there. For example, while acknowledging that Richmond lacks the energy of a big city such as Buenos Aires, an immigrant from Argentina appreciated the quiet and calm of the smaller city. Latinos continue to be happy with these facets of life in Richmond. Seventy-five percent of our respondents said they are either satisfied or very satisfied with life in the area; only 23 percent said they have plans to move elsewhere.

Latinos often express their satisfaction with Richmond by contrasting it with their experiences in large urban areas such as Washington, New York, or Los Angeles. A newly arrived Salvadoran commented on how life is more tranquil in Richmond than in an ethnic enclave. Even though he was surrounded by a larger Salvadoran community in Washington, he prefers Richmond's pace. The level of perceived safety he found in Richmond impressed another respondent. Unlike his experience of New York, in Richmond he feels he "can leave car windows down. There's more trust." He also argued that in the greater Richmond area, it is easier to better one's life, emphasizing a classic immigrant aspiration.

Although economic opportunities are the predominant factor cited by our respondents, it is clear that the move to Richmond per se meant also providing a different environment for oneself and family. One respondent explained his move there as motivated by wanting a better life for his children, especially his oldest daughter, because "life was rough in New York." Others discussed explicitly the need to move their children out of the larger urban areas they had been living in. Some respondents talked about urban crime levels; one recalled that getting mugged was a determining factor in the move to Richmond. A number referenced the better public school system in contrast to other metropolitan locations. Immigrant parents in the Children of Immigrants Survey cite similar concerns about their children, an unease with urban life related to the prospect of dissonant acculturation (i.e., acculturation into a downwardly mobile culture) (Portes, Fernandez-Kelly, and Haller 2005).

Another part of the satisfaction with Richmond stems from a perception of its friendliness, and by extension, the sociability that is peculiar to the South. Richmond strikes many of our respondents as friendly in two ways: they perceive locals as acting friendlier than elsewhere, and also assume that the friendliness in an indicator of nonprejudice. As one respondent put it, he has "never encountered racism in Richmond. Everyone was very friendly to everyone." Over and over the Latinos surveyed emphasized that locals do not treat them badly, and that they have not encountered much difficulty since moving to Richmond. They sense that people in Richmond are more welcoming, at least compared to other places they have lived in the United States.

Despite these perceptions of tranquility, safety, and surface friendliness, it is clear that the peaceful atmosphere does not translate into an equal measure of respect that also includes trust and acceptance. Latinos do not always feel that they are treated as peers by local Richmonders. About one-quarter said that they either probably or definitely disagree that Anglos accept Latinos as equals. As one Latino put it very tellingly, "I'm very happy with life in Richmond, satisfied with all aspects of my life. I have never experienced any discrimination, although I look Hispanic. People accept me, even though it may not be as an equal." Apparently, Latinos can become a part of Richmond life, but there are limits to the level of acceptance that comes with that offer. Latinos are aware that even as they are welcomed, they are not equal to those who are native to the area. Having lived for a while in central Virginia, we are used to stories about the surface gentility that masks a deep distrust, even of white residents. It is profoundly challenging *not* being marginal in an area where people who have been residents for thirty years might occasionally find themselves referred to as "newcomers to the area."

Historical Wounds in Capital of the Confederacy

Life in Richmond means becoming aware of the city's old wounds. It is striking how swiftly Latinos come to understand Richmond's connection with the Civil War and its consequences. Most of their perceptions are quite negative. A Cuban respondent who has lived in the United States for forty-three years and Richmond for eleven was quick to point out, "The Civil War consumes Richmond, and Richmond is a big backwards [city]. It's hard to be intellectually satisfied. Its proximity to D.C. is not a help, [as] it's for Yankees. Richmond is stuck in history. Richmonders are very proud, and don't see the need to move on. It has a misunderstood sense of importance."The way that Latinos connect Richmond's history to the racial fault lines that run deep through the community is ironic—Latinos, as outsiders, know more about being American, and the prospect of national unity, than some Americans do. "The city itself is divided," said one respondent. "Some revel in the Rebel flag. [I say,] accept being American together with all other Americans, since the only ones that truly belong here are the American Indians. If bigger cities can accept that, why can't Richmond?"

For Latinos of many hues who are not easily categorized racially, the racial divide—the importance of skin color in the United States and especially the South—is curious. Non-Latino residents, lacking a clear racial category for Latinos (who, after all, can be of any skin color), tend to blend them all into a single ancestry: Mexican. A sixty-year-old Puerto Rican, born on the mainland, who described his race as "brown," remarked, "For the Richmond area, people need to realize there are different Hispanic ethnic groups—not all are Mexican!" Another Puerto Rican, a woman, added, "It is irritating how the Americans in this area always think that anyone speaking Spanish is Mexican, and they don't like finding out they are wrong."

Moreover, unfamiliar with the conventions of Southern racism, some Latinos *do* find themselves facing harsher treatment, especially those who are dark-skinned. Many were unaccustomed to racism in their native countries, often because racial demarcations in Latin America are more ambiguous than in the United States, especially the South (see Rodriguez 2000). A Puerto Rican man recalled people making jokes about his appearance and dress with comments such as, "Where'd you get those shirt buttons, man? They're as big as hubcaps. Where'd you rip them off from?" Another Puerto Rican, a young woman immigrant, expressed frustration as she told us how her husband got charged with trespassing and spent a year in jail merely for walking alongside the road. This happened, she said, because he looks more obviously Latino, and she concluded her comments by lamenting Richmond as a "racist community." "Is that some sort of 'spic' name?" a police officer had asked one of our respondents a decade ago. This respondent, whose ancestry is half-Mexican and half-European, and who gives his race as white and his ethnicity as Hispanic, wants to leave Richmond because of the general narrow-mindedness of the local population as well as ongoing discriminatory encounters with the legal system and the police department.

Despite such treatment, we found willingness among those we surveyed, especially middle-class residents, to respond to these difficulties by educating locals in the benefits of cultural diversity. Some Latinos are willing to work hard to create that acceptance, meeting Anglos more than halfway: "It's a very exciting time to be a Hispanic in Richmond, a window of opportunity to not become a stereotype." A fifty-year-old Colombian with thirty years of residence in the United States explained, "Whites are skeptical of Hispanics in the area perhaps because [they are] unfamiliar—or ignorant. My sister is educating employers in relation to the Hispanic population, [in particular in relation to] education, safety regulations, and how to communicate with Spanish-speaking employees." This respondent thinks Richmond is starting to understand that "we're all consumers, Hispanics too." Such residents are eager to promote that Latinos have money to spend in the community and are a valuable asset to local businesses.

Other Latinos do not think that educating other Richmonders is a quick solution, since they perceive local friendliness as skin deep. Such superficial friendliness does not prepare the locals to move into a more multicultural era. In the harsh judgment of one respondent: "This town operates like a one-horse town. The thinking is small and the prejudices are big. Richmonders realize this and counter it with the 'Easy to Love Richmond' campaign, which makes me puke! It is easier to make friends with non-Richmonders. Attempts to put down social roots with Richmonders are only successful in the short term. Black, white, Asian—it doesn't matter for Richmonders. Consequently, Richmond does not embrace any cultural infusion," he said, giving examples such as the Latin ballet and a Kwanza celebration. For these Latinos, then, the lack of multicultural acceptance extends beyond the historical black-white divide to include other ethnic groups, especially Latinos.

Relating to African Americans

Adapting to the South also means discovering the world of a larger minority group, one with a long history in the city. For Latinos who are not familiar with African American culture, the process requires multiple layers of adaptation: interacting everyday with another minority group affected by previous racial divisions, understanding the distinct treatment African Americans receive from Southern whites, and struggling to place themselves within the preexisting system of racial stratification. Noticing discrimination, a forty-two-year-old chemical engineer from Venezuela commented quite astutely, "Wherever one goes, the largest minority is the one dealing with the greatest amount of racist stereotypes. In Richmond, the stereotypes are about blacks," although he had witnessed similar stereotypes about Koreans in northeast Washington, D.C., and directed at Latinos in Colorado and California.

Often, culture shock develops as a result of moving from areas with few African Americans. Latinos find black southern accents hard to understand, and reported that it is difficult for blacks to understand the respondents' own accents. Some respondents felt that African Americans treat them differently than whites do, including some racism directed at the most recent outsiders. Others observed that blacks, even those who had lived in Richmond for a long time, are subject to much more racist treatment by whites than Latinos are. "Why are [blacks] at a company for more years than any others, fifteen years or more, but they may not get paid as much?" queried a fifty-eight-year-old Columbian immigrant who worked in an eyeglass factory. "I have been to New Jersey, New York, DC, Miami, and 'los morenos' (the blacks) here in Richmond are more educated than other places." Despite these types of comments, there appears to be very little perception among Latinos that they occupy a "middle-man" minority position in the racial hierarchy (Bonacich 1973).

To be sure, in terms of social contact, Latinos spend fairly little time inter-acting with Richmond's African Americans on more than a superficial level. About 4 percent lived and worked in predominantly black neighborhoods or establishments, but most of our respondents had few black friends and seldom interacted with blacks socially or at their churches.

Since Latinos in our sample straddle the racial divide, ranging from those who describe themselves as white to those with very dark skin who identify as black Latino, it is difficult to place them easily on one side of the black/white binary. However, given the historical Southern antagonism between blacks and whites still prevalent in Richmond, Latinos of African descent could find the Latino community an easier place to be than they would the larger local community, especially if being Latino already carried a stronger identity than being black. For Latinos in those instances the Latino community may provide a bridge for a different form of interaction between the races.

At the same time, Latinos who identify more strongly with race than with ethnic identity might face the possibility of dismissal by Latinos in the community, especially if that race is black. Such migrants, as was the case for U.S.-identified Caribbean blacks interviewed by Waters, face the likelihood that they will be viewed negatively by the ethnic community. For example, one nineteen-year-old respondent we interviewed, a dark-skinned second-genera-tion Colombian, remarked that other Latinos at his high school felt that he had rejected *them* because he had a lot of African American friends. Assumptions about his character arise because he does not live in a Latino neighborhood and engages in behavior not considered "Latino enough." "People might be surprised about my character, since I've grown up in South Richmond and people think I am a thug by how I dress," he said. They think because he does not speak Spanish all the time, he is a traitor to Latino culture, although he himself classifies his race as Latino. This example exemplifies the fear of many Latino immigrant parents—that dark skin might condemn you to a minority culture, or at least the assumption that you belong to one. Although the number of dark-skinned Latinos in our sample is not large, those who are recognize that dark skin is perceived as a liability in Richmond.

Inter-Ethnic Relations

By the same token, Latinos moving into Richmond learn new ways of relating to other *Latino* groups, which sometimes means the rejection of certain behaviors and attitudes reflective of a marginal group. The process of creating a pan-ethnic identity in Richmond is still in its early stage (a topic we return to in chapter 8). When others see them as Hispanics, some respondents react negatively to this generic label—out of a sense of loyalty to a narrower identity, to avoid the negative stereotypes of Anglos, or merely because they do not wish to be lumped together. Some respondents denied having many things in common with other Latinos in the region; they share language, certainly, and perhaps some specific cultural values about family, but not much else. One respondent, looking to remarry, said that he would be satisfied with another Mexican American, or even an Anglo woman, but "he has nothing in common with a Cuban woman!" or any other Latin American merely because she is Latina.

Because there is a tendency among Richmond Anglos to assume that Latinos in the area are all Mexicans (the largest Latino group in Richmond, after all), and because Mexican immigrants and Mexican Americans are subject to particular disapprobation in Richmond, other Latinos sometimes demonstrate an anti-Mexican bias. A Colombian immigrant who has lived in the United States for thirteen years told us that he "tries to avoid associating with Mexicans because they are 'peleadores' and get into fights easily." Others conflate ethnicity with the difficulties faced by less-assimilated, low-wage recent immigrants: "Most of the Mexicans from my area are those involved in yard work or construction. Most have broken English," one had to say. A third-generation Mexican American himself, he was annoyed because the newer arrivals result in the employees at local convenience stores speaking loudly and slowly to *anyone* who looks of Latino heritage, because the employees expect they cannot speak English.

A number of our respondents commented on the lack of education and poor English of very recent immigrants, but rather than attributing these problems to structural conditions related to immigration, they blamed the immigrants for not trying hard enough to become assimilated. A Guatemalan white collar worker, fifteen years in the United States, said that "immigrants typically don't try as hard to get educated." A more sympathetic respondent, a second-generation Mexican skilled laborer, remarked that although immigrants are hard workers, he wished "they realized where they are and assimilated themselves more within the culture, [and] that they speak more English." Even recent immigrants commented on the failures of other immigrants. According to one Mexican immigrant who works as a roofer, four years in the United States, the Mexican immigrants from La Sierra "are not well educated, without good nutrition, and they are easily misled, misused. Often they speak dialects, and Spanish is not their first language."

Immigrant or not, another aspect that divides Richmond Latinos is whether Latinos should unite in a show of solidarity against Anglo prejudice and discrimination. Some see in such an effort a form of victimization, emphasizing poor treatment by Anglos rather than individual responsibility to adapt. Others remarked that certain groups, whatever the ethnicity, go out of their way to create a separate identity that distances them from others. This distancing is expressed in a fixation on the country of origin or a retention of the original culture at the expense of assimilating, something that was very troubling to some Richmond Latinos. "Many Hispanics come here and expect the U.S. to adapt to their wants and needs. For example, [in terms of] learning English, some families only teach Spanish in their home. If they liked it that much, stay there," remarked a thirty-year-old systems specialist, a woman who migrated from El Salvador when she was nine. Her words echo the thoughts of some of our country's more conservative white natives about the foreign-born.

The perceived differences between Latinos—immigrants versus non-immigrants, Mexicans versus other ethnicities, educated versus not educated, those who learn English versus those who have not—often reflect underlying class-based differences. Although most respondents did not categorize these differences by social class, one elderly Cuban woman who had fled her home-land four decades ago made this insightful argument. "There are many different kinds of Latinos. [But] it's a class level more than culture." Class-based distinc-tions are revealed when Latinos discuss the social status of non-immigrant Latinos (those who have been in the United States longer are seen as better off) or when they try to differentiate among narrower Latino identities. Moreover, a number of behaviors that respondents described as cultural "choices"— speaking English or not, becoming acculturated or not—reveal differential access to economic and other opportunities. Judging from the evidence, social station plays a greater role in differentiating Latinos than their perceived ethnic differences.

Settling in Richmond

Until recently, immigrant groups tended to cluster in the United States as close to their country of origin as possible. These clusters usually formed as large ethnic enclaves. That view is moderated by scholars who argue that professional and entrepreneur immigrants have greater mobility, being able to choose whether or not to move away from such ethnic enclaves. Their mobility serves as a prelude for the movement of other, less-well-off groups, who can then provide Latino elites with services related to their cultural roots.

What we find in Richmond, Virginia, is an unexpected and far richer set of migratory experiences. Although Richmond Latinos form primarily an immigrant community, paths to Richmond, length of stay, and reasons for coming to the area are diverse. Some of our respondents did indeed come from large urban enclaves. But some came to Richmond straight from their homelands. Others are long-term residents who lived in the United States for decades and moved around different regions of the country before settling in central Virginia. A few were actually born in Richmond.

The Latino community in Richmond differs considerably on a number of variables: length of time in the United States, length of time in Richmond, countries of origin, and regions from which they migrated in the United States. Some Richmond Latinos came to the United States for family reasons or to escape war and persecution back home, but economic reasons were the foremost motivation for most of the community, whether middle- or working-class. Similarly, occupational and educational opportunities attracted half of the respondents to Richmond itself, while only one-third came to the area for family reasons.

Southern newspaper accounts portray Latinos as laborers, usually of one particular ethnicity (most of the Hispanics working the chicken processing plants, as farm hands, or in textile industries are Mexican). As a result, the image of the Southern Latino experience is subsumed into that of one monolithic group. Instead, Latinos who settle in Richmond fall into several distinct segments: The first wave of Richmond Latinos was marked by professionals and business-owners. In the chapters to follow we demonstrate how they are more likely to exemplify the traditional model of assimilation, opting for dominant white middle-class values. The second wave of Richmond Latinos brought more middle-class along with working-class immigrants to the area. These individuals tend to be marked by the "selective acculturation" pathway, moving to Richmond for its economic opportunities, but aware of the desirability of preserving their cultural integrity. A much smaller group did move out of more discriminatory and problematic urban areas, seeking solace for themselves and their families while avoiding a minority-identified urban underclass life for their children. Recently, new immigrants have even moved in directly from their countries of origin.

Underlying the Latino resettlement experiences in Richmond is the unifying force of class rather than culture. Richmond Latinos, especially those who are middle-class, take pains to differentiate themselves from Southern whites, African Americans, and even new Latino migrants to the area. Relationships with others, as predicated by segmented assimilation theory, involve a careful adaptation of some values and avoidance of others related to skin color and ethnicity. In this way, social class unites Latinos rather than national origin or ethnicity, although only *within* social classes. In the next chapters we illustrate how these processes of differentiation are structural instead of based on overt class antagonisms or desires to differentiate, as predicted by segmented assimilation theory. Subtle class-based assimilation processes, rather than an explicit antagonism, separate Latinos.

Chapter 4

Living in Multiple Worlds

I am very proud of my heritage—in terms of getting a job, it has been an asset, not a liability. My parents had a rich background and I am proud of them.

—Forty-nine-year-old Cuban education consultant

Moving into a new area entails a series of adaptations: settling into another neighborhood, learning the local culture, finding new service networks (banking, schools, clinics, shopping), and establishing new social relationships. For anyone who grew up in the United States, the experience requires a series of usually small adjustments and the willingness to be sensitive to the cultural differences of a new region. For someone coming from another country, especially someone whose ethnicity or culture is not traditionally associated with the area, moving can involve a more complex series of negotiations, especially if you do not have the safe boundaries of an ethnic community to join.

While there is no clear theoretical framework that describes every path to immigrant incorporation, there are indicators to gauge how well immigrants negotiate their resettlement in a host area. Being in a new country means living in multiple worlds, at least for a time, with varying degrees of comfort in either the old or the new. Some of the issues at stake in this complex process include the use of the host versus the original language, the level of social distance one keeps from new neighbors and colleagues of other ethnic groups, and the preservation of the culture of origin at home, through practices such as the cooking of ethnic foods and listening to music in one's native language. These multiple worlds can overlap in some instances, while remaining perfectly detached in others. In this chapter, we examine several factors that predict the extent to which Latinos in Richmond adjust to living in two worlds—identifying with dominant values or minority values in the host culture (which means losing that first world), or selectively acculturating to life in the United States. As with other aspects of the immigrant experience, we argue that social class plays a predominant role in this determination (Negy and Woods 1992).

Latino Assimilation in Richmond

Acculturation is a multidimensional process. For example, Gordon (1964) distinguishes between cultural and structural assimilation. For cultural assimilation in the United States, he includes acquisition of the English language, dress, and outward emotional expression, and the adoption of dominant U.S. values. Structural assimilation, on the other hand, is related to an ethnic group's integration into the organizations and institutions of the host society. The more a group enters into primary group relations with members of the host society, the more structural assimilation has occurred.

In this section, we explore Latino cultural assimilation through three measures: language assimilation, media usage, and the resilience of ethnic customs, including ethnic food preparation. Each concept is measured in several ways. Latinos in Richmond show high levels of English usage and significant incorporation of Anglo customs. But unlike what is predicted by traditional assimilation models, these behaviors are not always accompanied by a simultaneous decrease in the use of Spanish or other cultural traits. After discussing the basic levels of adaptation, we look at the predictors of Latino assimilation, including social class.

Adoption of the host country's language is perhaps the strongest indicator of assimilation (Hoffman 1989), especially in the United States, where "English only" is the main requirement for full membership in society (Lieberson 1981; López 1982; Veltman 1983). Language use among Latinos in the United States varies considerably by nativity. In one study, immigrant Latinos reported speaking "limited English" 65 percent of the time, while only 30 percent said that they spoke English "very well" (Cafferty 2000:76). In Virginia, in particular, English usage is low for Hispanic residents, especially recent immigrants. For those who have lived in the United States fewer then five years, more than two-thirds do not speak English well, although this rate falls the longer immigrants have lived in the United States ("Hispanic Immigrants and Citizens in Virginia" 2007). About 60 percent of U.S.-born Latinos, however, predominantly speak English, while one-third are bilingual (Nieves 2002). Studies show that the majority of second-generation ethnic groups are fluent in English, to the point where one-half to three-quarters of the groups surveyed preferred to speak English over the parental language (Portes and Rumbaut 1996).

Measuring language assimilation requires examining two dimensions of usage, not just one: use of Spanish, and use of English. Language assimilation is neither one-dimensional nor a linear process of adaptation; high fluency in one does not rule out high fluency in the other (Cuellar et al. 1995). One could have a high fluency in both, only one, or even neither language. For respondents who are bilingual, use of both English and Spanish might be a necessary part of assimilation rather than indicate incompleteness along a path to being fully assimilated. For these reasons, we measure language usage in a number of ways designed to gauge its multidimensional nature among Latinos in Richmond.

Richmond Latinos are remarkably comfortable using English in everyday life, especially compared to the rest of the state. In fact, about half of the respondents said they speak English "extremely often or almost always." Some 14 percent said they do not speak English very often, but less than 1 percent speak no English at all. Speaking English, however, does not detract from the use of Spanish. Although one-quarter of those surveyed speak Spanish very seldom or not at all, 30 percent of the sample said that they almost always speak Spanish. Almost one-third said that they speak both English and Spanish either "most of the time" or "almost always" (that is, they are bilingually competent).

The fact that approximately 70 percent of our interviews were conducted in English is another indicator of high English fluency (respondents were able to choose the language of the interview). Of course, many native Spanish speakers were interested in practicing their English, but respondents who requested a Spanish interviewer may have been doing so to practice their Spanish (or perhaps to demonstrate to us or themselves the importance of their cultural heritage), rather than because their English abilities were low. Often our student interviewers had to remind one another to take both sets of survey forms to each interview, one in English and one in Spanish, because they did not always know which language would turn out to be the predominant language. Sometimes interviews begun in Spanish switched over to English when it was ascertained that both interviewer and respondent were actually more fluent in English.

Setting, of course, matters in language use. Language use can be an example of living in multiple worlds, perhaps using the predominant language as one associates with the larger Richmond world, while maintaining one's mother tongue in the intimacy of relatives. Immigrants may use a host language to economic advantage (in work, for example), but return to the native language for personal use. Thirty-eight percent said they speak only or mostly Spanish at home, and more than 50 percent speak only or mostly Spanish at family gatherings. With friends, however, the majority of Richmond Latinos (55 percent) speak English. Even within one setting, however, there is some fluctuation. Some immigrants speak English with family in the United States, but not with family when they visit "home." Married respondents might speak English with his family, but not with hers: "There [are] some family [members] who don't know English and they only know Spanish, there [are] some family who don't know Spanish and only know English." Such vast disparities in communication provide a distinct character to living the immigrant life.

Thus, we observe that Latinos in Richmond are slightly more likely to use English than Spanish in many settings, although neither predominates. We compiled the five measures of language use together—use of English (with values reversed), use of Spanish, language at home, language at family gatherings, and language with friends—into a language use index. The average score for the index is 3.2, where a score of one indicates most use of Spanish and a score of five indicates most use of English. In other words, it appears that Richmond Latinos tend to speak English and Spanish about equally, albeit with a slightly higher use of English, at least in the aggregate.

The language of one's popular culture choices is another strong indicator of assimilation, both of language ability and of the allure of a new culture compared to the old. When moving to a new country, immigrants face the process of learning not just another language, but the language of another culture. Even when using the host language in other arenas, they might hold on to native ways in their use of media and other entertainment, looking at their host society through a cultural prism they bring with them. Conversely, immigrants may begin to adopt the popular cultural tastes shared by the majority of U.S. citizens (Birman 1994; Negy and Woods 1992; Padilla 1980; Szapocznik and Kurtines 1980).

To measure that aspect of language assimilation—language of media use—we asked Richmond Latinos how they used English or Spanish in media-related activities: listening to music or the radio, reading newspapers and magazines, and watching television and movies. Respondents were hampered in their answers somewhat by the fact that although some types of Spanish media are available in Richmond, not all in the sample were aware of or have equal access to them. So, for example, although there are Spanish programs broadcast by a radio station in nearby Ashland and in a Latino station in Richmond, not all respondents have heard of them. Other media are available only under certain conditions (e.g., Univision, if one has a cable subscription, but then only in certain counties of the greater Richmond area). We have no way of knowing whether use of media in Spanish would have been higher had residents been aware of them and had access. So our results should be interpreted with a little caution.

Nonetheless, when we look at the one item where all respondents theoretically had equal access—music—almost half of our respondents said that they listened equally to music (tapes, compact discs, etc.) in both Spanish and English. For the other media, one-third or more (up to 45 percent for films) reported participating exclusively in English. The average for the five items indexed is 3.8, with a four indicating "mostly English." This demonstrates that in the aggregate English is the more prevalent language for these forms of media participation, slightly more so than for everyday face-to-face interaction.

To measure structural assimilation, we looked at social distance. Shibutani and Kwan (1965) describe social distance as a central measure of assimilation, a subjective state of physical proximity experienced among individuals of different groups. Greater social contact with Anglos rather than Latinos suggests greater assimilation into the dominant culture. The more social distance is reduced, the more structural assimilation takes place (Welch and Sigelman 2000). For instance, Welch and Sigelman found that modest contact with Anglos was positively related to other measures of assimilation, although Latinos were still more likely to mingle with members of their own ethnic group than with Anglos. For our social distance measure, we inquired with whom Latinos were more likely to associate (are they primarily Anglo, primarily mixed, primarily Latino, or something else?) in six settings: as friends, as neighbors, as co-workers, as church associates, as playmates for one's child, and at parties.

Latinos in our sample typically associate with a mix of other Latinos and Anglos, although there is considerable variation based on the setting (58 percent of respondents said the groups were "mixed" for friends, 53 percent for the places respondents relax and have fun, 52 percent for the friends of one's children, and 45 percent for work colleagues). Neighbors and fellow churchgoers, on the other hand, are likely to be Anglos (54 and 38 percent, respectively). When all six variables are indexed, the average value is 1.77 (values range from 1 to 3; a high value on the index indicates greater affiliation with other Latinos and less social interaction with Anglos). Richmond Latinos, then, are generally slightly more in contact with Anglos rather than Latinos, although given the small size and geographic dispersion of the Richmond Latino community, the amount of continued Latino contact is quite large.

Yet another way to look at the process of assimilation is to measure the resilience of an immigrant's ethnic customs (Waters 1990). Certain language and cultural activities may denote a necessary adaptation to the world of the host society, but daily routines provide an important measure of the newcomer's closer embrace (or the lack thereof) of his or her new nation's customs (Bernal and Knight 1993; Gil and Vazquez 1996; Martinez 1994). To measure the retention of ethnic customs for Latinos in Richmond, we asked the respondents about the dominant customs used in their homes. Their responses to this question indicate a less thorough assimilation process than language usage does.

When Latinos were asked whether the dominant customs in one's home are Anglo, Latino, a combination of the two, or some other set of customs, the most common response was Latino (about 40 percent of the respondents chose this option). Thirty-two percent said mixed, and about 26 percent said that Anglo customs dominate in their homes (although in some cases this may have meant more of a hybrid; as one respondent put it, "Anglo with a Latino flavor"). The remaining 1 percent said they had yet other customs—in one case black, and two others were unclear.[1]

What exactly distinguishes Anglo from Latino customs, for our respondents? People, for the most part, do agree that there are differences between Latin American customs and Anglo customs (or what one Puerto Rican respondent referred to as "the American Way"). Some feel these differences have to do with respect for one's elders, caring for others, or the meaning of friendship. For example, one respondent argued that friendship in the United States was based much more on short-term gains in a relationship. Respondents also discussed differences in more emotional or physical customs, such as cheek-kiss greetings. Personality traits are relevant: "Our liveliness is something we add to the American culture," stressed a Cuban respondent. "Even when taking on American traditions and customs, I hope we never lose our spice." Finally, the people we talked to played up the Latino/Anglo differences in family values, which we discuss more thoroughly in chapter 5.

Concern with preserving customs from one's homeland also means promoting Latino traditions, art, even a way of life. A good number of respondents complained about the lack of Spanish radio stations, or the lack of other media such as a newspaper or films in Spanish. For many respondents, however, safeguarding Latino culture does not come at the exclusion of incorporation. A Guatemalan who had migrated to the United States fifteen years previously told us, "I think keeping your culture is extremely important, but you must also accept the culture surrounding you. In other words, be open-minded and accepting." It is clear that many want to be, and feel it is possible to be, bicultural—a positive aspect of living in two worlds.

As a fifth measure of assimilation, we asked about one specific household custom, the cooking of foods from one's country of origin. Cooking foods from home is another important indicator of how Richmond Latinos often straddle multiple worlds. Ethnic cooking remains far after other vestiges of ethnic life are gone, ethnic cooking being one aspect of "symbolic ethnicity," the voluntary celebration of one's ethnicity (Waters 1990). Richmond has numerous neighborhood Latino grocery shops and supermarkets, and the availability of ingredients used in Latin American cooking has increased in the mainstream food shops in the city in the last decade. It is relatively easy for a Latino family to maintain a regular diet of traditional dishes. Indeed, cooking is a durable custom for Latinos in Richmond. Most of our respondents say that they cooked ethnic foods at least some of the time, with 60 percent reporting cooking dishes from their home regions much or all of the time. And yet we find Richmond Latinos also enjoying their fair share of whatever they perceive to be "American" foods. In the words of a Dominican immigrant, "I cook certain things from my home country, a mixture. I like both. Fifty-fifty....There are a lot of American dishes that I really like."[2]

As we predicted, all our measures of assimilation are positively related to social class, measured here with household income. The language use index is directly correlated to household income: the higher one's income, the more likely he or she is to use English rather than Spanish in these settings (r = .43). For media usage, those better off economically are more likely to use English over Spanish (r = .36). In terms of social distance, Latinos with higher incomes are more likely to associate with Anglos than other Latinos or a mix of groups (r = -.53). Those with higher incomes are the least likely to cook ethnic foods on a regular basis (r = -.24). All of these relationships are significant at the .001 level, which is to say that the observed relationships between each of the two sets of variables would be likely to happen by chance only one time in a thousand. For Richmond, presence in a higher social class is related to a greater familiarity with the dominant culture.

Examining Anglo, Latino, or some combination of the two, the dominant customs of a household vary considerably by income as well. Respondents with Latino-dominant customs have significantly lower incomes, almost a whole income bracket, than those who do not. However, this could be merely a function of length in the United States, a variable also significantly related to customs and other assimilation measures (for example, second- or third-generation immigrants are more likely to use English, and less likely to speak Spanish). Those who have recently arrived are significantly most likely to say that their customs are Latino, and very unlikely to choose Anglo (only 3 percent chose that response). Native-born Latinos, on the other hand, report just the opposite, with more than one-half labeling their household customs as Anglo. Those who have been here at least twenty years are about evenly divided among the three main types (Latino, Anglo and mixed).[3]

To understand the impact of income independent of this intervening factor, we ran three analyses: one for immigrants in the country fewer than twenty years, one for those here twenty years or more, and one for U.S.-born Latinos (Figure 4.1). Even when we do this, the original relationship between income and dominant customs holds true regardless of time in the United States. Second-generation Latinos have higher incomes than immigrant Latinos, but those with Latino customs, rather than mixed or Anglo, have the lowest incomes of the group. Similarly, even relatively recent immigrants with higher incomes are more likely to say that Anglo customs predominate in their lives.

To further examine the relationship between income and our assimilation measures, we ran several multiple regressions. We suspect that some of the observed relationship between income and assimilation could be a result of time in the United States (the longer one is in the country, the more opportunities both for greater cultural adaptation and for economic prosperity). Similarly, differing economic opportunities in one's home country might affect social status upon arrival as well as ease of acculturation once here. In either case, measures of assimilation that appear to be affected by income might in fact be the result of one's country of origin (or ancestry) and longevity in the host country.[4] Our regression results show that three of the assimilation variables are also significantly related to time in the United States, although country of origin (at least when examining the three largest ancestries—Mexican, Salvadoran, and Puerto Rican—using dummy variables for the presence or

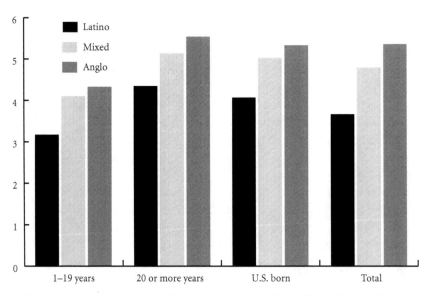

Figure 4.1. Average Income by Dominant Customs at Home, Controlling for Time in the United States

absence of those ancestries) matters less in explaining assimilation (Table 4.1). Even controlling for time in the United States and country of origin, economic status as measured by income affects adaptation to the United States for all the assimilation variables.

Ethnic Identification

The process of juggling multiple worlds while adapting to a new country may result in significant alterations to one's identity. Ethnic identity, in particular, involves issues regarding authenticity of self in social interaction. Migration requires developing a sense of self that allows for daily functioning in a new environment, while also struggling to preserve parts of a previous self. Clinging completely to the original identity might impede one's functioning in the host country, but giving it up would mean losing important personal resources, both psychological and social.

Assimilation theorists in the United States have historically posited that immigrant generations moved from identification with one's home country to a feeling of being (merely) "American." Gordon refers to "identity assimilation,"

Table 4.1. Unstandardized Coefficients from OLS Regressions of Socioeconomic and Demographic Variables on Assimilation Measures (Standard Errors in Parentheses)

	Language Use	MediaUse	Social Distance	Ethnic Cooking
Household Income	.142**	.113**	-.112**	-.152*
	(.027)	(.028)	(.014)	(.044)
Time in the U.S.	.774**	.457*	-.175**	-.112
	(.063)	(.064)	(.032)	(.102)
Puerto Rican	.072	-.028	.140*	-.001
	(.123)	(.132)	(.063)	(.201)
Mexican	-.163	-.274*	.184**	.179
	(.113)	(.118)	(.057)	(.185)
Salvadoran	-.387*	.098	.276**	.179
	(.152)	(.159)	(.077)	(.248)
Intercept	1.075	2.456	2.509	4.533
	(.150)	(.163)	(.076)	(.246)
R-Squared	.534	.299	.392	.068

*$p < .05$; **$p < .01$
Source: Latinos in Richmond Survey.

or gaining a sense of identity that is linked to the core society. Usually the process was assumed to be linear and one-way; for example, moving over the course of three or four generations from being Irish to being Irish American to finally becoming a generic "American" citizen (Waters 1990). The end result was that one's original ethnic identity was largely erased, except for a few occasions a year when celebrating ethnic holidays or consuming ethnic meals.

There are some notable and clearly problematic exceptions to this theory of ethnic adaptation, which is after all based primarily on white ethnic immigration. African Americans, for example, regardless of level of assimilation, have never been able truly to shed a nondominant identity, although the identity is a racial one, rather than of a particular country of origin. African Americans have never been "just" Americans. For recent immigrant populations, as well, it is not clear that the process will be quite as straightforward as in the past. Moreover, new theories of immigrant incorporation question the likelihood of assimilation at all. They inquire whether immigrants must give up previous identities in order to adapt, arguing for the possibility of maintaining original ethnic identity even in the pursuit of economic and social acceptance through the creation of a bicultural hybrid.

Latinos contend with socially constructed identities that are unique to being Latino in the United States (Fox 1996; Rodriguez 2000). The official governmental label for Latin America immigrants to the United Status and their offspring is Hispanic, although such an identity exists nowhere else in the world. Upon arrival, immigrants may also learn of the more politicized ethnic identity of "Latino," often chosen by people who do not identify solely with a Spanish ancestry. Or they may adopt or hold onto ethno-political identities specific to country or culture of origin (Mexican American, Chicano, Puerto Rican, Boricua, etc.). In a national survey conducted by the Pew Hispanic Center in 2002, researchers found that 54 percent of all Latinos preferred their country of origin when describing their ethnicity, while 24 percent said Hispanic or Latino, and only 21 percent chose "American" (Brodie et al. 2002).

We suspected the choice of ethnic label might vary by region in the United States, but were not sure what the new arrivals to the South would favor, as compared to other parts of the nation (although the Southern media invariably refers to those with Latin American ancestry as "Hispanic," not Latino). And in Richmond, "Hispanic" does appear to be the ethnic label of choice. When asked the open-ended question, "What do you consider to be your ethnicity?" 42 percent of the respondents gave this label. Just exactly what this created identity meant is unclear for some. "To be Hispanic is to be Mexican? What is it to be Hispanic?" queried an Argentine respondent, who gave his ethnicity as "mestizo." Only 13 percent choose "Latino," a term favored in western states, but not as common in the Southeast.

Some respondents, however, do not like either label, not wishing to be forced into an identity. One of our Peruvian respondents, for example, argued that "Latino" is itself an artificial label, because he believes that Latinos should be identified by their country of origin. Respondents feel these bureaucratic markers are incapable of allowing for individual differences or differences between Spanish-speaking peoples. A Puerto Rican man informs all of those who ask him that he is Puerto Rican, not anything else. He has hung the island's flag in both his apartment and his car. According to him, the terms *Latino* and *Hispanic* create potential stereotypes by consolidating all Latin American immigrants. His identity as Puerto Rican extends beyond ethnicity; once, a speeding ticket listed his race as white, which made him quite irate. His race, as he indicated on our survey, is the same as his ethnicity: Puerto Rican. His reaction to the police problematizes the bureaucratic separation of ethnicity and race. As for many of our respondents, race and ethnicity are the same, or much more complex than most administrative decisions allow room for.

Almost one-third (31 percent) of our respondents referred to themselves according to the ethnicity of their country of origin.[5] These Latinos think it is quite difficult to lump people from Latin America together indiscriminately, and make sure that we know it. "When [you] speak of Latin Americans, think of British / Australian / American. We speak the same language, but we're all different! We will even talk [i.e., negatively] about each other—we have internal pride, and our own ethnicities. Generalizing is tough," said a respondent from Colombia who emigrated as an adolescent. Independent of the particular choice, however, ethnic identity is of marked importance to Latinos in Richmond. More than 70 percent responded that their ethnicity (however they defined it) is very important to them.

If we were making assumptions about ethnic identity transition based on a traditional assimilationist model, we might predict that recent immigrants would identify most strongly with their home countries, and that "Hispanic" or "Latino" would be interim identities, adopted by those who have already negotiated some of the elements of the new culture, as they learn the term unique to our country for people of Latin American descent. The most assimilated Latinos, as their earlier European counterparts did, would become simply "American." But this is not the case for Richmond Latinos. Those who use either the Hispanic or Latino label are more likely to be immigrants, and among those immigrants, those who have been in this country the least amount of time (see Figure 4.2). In fact, more than 70 percent of those who have been in this country less than twenty years prefer the terms *Hispanic* or *Latino*. U.S-born Latinos *are* more likely to refer to themselves as "American" (around 20 percent) than either recent or long-term immigrants, but are even likelier to continue to identify as Hispanic/Latino (37 percent), or even by their country of origin (34 percent), than as American.

Ethnic identity is closely associated with time in the United States, suggesting a pattern of assimilation that resembles traditional assimilationist theory and yet negates it. Supporting the former, over time our respondents grow more likely refer to themselves as American (Figure 4.2). However, though Latino, and particularly Hispanic, labels *do* decline the longer one has lived in the United States, they remain strong even among second-generation Latinos (recall that when we asked respondents about the use of "Latino" customs in the home, this phrase was understood by most respondents and accepted as salient). Although one would expect allegiance to country of origin to disappear early on among immigrants, perhaps even as they adopt pan-ethnic terms such as "Hispanic," such a sense of self actually increases the longer one has been in this country. For instance, a Cuban respondent who came to the United States at the age of fourteen and has been here for forty-three years argued

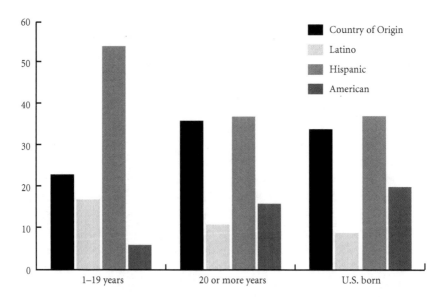

Figure 4.2 Ethnic Identification by Time in the United States

that he had "wanted U.S. citizenship to be a 'free man,'" but he feels first and foremost that he is Cuban. Second-generation youth, in particular, are more likely to shift away from early identification as Americans to a more ethnic or national identity (Portes and Rumbaut 2001b). Rather than a clear pattern of linear, one-way assimilation, what we see is a more selective acculturation pattern, with some people becoming more ethnically identified over time with their country of origin.

The choice of ethnic label does vary considerably by age (young Latinos are most likely to use Hispanic or Latino) and by ancestry. Figure 4.3 provides the percentages that choose each label for the five largest Latino groups in Richmond. Salvadorans and Guatemalans are the most likely to call themselves Hispanic or Latino (more than three-quarters do so). Cubans, on the other hand, most often refer to themselves as Cubans, while Mexicans and Puerto Ricans are about equally like to give their ethnicity as either Hispanic or their country of origin. Of all of the ancestry groups, it is "other Central Americans" who are the most likely to use the label "American," at 27 percent (not shown).

Tied to ethnic identity are our first three measures of assimilation, but in ways that again tweak at the expected pattern of greater assimilation over time,

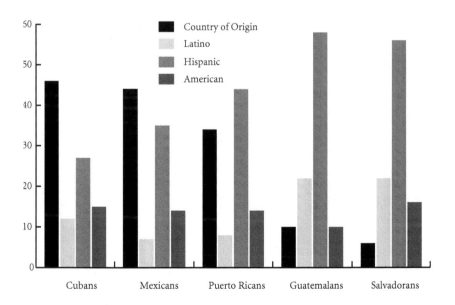

Figure 4.3. Ethnic Identification (in percentages) by Ancestry
for Five Largest Ancestry Groups

especially the notion that "becoming American" is central to such adaptation. Certainly, those most assimilated in terms of language use, media use, and social distance are more likely to call themselves "American," while "Latino" is used by those who were the least likely to use English over Spanish and the most likely to associate with other Latinos (Figure 4.4). Those using the country of origin labels or "Hispanic" fall in the middle when it comes to those measures of assimilation. However, there are not huge differences in levels of assimilation for any of the identity choices, which suggests no clear pattern between degree of assimilation and preferred ethnic label.

As an important and highly significant predictor of ethnic identity, income has a bit more extrapolative value than the assimilation variables do. Those who identify as Latinos have the lowest incomes, averaging $25,000 to $35,000. An entire income bracket above them are those who use the country of origin and Hispanic labels, while those who see themselves as American fall in the highest income bracket of all (averaging $50,000–75,000). These differences hold even if you control for immigrant status; even immigrants with higher incomes are more likely to refer to themselves as American.

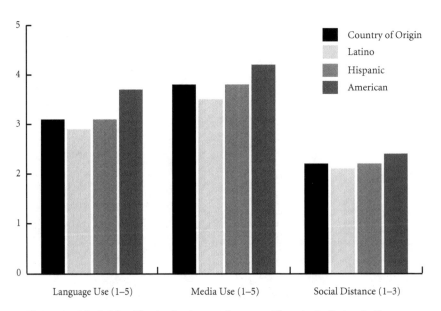

Figure 4.4. Ethnic Identification by Average Scores on Three Assimilation Indices

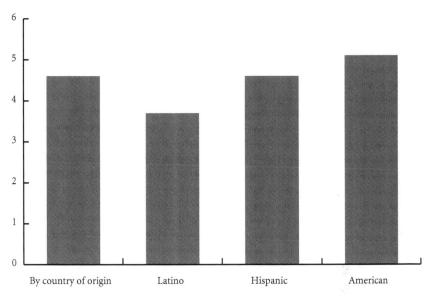

Figure 4.5. Average Income by Ethnic Identification

Racial Identification

In addition to the labels referring to ethnicity, immigrant adaptation in the twenty-first century must also contend with the additional connection between ethnicity and racial identification, as we already discussed somewhat in chapter 3. For many Latinos, race is a cultural and social term as much as it is a referent to biological traits such as skin tone (Landale and Oropesa 2002; Rodriguez 2000). Some Latinos adopt the dominant cultural dichotomy (black and white), while other assign color descriptors in Spanish to their sense of self, or identify their race as Hispanic or Latino. There appears to be a growing preference for pan-ethnic terms, especially among second-generation immigrants. Evidence from the third wave of the Children of Immigrants Longitudinal study shows that the children of immigrants prefer "Asian" or "Hispanic" when describing their race (Portes and Rumbaut 2006:258). Some Latinos adopt a racial categorization that shifts depending on social context or who is asking the question, identifying as white in some situations, Latino in others, or even black in a third (Rodriguez 2000:139).

Indeed, many of our respondents grapple with our question about race.[6] We asked an open-ended, "What ethnicity do you think of yourself as?"

followed by "Do you think of yourself as: white, black, or some other race?" with a prompt to define the third option. Respondents mix racial categories with ethnic or ancestry terms. Even "Hispanic" (or other "middle" categories more racially defined, such as color descriptors or "mestizo") does not work for some respondents as a catch-all term. A female respondent, who gave her race as "white" and ethnicity as "Cuban," suggested, not merely to us but as a general notion, "There needs to be a broader category than just black, white or Hispanic."

In the Richmond case, most respondents offered either "white" or "Hispanic/ Latino" when asked to describe their race. Even here, however, the evidence suggests that when compared to national data, Latinos in Richmond demonstrate a greater variety in their choices. Thirty-nine percent of our respondents chose "white." Although this is also the most common racial preference chosen by Latinos nationwide (Rodriguez 2000), the percentage of our respondents who chose white is considerably lower than in recent censuses (approximately 52 percent chose white in 1980 and 1990; even in 2000, when respondents could choose more than one race, almost 48 percent of Latinos gave their race as "white alone.") About 25 percent of our sample chose "Hispanic/Latino" when describing their race, and indeed, most in this group (more than two-thirds) chose Hispanic or Latino as both their race *and* their ethnicity. About 3 percent gave their race as black, 8 percent provided a color descriptor such as brown ("morena"), 7 percent said they are of mixed race or "mestizo," and 9 percent gave their nationality or ancestry as their race.

Living in Multiple Worlds

Richmond Latinos carefully manage the ways in which they develop familiarity with the customs and language of the dominant culture. It is not a matter of learning about Richmond alone (or even Southern culture!), but becoming assimilated (or not) into the broader U.S. ways of life: learning English with a Southern accent, adopting a new cuisine, or acquiring information about the world that surrounds them, to mention only a few aspects of the process. Whether through language use, media use, social distance, or retention of customs from country of origin, Richmond Latinos have negotiated the transition without losing sight of the dual resources of their two worlds. The majority of Richmond Latinos speak English and Spanish about equally in their everyday activities (showing a slightly higher use of English), and enjoy cultural aspects from both countries when available.

To be sure, there is evidence for more traditional assimilationist experiences. Recent arrivals are those least assimilated in terms of language usage, dominant customs, and ethnic cooking (although not ethnic identity), suggesting a straight-line process. Those who are the most assimilated in terms of language and other cultural elements are also more likely to see themselves as simply "American."

At the same time, not all segments react to adaptation in the same way. A large minority of our respondents speak both English and Spanish well rather than transitioning from Spanish to English. Those who do so are more likely to use Spanish, to cook food or retain customs from the country of origin, and to associate with other Latinos. Ethnic identity remains very salient for Richmond Latinos as is maintaining one's culture of origin. Preferences to self-identify with one's country of origin increase over time. This suggests far more attention to selective acculturation practices than previously understood. More assimilated does not automatically equal "more American."

Social class has a definite imprint on the process of transition that takes place in the lives of Richmond Latinos. Income influences our measures of assimilation, even accounting for other relevant variables, such as length of time in the United States and ancestry. There is a parallel between economic well-being and familiarity with U.S. ways and customs. Whether the path is a more traditional assimilation versus a more bicultural, selective acculturation, both are largely middle-class options. Especially for those Latinos who have the economic resources and social capital, experiencing life as Hispanic becomes more like a "symbolic ethnicity"—something pleasurable and voluntary, to be taken on intermittently.

Chapter 5

Richmond Latino Families
Migrating Globally, Living Locally

Touch is important to Puerto Ricans. Social relations are warm. [There is
a] tight family unit in my home and in the homes of most Hispanics.
—Forty-eight-year-old dental hygienist

Families can provide ethnic immigrants with crucial resources to aid in their
successful integration into the mainstream (Portes and Bach 1985; Tienda
1991). Operating as an important support system, families shelter members in
emotional and financial ways (Perez 1986; Sanders and Nee 1996). Latino families, in particular, contain more extensive interactions with relatives, depend
more on each other for aid than on organizations or institutions, and have
extensive visitation networks (Mindel 1980). Moreover, literature suggests that
familialism is an important value in Latino communities, resulting in "strong
identification and attachment of individuals with their nuclear and extended
families, and strong feelings of loyalty, reciprocity, and solidarity among
members of the same family" (Marin 1993:184; see also Baca Zinn 1978).

Familialism—the importance of preserving family connectedness and interdependence—is an issue addressed by theories of assimilation. The traditional
model of assimilation, for instance, assumes that second-generation members
adjust more rapidly to their new surroundings, creating tensions and struggles
between parents and children even when successful economic and social
adaptation occurs. Alternatively, segmented assimilation theory predicts that
immigrant parents worry that they will lose their children through assimilation into a downwardly mobile minority culture. Since familialism appears to
decline with economic success and adaptation to the U.S. value system, assimilation could mean not only the loss of family members who remain behind, but
also of important family values and mechanisms that support immigrants.

More so than individuals, immigrant families struggle to balance their
connection to two worlds (Portes and Bach 1985; Rumbaut 1997). While most
of their daily activities are related to adaptation to life in a new country, they
also work on sustaining ties to relatives and others back home (Martinez 1994;
Mindel 1980). In fact, a number of our respondents report that questions that

made reference to one's "home" are not easy to ask of an immigrant population. Does home refer to one's homeland? Does it refer to the city where one
currently resides, regardless of the level of comfort one feels there? Some still
talk with sadness about home as the place where they grew up: *home* is what
was left behind, perhaps even the place to which they may someday return.
Remember the Cuban immigrant mentioned in chapter 4 who will always feel
Cuban first. He suggested that he might like to retire in Cuba "if the political
ambience changes positively." For some respondents, no place is really home;
others, however, quite emphatically argue that they have made Richmond their
home.

In this chapter, we look at family life for Richmond Latinos. We explore
family composition, the effect of Anglo culture on child rearing, and how
immigrant status, ethnicity, and social class help predict the way Latinos feel
about the importance of family life. The balance between two worlds is clear
from the start: Richmond Latinos indicate the importance of raising their
children in their native culture. However, they also value U.S. education—both
for the positive consequences of educational attainment and for preservation
of their cultural heritage. Their support for bilingual education in the school
system, especially in light of perceived threats to family from life in the United
States and the possibility of downward mobility, demonstrates the salience of
the segmented assimilation model.

Latino Family Life in Richmond

We begin by providing some demographics to set the context for Latino family
life in Richmond. Richmond's Latino community is marked by two traits: many
families with children, and a sizable group of people living alone. Latinos have
higher rates of married couples with children under eighteen than non-Latinos
in Richmond (according to census data, almost half of the Latino population,
but only 40 percent of non-Latinos). Latinos in our sample have even higher
rates of families in that category, at 57 percent (see Figure 5.1). While the
Richmond census reports that female heads of households comprise 18 percent
of the Latino population of Richmond (though fewer than for Richmond
overall), we sampled only 8 percent (probably because these mothers are more
difficult to locate). We were more successful at locating households headed
by single fathers (9 percent of the sampled families, versus 13 percent in the
census report).

About 20 percent of Richmond Latino respondents live in nonfamily households or alone (according to census data, 19 percent of Latinos households

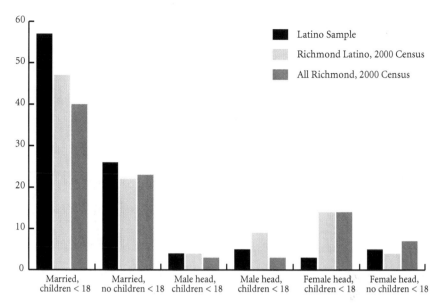

Figure 5.1. Family Composition for Richmond Latinos and All Residents
            (in Percentages)
Source: Latinos in Richmond Survey: Census 2000

nationally are nonfamily [Ramirez 2004]). Based on our data, these nonfamily households typically consist of single men; in some cases, but certainly not all, temporary migrants. Nonfamily households are almost twice as likely to house non-immigrants as immigrants. About two-thirds of these households are single males living alone, and most of the rest are two unrelated male room-mates. There are only a handful of respondents who live with several unrelated friends.

To some extent, economic factors, including household income, are related to the arrangement of households among Latinos in Richmond. Non-immigrant married couples, with or without children, have the highest incomes (averaging between $50,000 and $75,000), followed by female householders and then male householders (Table 5.1).[1] Nonfamily households have the lowest incomes in the sample (averaging on the low side of $35,000, especially for immigrants). Our research corroborates patterns found by Blank and Torrecilha (1998) that family composition varies by the immigrant status of the respondent: immigrants are more likely to live in married couple families with children. Even controlling for immigrant status, however, average incomes differ significantly for each type of family.[2]

Table 5.1. Average Household Income, by Household Type and Immigrant Status

	Average Household Income[a]	
Household Type	Immigrant* Mean	Non-Immigrant** Mean
Family Household		
Married Couple		
With children under 18	4.5	5.5
No children under 18	4.8	5.9
Male head of household	3.8	4.3
Female head of household	4.7	4.3
Non-family household	3.1	4.0
Total	4.5	5.0

[a]Income: $1 = <14{,}999$, $2 = 15{,}000–24{,}999$, $3 = 25{,}000–34{,}999$, $4 = 35{,}000–49{,}999$, $5 = 50{,}000–74{,}999$, $6 = 75{,}000–99{,}999$, $7 = 100{,}000+$.

*$f=5.49$, $p < .001$, $N = 97$

**$f=5.52$, $p < .001$, $N = 193$

Source: Latinos in Richmond Survey.

When we look at Latino households in terms of *generational* composition, we find a high number of extended families in the area (about 15 percent of our sample). They range from adult siblings living together, all the way to several generations of the same family residing in the same household (Figure 5.2). Quite a few of the extended family arrangements are not two or more direct generations. About three-quarters of the extended family category includes sisters, brothers, aunts, uncles, and/or cousins living together. There is also a tendency for Latino adult children to live with their parents (an additional 8 percent of the sample). Although technically those families would qualify as nuclear, the arrangement suggests a different form of family organization. The only reason we do not characterize these families as extended families is that the adult children have not yet had children of their own.

As with family composition, different generational living arrangements vary considerably, and significantly, by economic and cultural factors. Again, nonfamily households have the lowest incomes (in the $25,000 to 35,000 range), and nuclear families without children have the highest (the $50,000 to $74,000 range), differing on average more than two income brackets. Extended families tend to fall in the middle, with average incomes comparable to other types of arrangements that involve children. Also, the average income for extended families is not significantly different from the average household income for the

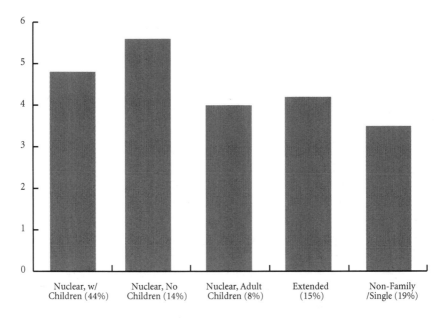

Figure 5.2. Average Household Income by Household Generational Composition

whole sample. Extended family arrangements may indeed be a survival strategy for newly arrived working-class migrants, supplying a family with additional earners to provide economic resources.

Respondents who are members of extended families all score significantly lower on our four ordinal assimilation variables, supporting earlier evidence that there is a relationship between family living arrangements and successful adaptation. Education and occupational prestige are related to whether or not Latinos in Richmond live in extended or nuclear arrangements. Respondents from extended families have the lowest levels of education and occupational prestige. Years lived in the United States and country of origin are also important: immigrants are more likely to live in extended families (18 percent versus 7 percent of non-immigrants), and among immigrants, those who are more recent arrivals are more likely to have such arrangements. Again, our findings substantiate those of Blank and Torrecilha, who argue that the extended family is a common survival strategy for recent immigrants. In terms of ancestry, Salvadorans (25 percent), Guatemalans (36 percent) and Mexicans (18 percent) are the most likely of the largest ancestry groups to live in extended families (results not shown), although married couples with children under eighteen are the most common arrangement for all ethnic groups.

Household size is another indicator of how family demographics differ for Richmond Latinos. The average Latino household in our sample consists of 3.4 people (compared to an average of 2.6 persons for U.S. families overall), but there is considerable variation in family size based on immigrant status (see Table 5.2). Recent immigrants have the largest households, with an average size of 3.7 family members (the average for Latino immigrants in Virginia overall in 2007 is 3.6, "Hispanic Immigrants and Citizens in Virginia"). Households headed by Latinos who have lived in the United States for at least twenty years are somewhat smaller, while Latinos born here average fewer than three inhabitants in their household.

Country of origin also affects household size. The most recent immigrants from Central America tend to have the largest families (close to four members), followed by Mexicans. Conversely, Puerto Ricans, Cubans, and Latinos from South America have family sizes closer to non-Latinos. On the other hand, family size appears to be unrelated to structural elements, such as social class. Neither household income nor occupation of the head of the household is significantly correlated to household size (results not shown).

Table 5.2. Size of Household by Time in the United States and Ancestry (in Counts and Averages)

	N	Average Size
*By Time in the US**		
1-19 years	101	3.7
20 or more years	101	3.5
U.S. Born	95	2.9
*By Ancestry***		
Cubans	27	3.0
Colombians	19	3.3
Guatemalans	31	4.0
Mexicans	75	3.7
Other Central Americans	12	3.9
Other South Americans	40	2.8
Puerto Ricans	65	3.1
Salvadorans	32	3.7
Overall	*301*	*3.4*

* f=6.0, p < .005

**χ2=2.9, p < .005

Source: Latinos in Richmond Survey.

Giving and Receiving Aid

Strong familialism in Latinos is connected with a deep sense of obligation to aid relatives, either nearby or in one's country of origin (Glick 1999; Lee and Autac 1998; Marin 1993). However, we find interesting patterns concerning the giving and receiving of aid among Richmond Latinos. A noteworthy trait is self-reliance when it comes to receiving help from other relatives. Despite the presence of some extended families among them, almost 50 percent of Richmond Latinos have no relatives outside of their immediate families residing in the area (Figure 5.3). Of those who do have relatives nearby, some 58 percent do not count on them for help at all (see Figure 5.4). Recall from chapter 2 that only about one in eight Richmond Latinos moved to Richmond to reunite with family. So compared to Latino trends in other regions of the country, this degree of self-sufficiency is quite unusual. Nevertheless, extended relations are still a hallmark of family life for some Latinos in the area, immigrants and non-immigrants alike. Almost one-fifth of our sample report having between six to twenty relatives within the greater area and a handful have more than fifty relatives in Richmond!

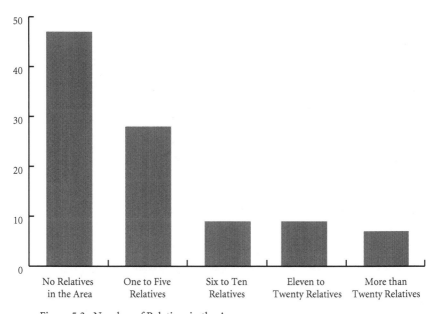

Figure 5.3. Number of Relatives in the Area

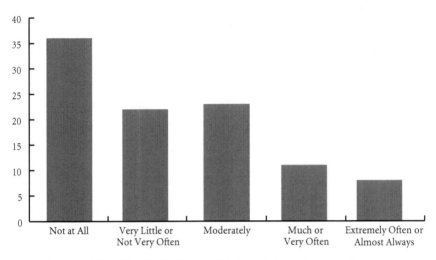

Figure 5.4. How Often Do You Receive Help from Relatives in the Area?
(N = 158)

When asked the question about receiving help, those with relatives in the area are more likely to reply by emphasizing the extent to which *they* help their relatives. One respondent commented, "Many of [my relatives] stay in my house when they move to Richmond until they can get on their own feet. I was the first to come here and brought them after I arrived here." Other respondents highlighted the reciprocity of the help given, with relatives supporting each other when needed: "When someone is sick or when I am sick, I call for advice or other help." But even those who reported enjoying this kind of help emphasized that the aid is often limited. Women were slightly more likely to report help from family members than men did (a difference that is nonetheless significant: women average 2.6 on a five-value item, with five indicating the most help; men average 2.2; the differences of means test is significant at the .05 level).

It may be that many Latinos in our study are helping family back "home," rather than in the Richmond vicinity. While our survey does not have questions on money transfers to Latin American countries (though a few respondents volunteered that information), a national survey conducted for the Multilateral Investment Fund of the Inter-American Development Bank indicates that Latinos in Virginia send to relatives back home an estimate of $586 million dollars a year. Money was sent on average thirteen times a year, in average payments of $240 at a time. The survey calculated that about 84 percent of Latin American immigrants in Virginia sent money home (compared to 61 percent for Latinos nationwide). When asked about why she sent money home, when she has to work two menial jobs to support her four-year-old son here, a single mother replied, "It's my obligation as a daughter" (Sheridan 2004).

Preserving Latino Culture in Richmond

Perhaps because of the lack of extended family connections, as well as the relative invisibility of the Latino population in the area, Richmond Latinos are strongly determined to preserve their cultures of origin for their children. Culturally, family can serve as a buffer against the mores of the external society. For immigrant parents and their children, the predominance of the language, lifestyle, and customs of the host society are especially hard to escape. When that group represents less than 5 percent of the population of an area, it is even more likely to feel encroached upon by those mores. Thus, it is not surprising to find that almost 50 percent of Richmond Latinos in our sample indicate that the U.S. way of life weakens the family.

When pressed to explain that feeling, respondents argue that life in the United States can weaken family relations in a number of different ways. Some see the extent of geographic mobility in the United States as a hurdle for keeping the family together and maintaining meaningful family relationships. One respondent made clear that familialism is reduced here; life in his home country was "about the closeness of the family. You grow up in a town or a part of town, and that's where you grow old and die in Argentina. Here everyone moves around like crazy, like nobody means anything." For these respondents, families often end up spread out over long distances in the United States, thus breaking down ties already weakened by migration.

Others complained about the deleterious effects of the pace of life in the United States, especially work-related stresses. They see the results of a culture overly oriented toward economic achievement, resulting in family members having less time to spend with loved ones. Parents in our sample particularly drew attention to the dangers of latchkey kids and too much television. They argued that popular culture in the United States runs counter to family obligations and the values of familialism, and suggested that Americans are too lax in raising their children. "Americans are too free in raising their children," reported a Puerto Rican woman in her twenties. "They should take more care [with them]. It's not interfering!"

On the other hand, some respondents argued that living in the United States has had the opposite effect—they proposed that their families are stronger since arriving here, finding that family members show a greater sense of unity against adversity and the trials of migration-related separation. Others focused on the improved economic situation of the family, even if some family members remained behind. For example, a Guatemalan construction worker, who has been in the United States for four years, argued that his family is stronger despite their separation *because* he is working here and sending his money to them in Guatemala. Thirty percent of our respondents said that living in the United States does not weaken the family (and indeed that it may be beneficial), while 23 percent said neither of these has happened.

Concern that U.S. culture weakens family life is not explained by Richmond Latinos' immigrant status, or the number of years they have spent in the United States, or even by ancestry. We did expect, as segmented assimilation theory would predict, that more recent immigrants and the most economically disadvantaged would be more concerned about preserving ethnic culture against inroads by the dominant society, but this is not the case. In fact, those *most* concerned about the erosion of family values have the highest incomes, as indicated in Figure 5.5, although the differences are not statistically significant. We propose that it takes economic integration and some familiarity with U.S. culture to become anxious about cultural modification affecting the family.

Ironically, part of the explanation comes from language use (Table 5.3). Latinos who are not likely to feel that U.S. customs weaken family life are also less likely to use English in everyday life. Again, at least some exposure to the

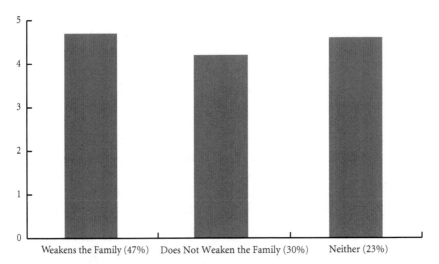

Figure 5.5 Average Household Income by Responses to "Do You Think
the U.S. Way of Life . . . ?

Table 5.3. Responses to "Do You Think the U.S. Way of Life . . . ?" by Language
Assimilation and Acceptance of Anglos Indices (Counts and Averages)

On Language Assimilation Index* (1 = Least use of English, 5 = Most)	N	Mean
Weakens the Family	121	3.2
Does Not Weaken the Family	79	2.9
Neither	62	3.3
On Acceptance of Anglos Index **(1 = Least Acceptance, 5 = Most)		
Weakens the Family	121	4.2
Does Not Weaken the Family	76	4.6
Neither	61	4.4

* f=2.7, p < .1, N = 262

** f=2.9, p < .005, N = 258

Source: Latinos in Richmond Survey.

United States is required for a negative perception of how life in the United States affects family relations. Parents who shelter their children, using Spanish language and media at home, do not see a problem with U.S. values. However, it is likely that continued contact with U.S. culture may eventually reduce this initial negativity, as it is related to acceptance of Anglo ways in general. People who are the most accepting of Anglos are the least likely to feel threatened by the influence of U.S. culture.

Anxiety about the conflict between family and U.S. culture is also reflected in the importance respondents assigned to raising Latino children in their own (original) culture (see Figure 5.6). The majority of respondents considered it *very* important for Latino children to be raised in the culture or country of origin of their parents (56 percent). Of course, some respondents acknowledged the difficulty of doing so: "You can't raise them in your own country when you don't live in it," a forty-nine-year-old Cuban father of four said poignantly. However, differences in opinion about the importance of cultural preservation for the next generation vary significantly by income. Those who felt the strongest about raising their children in their culture of origin tend to have the lowest incomes, while those with higher incomes thought that this was less important. Because levels of assimilation vary by income as noted in the previous chapter, these differences may indicate different rates of assimilation—as those who are least assimilated are the most likely to say they want to preserve their culture as well as have lower incomes.

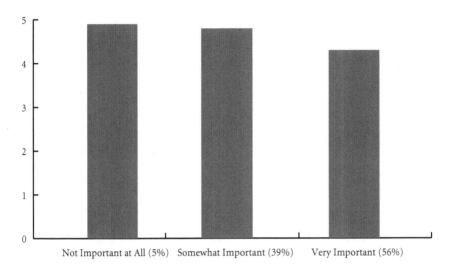

Figure 5.6 Average Household Income, by Importance of Children Being Raised
in One's Own Culture

Concern with preserving Latino culture is also evidenced by the ethnicity of Latino children's friends. Parents often make efforts to shape their children's choices of playmates, and Latinos are no exception. Although only 11 percent of parents argued that their children play exclusively with other Latinos, more than 50 percent noted that their children play with "mixed" groups of Latinos and Anglos, a percentage that is remarkable in a city with relatively few Latinos (Figure 5.7). Income is important in explaining this trend—lower-income parents are more likely to have children who have Latinos friends. Again, the desire to preserve culture in this manner is related to our language and cultural assimilation variables, which are also significantly related to income. However, immigrant status and ethnic identity are not relevant to this relationship.

At times, responses to this question indicate that parents are keen to project an image that their children are well connected to the Latino network of children in their neighborhoods, even if that is not fully the case. Often, children were present during our interviews. When a young girl responded to the question posed to her father about the ethnicity of her playmates by saying she played mostly with African American friends, her father quickly insisted that she played with both blacks and Hispanics. This was not the only occasion in which Latino parents expressed concern about black playmates. At any rate, whether through actual steering of children's acquaintances or merely

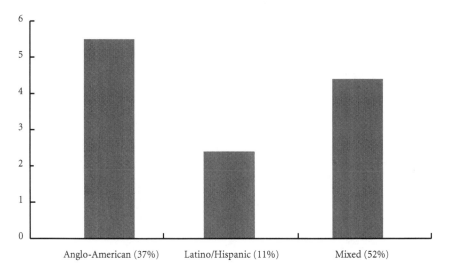

Figure 5.7. Average Household Income, by Ethnicity of Children's Friends

by emphasizing this fact to researchers, the preservation of Latino social ties through a variety of means is clearly important to our respondents.

Cultural Preservation, Bilingualism, and Education

Bilingualism is an important component of cultural safeguarding, often manifesting as a family issue because of struggles between immigrants and their children over language usage. Parents understand the important of mastering the dominant language for the future success of their children, and usually go to great lengths to provide such opportunities. Educational success can be a significant first line of defense for parents. School achievement (measured, for example, by high school drop out rates) is determined by English ability and whether or not English is spoken at home (Garcia 2001).[3] However, learning English in our school systems can prove a daunting task given the lack of sufficient classes and trained teachers, as well as an ideology that acquiring English necessitates loss of the first language (Bayley 2005:283). What passes for bilingual education in the United States is often more like remedial instruction in English (Portes and Rumbaut 2001b).

In true selective acculturation fashion, parents are also concerned with the safeguarding of their mother tongue. In fact, almost two-thirds of Richmond Latino parents reported that their children speak Spanish, while only one-third have children who do not speak the language at all. Parents are not the only purveyors of Spanish usage, of course. "My grandson speaks English but I'm trying to teach him Spanish. When he talks to me in English I tell him to tell it to me in Spanish. He is the only one who speaks English in my house when he is there," related a sixty-three-year-old Mexican who migrated to the United States as a teenager.

Moreover, Latino parents in Richmond see their children's fluency in Spanish as intimately connected with their own desire to pass on their original culture to them. Spanish fluency is strongly related to the importance they attribute to raising children in their culture. Forty percent of the parents who think that it is not important at all to do so have children who speak no Spanish, while 60 percent of those who think preserving the culture is very important note that all of their children do speak Spanish.[4]

Immigrant status helps predict the likelihood that one's children will speak Spanish. About 75 percent of Latino immigrants have children who speak Spanish, while only 36 percent of those born in the United States do. Income is also significantly, and negatively, related to the likelihood of having children who speak Spanish (Figure 5.8). An entire income bracket separates parents with children who speak no Spanish (income bracket with a midpoint $62,500) from those that do (income bracket with a midpoint of $42,500), indicating

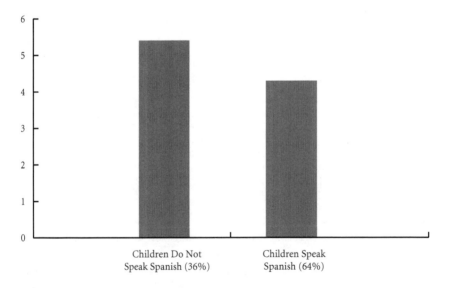

Figure 5.8. Average Household Income, by Number of Children Who Speak Spanish in the Household

that significant economic assimilation leads to a decrease in Spanish usage among the second generation. Even controlling for immigrant status, substantial differences in income remain between the two groups of parents.

Education is one of the processes by which ethnic groups may find easier access to the dominant culture and to economic opportunities. Educational opportunity and family cultural cohesion come together for many Latino families in Richmond, especially for those Latino parents who have already benefited from such educational advantages themselves. Respondents are almost universal in their agreement on the importance of a good education for getting ahead in life. Ninety-seven percent said that education is very important in order to succeed in life.

Educational and economic gains connected with acquiring the mainstream culture can, of course, run counter to cultural preservation. They may create tensions between parents and children, especially if parents perceive that assimilation is happening too quickly. Family cohesion and better school performance lead to consonant (i.e., successful) acculturation, but the reverse is true for dissonant acculturation (Portes and Rumbaut 2001b). Parents may worry over a diminished emphasis on schooling among those who become oriented toward a downwardly mobile subculture. Finally, selective acculturation leaves room for the possibility of achieving economic integration without sacrificing cultural preservation, as well as the prospect of rejecting the dominant culture altogether.

In the case of Richmond Latinos, 43 percent of the respondents' families have school-age children, mostly in the public school system. Most of these parents reported great involvement with their children's schools; one is even on the school board. More than two-thirds indicated that they are "involved" or "very involved" in the school that their child attends. As an additional measure of their commitment, 37 percent are members of the Parent-Teacher Association (PTA) at their children's schools.

Parental participation shows the importance that Latinos in Richmond place on educational opportunity, but parents bring another major concern to the Richmond school systems. Latino parents in the area are eager to see the public school curriculum addressing their children's native cultures as a way of balancing their overall education. As a result, they are concerned about the extent to which Spanish is taught in school. Many parents could recall the school systems of their childhood, when speaking Spanish was entirely discouraged, and they do not wish this for their own children. For example, one respondent who grew up in a very Hispanic area of New Mexico recalled his Anglo teacher smacking children's knuckles with a ruler if they were speaking

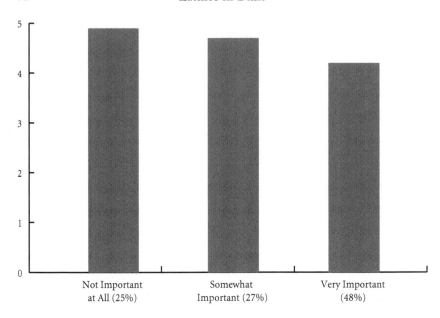

Figure 5.9. Average Household Income, by Importance of Teaching Spanish to Children

Spanish. Not surprisingly, 48 percent of all respondents (not just parents) said that it is very important that Spanish-speaking children be taught in Spanish at least part of the time, while 27 percent suggested it is of *some* importance. This belief varies by class status: those with lower incomes are more likely to be concerned with the preservation of Spanish language use in schools. This relationship holds even if when we control for immigrant status; even among immigrants alone, those who argue that it is least important that Spanish-speaking children be taught Spanish in school are more likely to have higher incomes.

Given the recent arrival of Latinos to the greater Richmond area, however, classes in Spanish or even English as a Second Language (ESL) classes are not perceived as a uniform need across the board by the school systems that make up Richmond's educational structure. The fragmentation of the area into nine counties and four cities makes it hard for local school systems to adjust to the curricular needs of immigrant Latino children. Multiple schools systems have different adoption policies and resources when it comes to implementing Spanish, so it is difficult to generalize. Efforts to create special language classes have happened in a haphazard fashion (or not at all), depending on which schools received the largest Latino populations first. For the most part, parents have few school options when it comes to keeping their children fluent in their mother tongue.

The opinions of our respondents about Spanish or bilingual education reflect this lack of options (see Figure 5.10). They are divided, too, on exactly *how* they want to children to be taught Spanish. When we asked specifically, "How should children who don't speak English when they enter school be taught?" more than 50 percent of all respondents said that non-English speaking children should only be taught in short-term ESL classes in the public schools (the programs that currently exist). One respondent, a third-generation Mexican American, is not atypical in his passion for English education. His response indicated an understanding of straight-line assimilation often articulated by white Americans: "We live in the U.S., where the official language is English. Therefore, English should be the language in which children are taught." A recent immigrant from El Salvador also emphasized the importance of English acquisition. "[Latino children] will be with American children, you have to learn how they learn. After school, and in college, [there will be] no more Spanish. [Children] have to learn this, because this is America." Many of those who favor English-only education still believe in the importance

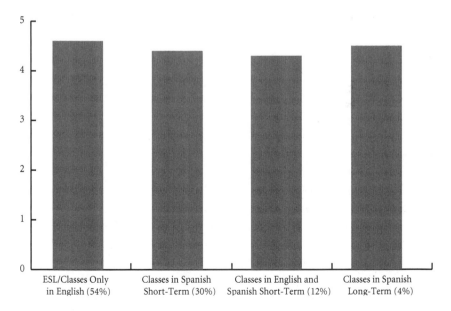

Figure 5.10. Average Household Income, by Preferred Method of Teaching Non-English Speaking Children

of cultural preservation and learning Spanish, but feel that it is the parents' responsibility to provide this education at home.

At the same time, a vocal minority of respondents feels very strongly that the school systems should be responsible for some increased level of non-English education. Thirty percent of the respondents argued for classes taught in a native language in the short term—a year or two, or in some cases only a few months—until the students can pass an English proficiency test. Many were adamant about the importance of this method as a means of transition only. A Mexican respondent related a story about how adolescents with limited English ability were put back in the second grade because they were unable to pass the grade. He said, "I understand the problem, but I don't want to prolong the problem by encouraging bilingual education or classes in Spanish."

Others, about 12 percent, thought that non-English speakers could be eased into the school system by having courses taught in both English and Spanish (or in primarily English with a Spanish-speaking teacher around to provide explanations in their native language). For example, one of our younger respondents, not yet a parent, said that students need, "a Latino teacher, because how can you teach biology in English? If the Latino has a question, how can they ask the teacher? I think that they should have some people in the schools that speak Spanish."

Finally, a very small group (4 percent) suggested that children be offered the option of taking classes in Spanish for an indeterminate amount of time, up through the high school level if necessary. While this may seem like an extreme approach, for those respondents knowledge outweighs fluency. Getting an education or the knowledge skills that prepare students for life is more important than simply learning English. That the group is a very small segment of the Richmond Latino population indicates that the majority are quite convinced of the utility of mastering the dominant language, but also reflects the lack of bilingual options in Richmond schools.

Quite a few of the respondents saw danger in bilingual education. While they sympathized with the students' needs to be taught for a time in Spanish, they also realized that students can remain in ESL classes far longer than they need to, which they find detrimental to the child's future. "Prejudice starts with difference," said a Cuban respondent, "and language is one of the things that differentiate—it's the first impression." Moreover, sometimes students can be assigned the ESL or Spanish classes based on factors unrelated to actual language skills. A Puerto Rican man who had lived in Texas and Colorado referred to the "segregation by last names" that his daughter faced in those school systems, based solely on her Spanish surname. School officials wanted to place her in all-Spanish classes, "even though she could speak English perfectly fine." He argued that classes should be bilingual, but applied according to the students' own language ability, and that students "should be moved up and into regular classes ASAP!"

The remarkable thing here is that opinions on bilingualism in schools are not explained by any of the factors one would expect. Parents are no different than non-parents when it comes to this matter. Immigrant status does not predict how one feels about bilingual education, nor does the number of years lived in the United States. Level of education is not a predictor. None of our assimilation variables are related to how one feels about this subject, including the extent of English and/or Spanish used in everyday life. Social class, as operationalized by income, is also not connected to one's approach to bilingualism. Neither is one's political orientation.

In fact, the only variables that predict our respondents' attitudes toward bilingualism are ancestry (but only to a certain extent), and the importance one places on teaching Spanish to one's children. For the former, Colombians and other South Americans are those most likely to favor classes taught only in English. Puerto Ricans, Salvadorans, and Guatemalans are more likely to favor at least some degrees of opportunity for learning Spanish in school. Not surprisingly, the respondents who feel that it is important for Spanish-speaking children to learn Spanish are also the most likely to believe that the schools should provide this opportunity either in the short or long term. Overall, although parents and other respondents are concerned with preserving the native culture, and many believe this should happen through language instruction in the public schools, they are not in agreement on how students' education should combine Spanish and English (more than 40 percent of those who said Spanish instruction in school was very important nonetheless said students should mostly be taught in English). Of course, true bilingual instruction, offering fluency in both English and Spanish, is not yet an option in Richmond.

Living in Multiple Worlds

For some Latino families in Richmond, who endeavor to lead lives well integrated into U.S. culture, the desire to achieve educationally and acquire the tools necessary for success in this country is paramount. Nevertheless, there are moments when one catches a glimpse of a deeper longing—that search for the balance that is just not realized when one lives between two worlds. It is a desire that is difficult to translate into action, given the large chasm—both geographic and emotional—that often separates the two cultures of these families. Celia Falicov argues that the loss experienced by immigrant families is quite unique and ambiguous, a space neither here nor there:

> Migration loss is . . . not absolutely clear, complete, and irretrievable. Everything is still alive but is just not immediately reachable or present . . . . A social community and ethnic neighborhood reproduce in pockets of remembrance the sights, sounds, smells, and tastes of one's country. All of these elements create a mix of emotions—sadness and elation, loss and restitution, absence and presence—that makes grieving incomplete, postponed, ambiguous. (2002:274)

Our group described with regret their exclusion from the world of their ancestors. In those cases, especially for second- and third-generation Latino respondents, there is a sense that something very important has been lost. Some cultural spaces are forever frozen in time and space for those who leave their home countries behind. One respondent remembered fondly the kind of Spanish that was spoken in his childhood home. Nowadays he longs for a Spanish radio station in the Richmond area that would play the "old tunes" he remembers from his grandmother's house. Some spoke with sadness about never being allowed to learn Spanish at home while they were growing up, even though their parents were fluent speakers. A third-generation Dominican woman verbalized at length about realizing too late the importance of cultural heritage now as a consequence of never having it:

> I do not consider myself Hispanic because my grandfather did not pass on his heritage because of discrimination among Anglos and other Hispanics. It is only in recent years that he started telling us stories of his life as a boy on a sugar cane farm and speaking some Spanish. I think he feels it is safer now to be Hispanic, and if he was just coming to this country today, I believe our family would be more in touch with our Hispanic heritage... [but] I am glad they do not suffer the discrimination that my grandfather did before [World] War II (if they suffer at all).

Still others spoke with regret about the tradeoffs made in the pursuit of economic assimilation. "I must honestly say that I have done a poor job keeping in touch with my cultural identity," said a young man, a third-generation Mexican American. "I have found that participating in educational pursuits followed by vocational pursuits, it has been easy to align myself with a diverse racial [community], much decreasing my ability to remain true to my culture." These comments substantially illustrate both the gains and the losses of a traditional assimilation pattern.

At the other end of the spectrum are Latino residents who feel a tremendous yearning to preserve a space in family life—through family unity, language use, and even in public school education—for the way of life known from abroad. For example, the woman whose quote we highlight at the beginning of this chapter made a connection between family relationships and culture unity that is common, she argues, not just among Puerto Ricans but also among Latinos.

Familialism—the care and support of family members—is weakened when families are more isolated. We have provided evidence here of separations between family members, as well as a set of complex family forms that result from external and internal migration. There is a tendency for family connections to decline with greater integration, as indicated by fewer extended family relationships and smaller family size over time in the United States. Richmond families do not receive as much help from family members; indeed, in many cases there is no extended family nearby. They seek family inclusiveness and interdependence, but there is a lack of it in Richmond (perhaps this is why they seek it in the community, as we discuss in chapter 8).

In numerous ways—the teaching of Spanish, maintaining the ties to relatives in the area or in the country of origin, engaging in family rituals, preparing favorite ethnic foods, or listening to music from back home—these Latino families in Richmond engage in a continuous balancing act, trying to safeguard Latino culture, and along with it, their children. They stress the importance of Latino family values, particularly in contrast to the toxic effects of U.S. culture. They lament the encroachment on family life that is the result of the assimilation of Anglo values such as competition or overachievement. They encourage doing well in school as a means to upward mobility in our society, but find it also important to promote learning Spanish in these schools so that the original culture will not be lost. Parents perceive that limiting the extent of assimilation has a protective effect. These actions provide strong evidence for the segmented assimilation framework, both because they reflect the assumptions of the bicultural third way, approaching adaptation through selective acculturation, but also because such efforts are directed at avoiding a minority-identified oppositional culture.

Chapter 6

Blue Collar Latinos, White Collar Latinos

Discrimination and Work Opportunity in Richmond

Hire me because I'm good, not because I'm Latino.
—Sixty-year-old Argentine small business owner

Work supplies a major source of identity in the United States. A high-status occupation can bring a degree of financial stability and even social influence into one's immediate community (Bond and Rosen 1980; Hezberg 1959; McIlwee and Robinson 1992; Nelson 1996; Ouellet 1994; Riemer 1979; Stewart and Cantor 1982). In the Unites States, having a decent, full-time job also translates into the pursuit of the "American Dream"—achieving a middle-class standard of living, the acquisition of consumer goods, and home ownership. Regardless of occupational status, working is a strong measure of a person's ability to become more incorporated into his or her community.

For ethnic groups, especially for immigrants, work has even greater potential to facilitate economic integration. It means having a stake in the host country's economy, adopting work habits that are part of the cultural mainstream. According to Portes and Rumbaut (1996), the resources that immigrants bring with them may not immediately translate into highly paid jobs—because of language or cultural differences, or lack of job-seeking experience in the United States—but in the long run, education and professional training can give them a significant edge, depending upon the type of community and labor market into which they settle.

Nationwide, Latinos lag behind other U.S. residents on multiple dimensions of economic success. In 1999 the Latino median household income was $33,676, compared to $41,994 for all U.S. residents (Census 2000). Latinos are less likely to find stable employment in core industries, to be in professional and managerial positions, and to own businesses. Moreover, Latinos are overrepresented in low-skilled, low-paid occupations, which translates into greater financial hardship. In part, differences in financial rewards and occupational status are the result of the educational attainment gap between Latinos and non-Latinos in the United States (Enchautegui 1995; Hogan, Kim, and Perrucci

1997; Kim and Perrucci 1994; Padilla 1997). For example, in 2000 52 percent of Latinos between twenty-five and thirty-four years of age had finished high school, compared to 80 percent of non-Latinos of the same age (Census 2000).

Recent arrivals in the South are often concentrated in operatives and laborer positions (Smith and Furuseth 2004). Work on the domestic side of the global economy of the New South is a double-edged sword: the jobs are plentiful, with flexible working conditions, and Latino workers are highly valued by employers, but the demands of such jobs often lead to worker exploitation, including poor working conditions, chaotic schedules, few benefits and no collective bargaining. "New immigrants . . . particularly those who are undocumented, are socially transitory, legally vulnerable, and overwhelmingly motivated to work—all of which predispose them to respond to the fickle labor demands of employers" (Ciscel, Smith, and Mendoza 2003:334).

Against the backdrop of national trends, the socioeconomic experiences of Richmond Latinos stand in stark contrast. Recall that census data for Richmond metro indicate that Latinos there are more likely to have higher average levels of household income and education, to be employed, and to be employed in high-status occupations, than do U.S. Latinos generally. The findings specific to our sample are similar: 86 percent are employed. More than 50 percent make over $35,000 a year in personal income, and when household income is taken into account, almost one-third of the households take in $75,000 a year or more (Figures 6.1 and 6.2).[1] At the other end of the spectrum, fewer than 10 percent of the Latino households in our sample fall below the poverty line. Even Latinos in working-class occupations tend to fare better economically than Latinos in other areas of the United States, although average earnings in each occupational category are still lower than for whites.

Richmond Latinos also have higher levels of educational attainment than Latinos nationwide. Latino college enrollment nationally lies well below that of non-Latinos (Tienda and Mitchell 2006), but data from the 2000 census for Richmond indicated that 68 percent of Latinos have graduated from high school, and 26 percent have a college degree or higher. In comparison, 29 percent of all Richmond residents have at least an undergraduate education. In our sample, 84 percent of our Latino respondents have graduated from high school, higher than the national average for all U.S. residents. Almost 40 percent of our respondents have attained a college degree or higher (Figure 6.3).

Our sample of Richmond Latinos also tends to be overrepresented in executive, managerial, and professional occupations compared to Latinos elsewhere. Thirty-six percent of our respondents are executives, managers, or

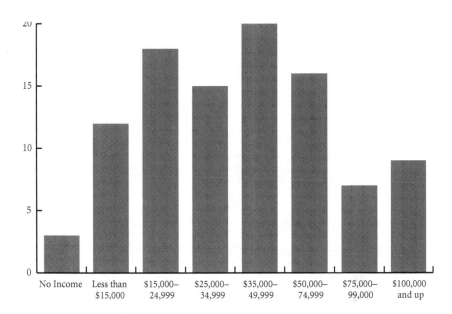

Figure 6.1. Personal Income of Richmond Latino Respondents

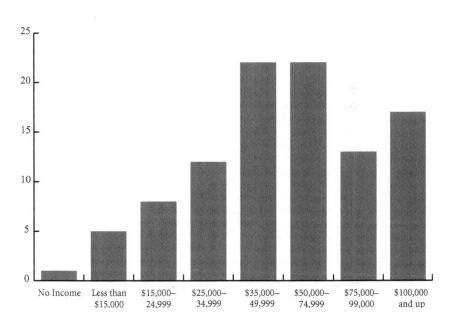

Figure 6.2. Household Income of Richmond Latino Respondents

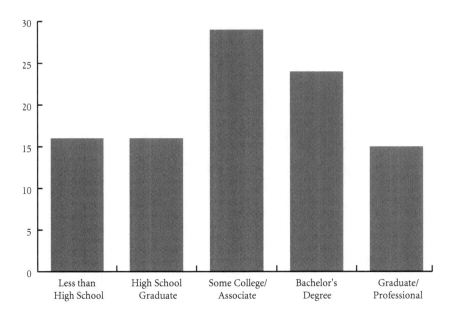

Figure 6.3. Education Levels of Richmond Latino Respondents

professionals (compared to only 17 percent of Latinos in the United States, according to census data). Eleven percent report employment in service occupations (24 percent of Latinos nationally) and a little over one-quarter of them work in traditionally blue-collar occupations (about 35 percent of Latinos nationally) (Figure 6.4). Thus, we can contrast our data with other studies of Latino workers in the South, where the focus is predominantly on working-class Latinos (Murphy et al. 2001). In terms of industries, Latinos in our sample are concentrated in service industries, but also work in manufacturing and construction (Figure 6.5).[2]

Considering the way social mobility can serve as a mechanism for families to become part of the economic mainstream (Blau and Duncan 1967; Bowles and Gintis 2002; Nam 2004; Portes and Bach 1985; Portes and Zhou 1993; Solon 1992), we thought it important to examine whether Richmond Latinos have experienced social mobility, and if so, which segment of the Latino population benefits the most from it. Clearly, access to an area where Latinos experience greater rates of employment and occupational opportunity might impact how Latino families in Richmond would fare in the long run.

A little more than one-quarter of Richmond Latinos experienced intergenerational upward mobility in relation to their parents. We measured mobility

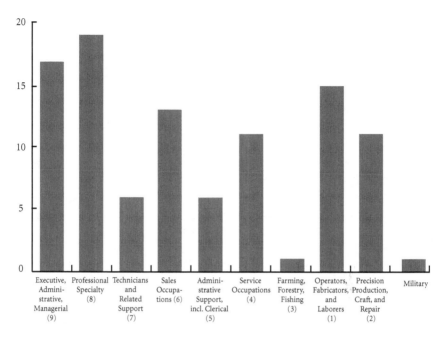

Figure 6.4. Occupations of Richmond Latino Respondents (with Ordinal Value Codes)

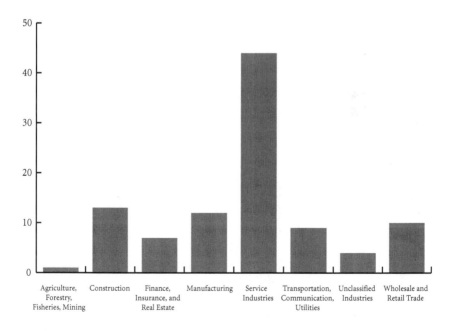

Figure 6.5. Industry Distribution of Employed Richmond Latino Respondents

by comparing the occupational status of both parents to the respondent, and describing the respondent's mobility as "upward" if the respondent's occupational status exceeds that of one or both of his/her parents, as "downward" if it is lower than one or both of the parents, and "none" if the occupational statuses are the same. The large bulk of Latinos in our sample (60 percent) have experienced little to no intergenerational occupational mobility. This type of mobility, however, becomes far more visible when one breaks down the Richmond sample into immigrants and non-immigrants (Figure 6.6). Immigrant status affects social mobility outcomes. Compared to their non-immigrant counterparts, immigrant Latinos in Richmond are twice as likely to have experienced intergenerational upward mobility (41 versus 22 percent, respectively). Of course, numerous respondents experienced occupational upward mobility when they moved to Richmond from elsewhere in the United States. For instance, a Colombian immigrant making five dollars in a factory in New Jersey recalled getting fifteen dollars an hour working in construction when he moved to Richmond.

This finding should not be too surprising, as many immigrants come to the United States and even to Richmond in order to improve their occupational status. Moreover, some respondents who immigrated as children were able to

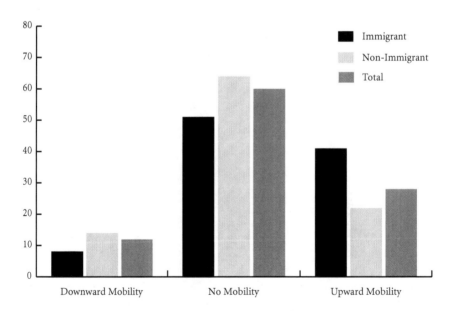

Figure 6.6. Intergenerational Mobility by Immigrant Status (in Percentages)

achieve upward mobility because their parents had first experienced downward mobility upon arrival in the United States. A number of respondents related stories of their professional parents being required to take menial jobs when they first arrived, although their children were eventually able to move up the occupational ladder even if their parents never did so. More typically, a respondent's occupational status eventually matches that of his/her parents *prior* to migration. For example, the parents of a Richmond architect had been well educated professionals, a nurse and a banker, in Mexico before migrating, but became workers in sportswear factory after arriving in Texas.

Given the unusual representation of Latinos among well-paid occupations in the Richmond labor market in both the census and our sample, especially in contrast to the national data, we suspected that the apparent success of Richmond Latinos actually masks a community split by social class. Moreover, we have already noted the role played by social class, and income in particular, in terms of different assimilation processes among Richmond Latinos. But to what degree is social class relevant to economic and occupational integration in the city? Perhaps a higher median income merely means that the Richmond Latino community includes a relatively small number of very well-off individuals, while the remainder is more economically marginal, rather than a strong middle class. Even knowing the answer to that question does not tell us if successful Latinos were sharing opportunities in the community with recent immigrants who are not so well off, have weaker English skills, and work in more fragile, lower-status settings, or even whether the two groups are much involved at all.

Instead of income, to test differences based on social class and acculturation experiences in this chapter we divide the sample into two occupational categories: middle-class, white-collar workers, represented by executive, managerial, professional, and sales occupations; and working-class, represented by low-level clerical, service, production, and operative occupations. Again, we note the predominance of middle-class Latinos in our sample (56, versus 44 percent in working-class occupations). This allows us to make a more direct contrast between the two classes than we could in communities dominated by mostly recent blue-collar migrants.

Once we dichotomize class along occupational lines, the image is very different from one of uniform prosperity. Blue-collar and white-collar Richmond Latinos vary significantly along several important dimensions. White-collar Latinos have higher educational attainment than blue-collar Latinos. The fathers of the white-collar respondents, too, were more educated, suggesting that class is often an important independent variable in the migration process (Figure 6.7). Those in white-collar occupations are less likely to be immigrants (62 versus 76 percent for blue-collar), and have been in the mainland United States an average of eight years longer than blue-collar workers. They are more likely to be Cuban, Puerto Rican, or Colombian (results not shown).

White-collar workers are more assimilated in terms of the language use, media use, and social distance indices introduced in chapter 4 (Figure 6.8). White-collar workers are more likely to say they use English over Spanish (an average of 3.5, compared to a blue-collar mean of 2.8, although both averages indicate fairly high English usage), and more likely to use English when listening to music, reading, and so forth (an average for 4 for white-collar workers, and 3.6 for blue-collar). Finally, white-collar workers are more likely to say that their colleagues, friends, and neighbors are Anglo rather than Latino (1.6 for white-collar workers, and 2.0 for blue-collar, where 1 indicates "mostly Anglo"). The causal connection between language use and other assimilation measures is recursive—those who spoke more English before migrating to the United States, all other factors being equal, will face more advantages finding employment in high-status occupations; however, those with a high occupational status in their country of origin may be more likely to have acquired English skills in the first place.

However, class does not predict a completely traditional one-way assimilation for white-collar respondents. In terms of ethnic identity, white-collar

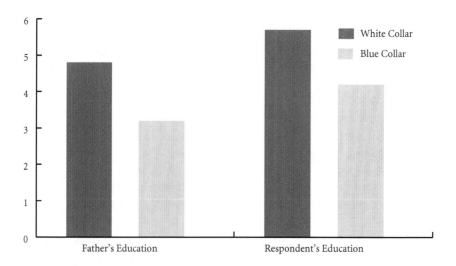

Figure 6.7. Father's and Respondent's Educations as Predictors of Occupational Status

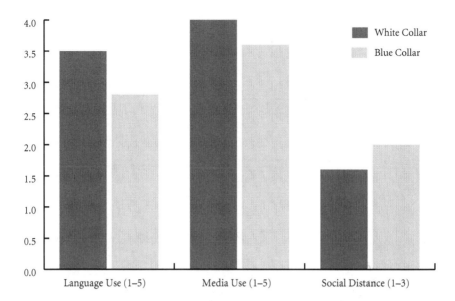

Figure 6.8. Three Assimilation Variables as Predictors of Occupational Status

Latinos are no less likely to refer to themselves as Latino or Hispanic. Fifty-two percent identified themselves as either Hispanic or Latino (versus 59 percent of the blue-collar workers) while 14 percent identified as "American." White-collar Latinos *are* more likely to refer to themselves by country of origin (34 versus 27 for blue-collar workers), which is surprising given how much more assimilated to dominant U.S. customs they are in other respects. Still, social class often allows a greater freedom of choice in terms of defining one's ethnicity.

Discrimination in Richmond

While Latinos in Richmond are well represented in high-status occupations (especially when compared to Latinos in other communities), they still face earning penalties when compared to non-Latinos (see Figure 1.4 in chapter 1). According to the 2000 Census, the average household income for Latinos in Richmond was $40,068, while for white households the average was $53,192. Moreover, although their levels of education are similar to non-Latinos, their educational attainment does not always lead to comparable incomes or occupational ranks. That is, they have a lower income or occupational prestige than their educational levels would suggest. One possible explanation for these income and occupational disparities are discriminatory practices Latinos have faced in the labor market prior to Richmond or in Richmond itself. However, since many respondents came to Richmond because of expanded occupational opportunities, it is likely that they expected to experience, and perhaps do experience, less discrimination than in other locations.

Research on the occupational experiences of Latinos in the United States indicates that they still do face issues of discrimination in the workplace (Catanzarite 1998; DeFreitas 1991; Grenier 1984; Portes and Rumbaut 2001b; Tienda 1995). For example, Latinos, especially males, experience less favorable treatment in the hiring process about 20 percent of the time (Bendick et al. 1992). Another study, based in Los Angeles, reports Latinos experiencing some form of personal discrimination in the workplace in the past year about 30 percent of the time, with 16 percent saying they had been refused employment as the most frequent example (Bobo et al. 2000). Even middle-class Latinos experience occupational discrimination (Aranda 2006). Better educated and more assimilated Cubans and Mexicans are more likely to report occurrences of discrimination. Perceptions of discrimination actually increase with tenure, which suggests that the longer Latinos live in the United States, the more likely they are attuned to life here as it is, with continued experiences of discrimination against those of minority status (Portes and Rumbaut 1996).

Among our respondents, however, there is little perception that they face discrimination in Richmond as Latinos, while the evidence of actual discrimination is mixed. When asked about occupational discrimination facing Latinos in Richmond *in general*, respondents were unlikely to identify much ethno-racial discrimination. We asked, "How difficult is it for a Hispanic to get a job or a promotion?" Thirty-four percent said, "not difficult at all," 39 percent said, "rarely," 15 percent said, "occasionally," and only 11 percent answered, "frequently." Respondents were even less likely to report *personal* occupational discrimination: 70 percent believe that they have never been treated unfairly because of being Latino when applying for a job, and 76 percent said the same about going up for a promotion.

Given such overwhelming agreement, it is not surprising that these questions are not related to either class status (as indicated by the blue/white-collar measure) or by respondent's personal or household income.[3] Instead, this perception is related to the respondents' confidence in Richmond relative to other places people have lived. For example, a forklift operator in his forties, who migrated from the Dominican Republic almost twenty years ago, told us, "I still don't feel this [discrimination] here, no; but in other places, yes. In New York there are many Hispanics, and there is a certain degree of discrimination."

It is possible that levels of discrimination in Richmond just do not compare to what respondents have faced in other cities, and thus respondents downplay its presence here.

Interviewees responded somewhat differently when we asked them to compare themselves with equally situated workers, although they were still more likely to see equity in employment. When asked if their income is comparable to that of their fellow employees, almost 50 percent said that it "definitely is," and another 30 that it "probably is." Similar numbers agreed that their skills and abilities are indeed reflected in their likelihood of receiving a promotion. People were less certain about whether their educational levels correspond to either their income levels or occupational status. Only 64 percent agreed that their present occupation "definitely" or "probably" "reflects their educational level," and 59 percent said that their income does so. In general, however, despite the aggregate income disparities we found, when we questioned our respondents about their direct experiences with discrimination in hiring or promotion, they do not see much of it.

The respondents' feelings about the match between their own skills and their chances of success in their workplace do vary significantly by type of occupation, however (see Figure 6.9). White-collar workers are universally

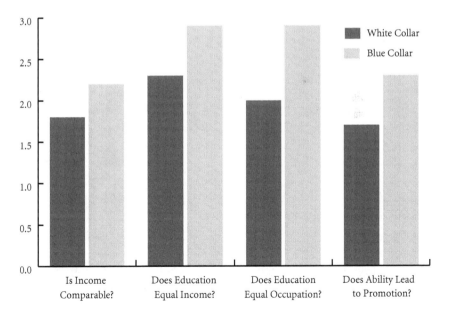

Figure 6.9. Average Responses on Four Measures of Occupational Discrimination by Occupational Status (N = 146)

more likely to think that their incomes are comparable to those of their fellow workers, that their incomes and occupations are appropriate to their educational achievement, and that their chances of being promoted at their current places of employment reflect their abilities. An index of these four items reveals an even more significant difference between white- and blue-collar workers. White-collar workers have an average of 1.9 (values range from 1–5, with 1 signifying the most fairness in their employment situations), while the blue-collar mean is 2.5. In terms of specific blue-collar occupations, factory workers are usually the least likely to think these statements are true, but sometimes clerical and service workers feel this way as well.

Class, as measured by income, is a significant predictor also: the higher one's income, the more likely a respondent is to agree with these statements of equity in employment. However, neither the respondent's gender nor self-described race is an indicator of how people feel about any disparate treatment in their occupational settings.

The qualitative evidence that respondents gave us as asides or in the discussion period after the formal interviews presents a more nuanced picture of occupational discrimination based on race or ethnicity. In some cases interviewees who answered survey questions about individual or group discrimination in Richmond in the negative finished the survey with anecdotes about experiences encountered by themselves or loved ones that sound like discrimination to us. In other words, respondents were not always aware of what constitutes discrimination in a work setting when answering the survey questions.

For example, one respondent told a Horatio Alger–like story about coming to the United States twenty years ago with fifty dollars in his pocket. He cleaned bathrooms for a living before eventually working his way up to owning a construction company. He claimed there is no discrimination against Latinos in Richmond, but then went on to relate an experience of bidding for a construction job. Once he talked on the phone with the apartment complex he was to work for, he never got a call back, "perhaps because of my accent." Although he was reluctant to attribute negative outcomes of his employment experiences to racism, he nevertheless felt it was important to provide us this account as a "Who knows what was really going on?" story.[4] Respondents also mentioned a disparity between the professional training they acquired in their country of origin and the lower occupational status opportunities that were available to them here in the United States. For example, one respondent's husband was a banker in Cuba and had to start over at Lynchburg as a Spanish teacher. When he tried to get a job at a bank, he was asked if he could "count

U.S. dollars." Another respondent worked as a bank manager and was a colonel in the navy in Paraguay, but now works at an electronics store as a bilingual customer service representative.

Compensation can also provide an arena for potential discrimination. One respondent reported that his wife had been in the same position in her organization for twenty years and she got paid less than seven dollars an hour. However, when the couple went on vacation to Mexico, the company paid her temporary replacements thirteen to fourteen dollars an hour. Most of these stories were related matter-of-factly, rather than in terms of indignation about treatment; however, they often came up during the portion of the interview when we asked the quantitative questions about occupational disparities discussed above.

Many other respondents replied in a similar fashion, first in the negative to questions about whether they have faced individual discrimination in applying for a job or a promotion, but then appending comments such as, "You never know," "It's hard to know," or "Where is the proof?" Their acknowledgment that they did not have the evidence to know for sure, but still thought discrimination possible or likely, suggests that the prospect had occurred to them even though they had no concrete proof. In Feagin's study of middle-class African Americans, one woman refers to this phenomenon as the subtle racism of "little murders" (1991:108). Each incident is potentially minor, but over the course of a lifetime the daily strain of suspecting discrimination but not knowing for certain creates great stress on people of color, pressures that would not have to be there if one was not constantly subject to racist treatment. Feagin's respondents, like Latinos in our study, typically err on the side of exercising caution before defining incidents as discriminatory; however, the work it takes to evaluate each situation and to decide on an appropriate response is considerable.

In another area of the survey, we asked a question that does not measure workplace discrimination directly, but does address inequality between Richmond Latinos and Anglos. We asked how much respondents agreed or disagreed with this statement: "In this geographic area, Hispanics have to work a lot harder to get ahead than Anglos." Our respondents indicated overwhelming support for this statement: more than 70 percent agreed or strongly agreed. These data, then, indicate less overt racial discrimination, but a greater possibility of structural barriers to economic success for Latinos in Richmond—factors much more difficult to see or prove.

Indeed, our respondents themselves, even those who acknowledged the possibilities of discrimination, found it necessary to offer up rationales for why some Latinos experience discrimination and some do not. Latinos are acutely aware of the areas in which they think they "fall short" *as individuals*, but rarely offer structural explanations for occupational discrimination. Many argued that cultural values determine how successful one will be, and that some Latinos thrive because they have a stronger work ethic. Respondents offered variations on the following statements: "It gets difficult for those who don't want to work." "If you want to work, you can." "I've never experienced difficulty [finding work] because I work hard," or, "People will treat you accordingly to how you conduct yourself."

Of course, many respondents argued that either the use of English and/or the lack of an accent lead to greater work opportunities; in fact, language usage is the typical explanation given for why some Latinos experience discrimination. But the use of non-accented English over Spanish carries a moral implication rather than a structural one. Adherents to this concept argued that learning to speak English is (or ought to be) part of one's work ethic; the assumption is that if people want to learn English, they will find a way to do so, and thus be successful in the labor market. An immigrant has a responsibility to master the host country's language in order to do well; not speaking English, then, is an acceptable rationale for discrimination. These assumptions not only dovetail with traditional straight-line assimilation, but attribute assimilation to individual choice. Respondents assumed that job barriers are mostly correlated with language or education alone, without realizing how bilingual or educational opportunities may themselves be exacerbated by preexisting racial and ethnic inequalities.

A few respondents *did* acknowledge that structural barriers exist in the workplace by suggesting that success is tied to the shade of one's skin. A number of respondents told us that they have never felt discrimination specifically because they do not look Hispanic. One respondent said that looking Hispanic can cause people to "accept" someone's presence at work, but not him or her as an equal. Another suggested a connection between skin color, nativity, and legal status by remarking that Anglos and blacks can more easily defend themselves in local companies because they can and will sue for discrimination, while Latinos (especially if undocumented) do not.

Still others equivocated about discrimination—it cannot be determined definitively because opportunities vary so much based on industry or geographic location. Further elaborating on this concept, a number of people suggested that *finding* a job is not as difficult as *keeping* a job or getting promoted. The issue of the glass ceiling is part of Richmond Latinos' perceptions of workplace inequities. There is always entry-level work for those who need it, they suggest, but moving into middle-class management positions is much more difficult for Latinos, especially those who do not have access to credentials or social networks. One respondent did file a racial discrimination report, and was eventually promoted, he argued, but not adequately compensated for his lost income.

Finally, it should be noted that fluency in Spanish can operate as a core work expectation, either to the benefit or detriment of Richmond Latinos. On the one hand, a number of white-collar respondents felt that speaking Spanish (and even being Latino) is advantageous in their line of work. "I am very proud of my heritage. In terms of getting a job, it has been an asset, not a liability. . . . I am very animated and outgoing and most people in my industry are boring." This quote comes from a forty-nine-year-old Cuban woman who works as a public policy consultant. Having come to the United States as a child, she feels at home here and has taken advantage of the country's educational opportunities, completing a graduate degree. Being an educated professional Latino, especially one who knows two languages, can be very beneficial in Richmond. Some respondents complained, however, that because they are the only people who spoke Spanish in their workplace, they are expected to work as translators for everybody else, but then do not get a chance to concentrate on developing other work skills. Bilingualism should, and often does, confer advantages on workers, but in cases where people must perform translations without added compensation it can be detrimental.

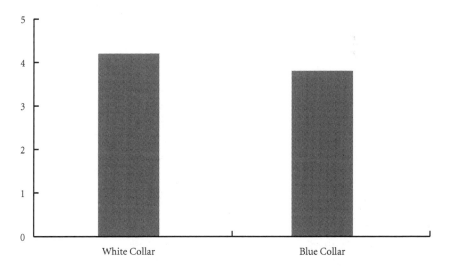

Figure 6.10. Average Job Satisfaction by Occupational Status (N = 142)

Perhaps as a result of their occupational expectations and experiences in Richmond, most Latinos in our study showed high levels of satisfaction with their jobs (Figure 6.10). Forty-two percent of the respondents agreed that they are "very satisfied" with their current employment, while 31 percent are "satisfied." Only 5 percent said that they are very unsatisfied. This job satisfaction does vary with occupational status, however, even though it is so favorably skewed. More white-collar workers would argue that they are very satisfied with work in Richmond than blue-collar workers.[5] Moreover, job satisfaction is correlated with another class measure, personal income. The higher one's income, the more satisfaction with one's job (r = .19, which is significant at the .005 level).

Work and Assimilation in Richmond

Work opportunities are central to Richmond Latinos' reasons for migrating to the area. Many of our respondents migrated from fast-paced, larger urban areas, where they faced high stress related to commuting and other work demands. Working in Richmond is not only economically positive, but it is something that enhances day-to-day living. A respondent compared life in Richmond favorably to a "fast market like Dallas, where I faced long commutes, I saw a lot of time slipping away. The cost of living [here is better]; it was expensive in Dallas, and this allows me to focus on family. . . . Looking back, I don't regret the move."

In terms of employment levels and occupational status, the measures show a population that overall is quite integrated into the local job market. Middle-class Richmond Latinos are very much aware of the contributions they make to the area. As one knowledgeable respondent commented, "Richmond is *starting* to understand that we're all consumers—Latinos too. There's a huge employer's need for service-oriented Spanish speakers." Professional Latinos are central to this process, highlighting the opportunities for Latino architects, builders, and entrepreneurs. Job satisfaction among them is uniformly high.

Working-class Latinos have not experienced quite the same level of success. Blue-collar workers are less assimilated in terms of language use, media use, and social proximity to Anglos, and are less likely to be satisfied with their work situation. Although we find a bifurcated community, however, we do not find quite the levels of difference that we might have predicted. Even in the area of work discrimination, where Richmond Latinos still face income inequalities in comparison to Anglos, we found very little evidence of outright discrimination, at least in terms of the quantitative data. Respondents argued that they rarely if ever experience discrimination in Richmond in terms of hiring or promotion, and feel adequately compensated. The qualitative data paints a more nuanced picture, suggesting that respondents who experience discrimination in the workplace are not very likely to label it as such or are willing to assign individual blame for unfair treatment.

There is little evidence that any in our group are developing an "adversarial stance" that emphasizes the discrimination faced by ethnic minorities in the United States, as exhibited by the minority-identified second generation examined in studies by Waters (1999) and Portes and Zhou (1993). Instead, their characterization of some (other) Latinos as lazy and not interested in learning English to find better employment is typical of the values of segmented assimilation adherents. They are actively distancing themselves from such a depiction of underclass Latinos.

At the same time, especially among our white-collar respondents, there is some substantiation of traditional, linear assimilation. Some white-collar respondents choose to de-emphasize their Latino heritage by speaking English without an accent and assimilating seamlessly into Anglo life. The epigraph to this chapter, "Hire me because I'm good, not Latino," is one way of subtly discounting Latinos who do call attention to their heritage and language skills as a way of finding jobs or clients. In some cases, it even indicates indignation at affirmative action efforts directed at Latinos.

Still, many respondents describe the occupational benefits of a more selective form of acculturation, one wherein migrants can use their ethnicity to their advantage. We find evidence of numerous white-collar Latinos who are successful *as* Latino workers, using Spanish to good effect in the workplace, maximizing Latino social networks, and emphasizing the importance of Latino consumers and businesses. The stories of these respondents show Richmond Latinos can achieve upward mobility without sacrificing cultural ties and values. As segmented assimilation theory predicts, full acculturation is not the only route to economic advantage, and can in fact be disadvantageous when maintaining cultural traits or language actually works to economic gain.

Chapter 7

Religion and Secular Assimilation in Richmond

> I struggled with religiosity questions . . . I am still spiritual, but I don't
> practice a religion.
>
> —Fifty-seven-year-old Bolivian woman

Newcomers face many options as they negotiate ties with a new community. One of the most important can be whether or not to join an existing religious organization. Historically, religion has played a major role in assimilation. Ethnic places of worship can provide social and cultural ties to the country of origin as well as adaptive mechanisms and informal networks leading to adjustment in the host country (Ebaugh 2003). Immigrants can bring their own religious organizations with them, join local congregations, or simply take on a nonreligious stance as they adapt to local living conditions. To what extent is religion still an important factor in the assimilation process? Are current ethnic groups relying on religious participation to become part of their host societies?

We contend that the connections between class, religion, and assimilation are not fully explored until one takes into account of all the options available to immigrant groups. Segmented assimilation theory suggests a variety of ways of adapting, and would lead us to expect more than the traditional patterns. Some immigrants may see comfort in maintaining the original religion—Catholicism for many Latin Americans. Selective acculturation adherents would likely remain in these beliefs rather than converting to Protestantism. Rather than complete assimilation, the church now incorporates Latinos into the Anglo-dominated institution without requiring that they shed ethnic identity; indeed, the church may even encourage Latino members to remain ethnically apart through Spanish masses and so forth (Levitt 2002). Those most assimilated might have become so by choosing a Protestant or even a secular path.

We expand on previous literature here by examining Latinos who are nonreligious as well as Protestant or Catholic. In the case of Richmond Latinos, we investigate whether the pattern of assimilation for secular immigrants is any different than for immigrants who retain their faith of origin or convert.

Furthermore, we ask whether social class affects assimilation through religion in the same manner that it affects other aspects of the assimilation process.

Studies of earlier twentieth-century ethnic groups who immigrated to the United States highlight the importance of religion in assimilation. Religion provided immigrants with a familiar space in a host society where they could hold on to their ethnic identity even as they and their children became part of the larger culture (Alexander 1987; Dolan 1975; Mor 1992).[1] The "triple melting pot" of religious faiths represented at the time (Protestant, Catholic, and Jewish) came from a common base and were not remarkably dissimilar, yet encompassed the diversity of the immigrant population. The process remained in place for much of the twentieth century; as late as the sixties, Herberg was still confirming the centrality of religion in ethnic assimilation (Herberg 1960).

Current research also documents the role of religious practice for more recent immigrants. Two issues make the post-1965 immigrant wave distinct from the previous one. First, it is a more racially diverse wave, with large proportions of Latinos and Asians who are not as easily absorbed into Anglo society (Kazal 1995; Rumbaut 1997). Second, changes in immigration law since 1965 bring an array of non-European populations to the United States, with religious options that go beyond the Judeo-Christian panoply. The greater variety of faith experiences is reorganizing the religious landscape (Ebaugh and Chafez 2000; Eck 2001; Kivisto 1992; Lawrence 2002; Warner 1998).

While religion continues to provide an important connection to an immigrant's country of origin, offering social and cultural support to ease adjustment to a new country, the variety of transplanted faiths (Buddhism, Hinduism, Islam, Sikh, the indigenous faiths of Latin America) filter the U.S. experience in radically different ways (Gregory 1999; Haddad and Lummis 1987; Kurien 1998; Lin 1996; Murphy 1994). Recent groups must negotiate a valid space for their faiths in the United States while coping with the demands of a new culture (witness the creation of networks of Buddhist and Islamic houses of worship in various parts of the United States). Their presence breaks the monolithic hold of Christianity on the nation's religious scene, allowing greater freedom not only for alternative religious practices but greater acceptance of conversion and even secularization.

The bulk of the literature on religion and assimilation for the post-1965 wave of immigrants spotlights how religious practices affect cultural and social adaptation. Immigrants who maintain their religion of origin often find their faith transition to the United States less problematic. The consistency between religious life back home and here aids their transition to the new country. A negative consequence, however, is that maintaining their faith may hinder their assimilation into other aspects of U.S. culture compared those who do not keep original religious practices. Since language and culture can remain intact in these religious settings, immigrants are less likely to learn English or adopt U.S. customs.

Some immigrants, of course, convert to Protestantism, often joining ethnic Protestant congregations but still moving closer to the nation's general religious culture. Conversion allows immigrants to reaffirm their ethnic identity, while giving up ancestral gods and traditions less adaptable to U.S. life (Chen 2002; Chong 1998; Marin and Gamba 1993; Ng 2002; Yang 1999). The new Protestant identity facilitates the crossing of cultural barriers with a degree of ease that often eludes those who remain committed to non-Protestant religions of origin.

Converts to U.S. Protestantism find in their religion a conduit to many aspects of the larger culture, even as it affirms ethnic solidarity. Among Chinese immigrants in California, conversion to Protestantism increased levels of cohesiveness, while also exposing them to aspects of mainstream culture. Congregants were more likely than non-converts to listen to and speak English, were more exposed to U.S. cultural mores, and celebrated Christian and U.S. festivals (Ng 2002). Comparable studies have found that conversion fosters both ethnic reproduction and assimilation for other ethnic groups, even more so than for those who maintain their religion of origin (Min 1992; Yang and Ebaugh 2001).

For Koreans, especially second-generation Koreans, the practice of Protestantism dovetails with a high level of ethnic religious participation as well as considerable economic integration (Chong 1998; Hurh and Kim 1990). Warner also observes that religious participation in Korean Americans tends to be accompanied by an unusually high degree of ethnic identity and self-consciousness (1990:261). That fact challenges assimilation theories that associate upward mobility with the loosening of ethnic ties (Warner 1953; Whyte 1943).

Social class is an important mediator of the relationship between religion and assimilation. For disadvantaged groups, conversion provides a buffer between immigrants and an alien dominant culture. Among Salvadorans and Peruvians living in the United States, Vazquez (1999) found that Pentecostalism provided a variety of survival strategies as they struggled with increasing poverty, ethnic community disintegration, and a hostile political environment. Pentecostalism has greater appeal among recent working-class immigrants with low levels of educational attainment (Vazquez 1999:630).

Among Latinos more generally, conversion to mainline Protestantism means a shift toward a culturally dominant religion that offers the prospect of faster cultural adjustment, if not greater economic integration. A major effect of non-Catholic affiliation for Latinos is the lowering of "the salience of Hispanic identity" (Hunt 1998:842), but there is no conclusive evidence that converted Latinos have higher socioeconomic status than their Catholic counterparts. Contrary to the Asian example, Hunt concludes that Protestantism "probably does not represent a new institutional path toward assimilation and upward mobility" for Latinos (1998:828).

Reviewing the relationship between religion and immigrant assimilation, Ebaugh argues that little is known about immigrants who adopt a nonreligious stance in this country (2003). We suggest here that not being religious is a valid third option for new arrivals, one not examined by current investigations of religion and assimilation. Studies of post-1965 immigrants have focused on all the other possible ways in which religion might be related to assimilation, but we know of no single study that directly compares the effect of the three options—remaining faithful to one's religion of origin, converting to the dominant religion, Protestantism, or becoming nonreligious—on assimilation for second wave immigrants.

The adoption of a nonreligious lifestyle is obviously a more marked change than conversion, since it may mean losing ties to religion of origin or to ethnic roots altogether. Still, a nonreligious or even secular lifestyle is easier to choose now than at the beginning of the last century. Despite the persistence of religion in U.S. society, there is a much greater tolerance for a secular lifestyle today (Falk 1995; Roof 1993, 1999).[2] If leaving religion behind is a possible choice for immigrants or their children, how would this choice affect assimilation in the United States? Would it hinder, facilitate, or have little effect on the pace and process by which one becomes part of U.S. society?

Given Richmond's quite traditional and religious outlook (Dabney 1990), the city is a fascinating setting for the study of religion. Being part of a religious community in Richmond immediately provides newcomers with a network of meaningful associations. However, the Latino population of Richmond is not as homogenous as one would expect when it comes to religion. Richmond Latinos typically come from a traditionally Catholic background, but in our sample we also find converts to Protestantism as well as nonreligious Latinos, as we discuss below.

Measuring Religion and Assimilation

To gauge the effects of religion on cultural assimilation we employ three variables—the two language assimilation variables discussed in chapter 4 (everyday language use and language used for various media), and a third variable designed to measure value similarity. In this case, we use one's approach to work, using agreement or disagreement with the statement "A job is just a way of earning money, no more." To the extent that the centrality of work reflects a cultural value of Anglo-Americans, disagreement with this statement indicates a greater acceptance of the dominant ideology.

For a structural assimilation measure, we use the social distance variable discussed in chapter 4. Alba and Nee (1997) argue that for the post-1965 wave of immigrants certain additional factors should be critical when talking about structural assimilation: level of socioeconomic attainment and participation in the open labor market, among other things. Social class variables, in particular, also play an integral role in the assimilation and religion literature. Following their suggestion, we also include variables concerning the Latinos' level of socioeconomic attainment and occupation to measure structural assimilation.

To the variables suggested by the literature, we add a political measure as a control, since participation in the political arena is an important sign of becoming part of the U.S. society. Here, we use a political participation scale of four items: voting in presidential elections, voting in local elections, contributing money to political parties, and attending political rallies (we discuss political participation further in the next chapter).[3]

When we compare the experiences of three Latino groups in Richmond— Catholics, Protestants, and the nonreligious—the first thing that stands out, not unexpectedly, is the size of the Catholic population (Figure 7.1). We ask respondents, "In what religion were you raised?" and "What is your current religious preference?" Catholicism has been a prevailing force in the lives of our respondents, whether immigrant or not, and whether discussing current or youth religious affiliations. More than 80 percent of Richmond Latinos were raised Catholic. Although the majority are still Catholic as adults (57 percent), a substantial number of Richmond Latinos have switched religious identification since childhood (Figure 7.2). Current mainline and evangelical Protestants both acquired new converts once our respondents became adults, and together make up one-quarter of our sample. Most telling for our purposes, however, is the change over the life course to no religion. More than one in ten Richmond Latinos has no religious preference as an adult, although very few were nonreligious as children (these findings hold true for women as well as men).

Our findings are very similar to those of the American Religious Identification Survey (ARIS/PARAL) (Keysar, Kosmin, and Mayer 2001). Looking at a subsample of Latinos in a national study of U.S. religious identification, the authors find almost the same numbers for religious affiliation: 57 percent of Latinos were Catholics, 26 percent were Protestants, and 13 percent are

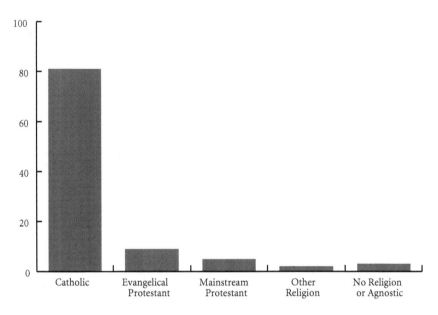

Figure 7.1. Religion of Origin for Richmond Latino Respondents

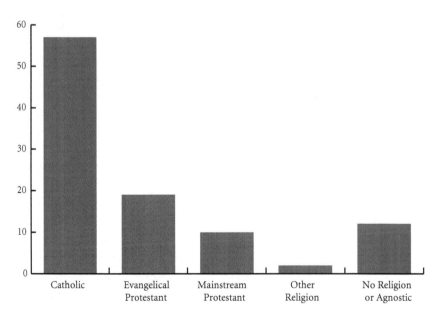

Figure 7.2. Current Religious Identification of Richmond Latino Respondents

nonreligious (we thus feel quite confident that our sample is comparable to the national population). Furthermore, the nonreligious population appears to be growing: according to the ARIS/ PARAL study, the number of Latinos who identify as "no religion" increased from 6 percent in 1990 to 13 percent in 2000 (Keysar, Kosmin, and Mayer 2001:6).

How do levels of assimilation vary for the Latino groups? Our data show that mainline Protestants and nonreligious Latinos score highest on both of the language indices, meaning that each group is more likely than Catholics or Evangelical Protestants to use English rather than Spanish in everyday life (Table 7.1). Both variables are scaled from 1 (most use of Spanish/least use of English) to 5, with an average of 4 indicating "mostly English and some Spanish." Mainline Protestants and the nonreligious use significantly more English in everyday life (about 3.5) and when using various media (over 4) than do Evangelical Protestants or Catholics. The universes of the former groups, at least linguistically, are more defined along English-speaking lines.[4]

The social distance index renders similar results. A high value on the index indicates greater affiliation with other Latinos (and less social interaction with members of the dominant culture); the implication of social contact with Anglos rather than Latinos is one of greater assimilation. Again, nonreligious Latinos and mainline Protestants are those more likely to associate with Anglos in their everyday life (although Catholics are here not too dissimilar from the other two). Evangelical Protestants are the least assimilated in terms of social distance, with greater contact with other Latinos.[5] Indeed, many Evangelical churches in Richmond have begun to minister extensively to Latino migrants and refugees, offering masses, social services, and even legal advice in Spanish. Evangelical Protestantism, then, serves as a force of unity for Richmond Latinos, but not one that provides much structural assimilation into the dominant culture.

The socioeconomic well-being of Richmond Latinos also varies significantly by religious preference (Table 7.1). Evangelical Protestants have the lowest levels of educational attainment (an average score of 4 indicates education at the high school level) and are the least likely to have jobs at the top of the occupational hierarchy (occupational status values range from 1 to 9; the higher the occupation score, the closer to the top of the occupational ladder). Catholics are somewhat average in occupational and educational attainment. The difference between nonreligious Latinos and mainline Protestants is more distinct: here, mainline Protestants average more education, while the nonreligious are more likely to be employed in higher occupational echelons. Both groups, however, indicate high levels of socioeconomic attainment.

Table 7.1. Analysis of Variance for Religious Preference,
by Cultural and Social Assimilation Variables

	Language Use[a]	Language of Media Use[a]	Social Distance[b]	Work Attitude[c]	Education[d]	Occupation[e]	Political Participation[f]
Catholic	3.04	3.69	1.75	2.00	5.09	5.58	.58
Evangelical Protestant	2.99	3.63	1.92	2.26	4.34	4.02	.49
Mainline Protestant	3.54	4.03	1.70	1.87	5.55	5.70	.59
No Religion	3.53	4.09	1.69	1.74	5.34	6.89	.58
Average Total	3.14	3.76	1.77	2.01	5.02	5.46	.56
F	3.97**	2.85*	2.83*	2.73*	5.34**	8.32**	2.61*
N	294	261	294	288	296	256	198

* $p < .05$; ** $p < .01$

[a] Language Use/Media Use Index ranges from 1–5, where 1 = more use of Spanish, 5 = more use of English.
[b] Social Distance Index: ranges from 1 to 3, where higher values meaning closer affiliation to a Latino community.
[c] Work Attitude ranges from 1–4, where 1 equals most disagreement.
[d] Education ranges from 1–7, where 1 = equals least education, 7 equals most education.
[e] Occupation ranges from 1–9, where 1 = lowest status, 9 = highest status.
[f] Political Participation Index ranges from 0–1, where 0 = least participation, 1 = most participation.
Source: Latinos in Richmond Survey.

In contrast to our findings, the ARIS/PARAL study finds no national differences in education between Latino Catholics, Protestants, and those with no religion. In terms of employment, nonreligious Latinos are less likely to be employed at all (though no other measure of occupational status is given). Moreover, income levels for the nonreligious are lower than for other groups. However, the authors note the nonreligious in their study tended to be younger and "might not have established themselves economically" (Keysar, Kosmin, and Mayer 2001:10). The authors find that more than half of the nonreligious Latinos were under thirty (2001:8). Our respondents, on the other hand, tend to be older (with an average age of forty-two), even the nonreligious. In that sense, our sample, though smaller, may be better at capturing the effects of the no religion option for Latinos who are older and more economically settled.

The findings in Table 7.1 also show that value similarity differs by religious preference. Higher scores here indicate agreement with the statement, "A job is just a way of earning money, no more," with a value range of 1 to 4. Evangelical Protestants are the most likely to agree with the statement (2.26), followed by Catholics next, then mainline Protestants. Nonreligious Latinos average a response of 1.74 (a one meaning the least agreement with the statement).[6] For nonreligious Latinos, at the top of the occupational hierarchy as noted above, it is much more likely that work is a source of more than just income, so it is not surprising that they have the lowest score.

Political participation is also significantly related to religious practice among Richmond Latinos. The political participation variable is an index of four behaviors: voting in local and presidential elections (U.S. citizens only), contributing money to political parties, and attending political rallies. Scores range from zero (meaning no participation at all) to one (meaning strong participation). Nonreligious Latinos are as politically involved as mainline Protestants or Catholics (averaging about .6), while Evangelical Protestants participated in politics significantly less than the other groups.

Religious Change and Assimilation

The data in the previous section are static: they merely show the relationship between the respondents' *current* religious preferences and measures of cultural and socioeconomic assimilation. Included are foreign-born and U.S.-born Latinos who have converted from Catholicism to Protestantism or to other options, as well as those who have retained their original religion, even after one or more generations of life in the United States. Does religious conversion affect the assimilation process, and if so, in what ways?

Since we can compare religious identification in childhood to that in adulthood, we can track religious changes that may be related to assimilation. The reduced number of Catholics in adulthood indicates that many convert from Catholicism, but to what degree exactly? In Figure 7.3, we show that 58 percent of respondents have remained Catholic from childhood, while 11 percent remained Protestant. About 16 converted to either mainline or evangelical Protestantism from Catholicism, and 9 percent adopted a nonreligious orientation. About 5 percent experienced other religious changes (e.g., from Catholicism to some other religion).[7] Because these last individuals are few in number and represent mostly idiosyncratic cases, we do not consider them in the remaining analyses.

We have limited evidence that the turn to no religion deepens the longer immigrants (or their families) live in the United States. First-generation immigrants are more likely to remain Catholic (Figure 7.4). Sixty-four percent of the foreign-born have stayed Catholic, while only 54 percent of the U.S.-born Latinos have done so. Second-generation Latinos, on the other hand, are

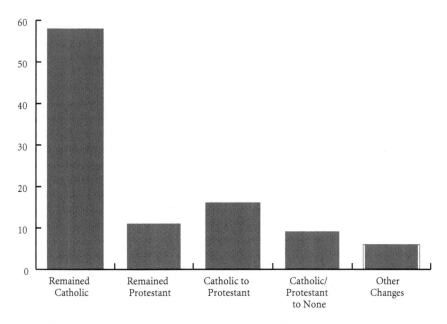

Figure 7.3. Religious Conversion among Richmond Latino Respondents

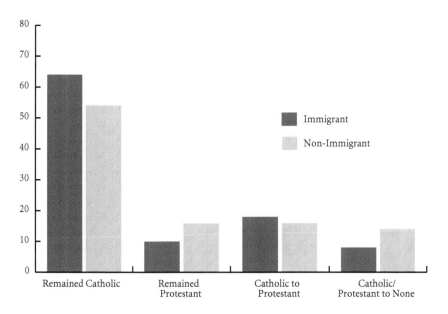

Figure 7.4. Religious Conversion by Immigrant Status (in Percentages)

more likely to be nonreligious. Nonreligious Latinos increase from 8 percent of first-generation immigrants to 14 percent of second-generation Latinos. Further, those who now have no religion (either former Catholics or Protestants) are more likely to be at least second-generation (or more) respondents. Although our data are cross-sectional rather than linking specific generations, there does appear to be a trend whereby the no religion option goes hand in hand with length of time in the United States.

Measuring religious change over the respondent's life rather than a stationary religious identification yields a more complex picture of the relationship between religion, assimilation, and social class. When we add religious change to the equation, many of the variables relating religious preference with cultural and structural assimilation are no longer significant (Table 7.2).

The relationship between religion and acculturation, especially in this second wave, is complicated by the presence both of converts to Evangelical Protestantism *and* those who move from Catholicism to no religion. Evangelical Protestant Latino groups are growing quickly as well, in terms of both new arrivals with already-established Evangelical affiliations, and converts once in the United States (Hunt 1998). Evangelical Protestants, however, typically maintain ethnic and cultural ties through religion, while other Latinos change religious preference during the process of acculturation, potentially concealing

Table 7.2. Mean Scores for Selected Assimilation Variables, by Religious Conversion

	Language Use[a]	Occupational Status[b]	Political Participation[c]
Remained Catholic	3.04	5.59	.58
Remained Protestant	3.22	4.86	.52
Catholic to Protestant	3.23	4.56	.52
Catholic/Protestant to None	3.54	6.64	.61
Total	3.14	5.43	.56
F	1.95*	3.29**	2.13*
N	279	244	188

[a] Language Use Index ranges from 1-5, where 1 = more use of Spanish, 5 = more use of English.
[b] Occupation ranges from 1-9, where 1 = lowest status, 9 = highest status.
[c] Political Participation Index ranges from 0-1, where 0 = least participation, 1 = most participation.
*$p < .1$;   **$p < .05$

Source: Latinos in Richmond Survey.

relationships between religious change and assimilation unless we consider the nuances of those changes.

Nevertheless, the relationship between religious change and language assimilation (although only significant at 0.1), does show results in the predicted direction: Latinos who became nonreligious have the highest average language assimilation score, indicating those who change to no religion are the most likely to use English in a variety of contexts.

Two other relationships are noteworthy. Religious change is significantly related to both occupational status and political participation. Those Latinos who have changed to no religion have a higher occupational status than either religious converts or those who remain Catholic (this difference is significant at .05). In terms of political participation, nonreligious changers appear to be more likely to vote and be involved in other ways, especially compared to Protestants and converts to Protestantism (the relationship is significant at 0.1). We suggest that these changes go hand-in-hand rather than being causally related—respondents who are politically involved, more assimilated, and so forth, are also more likely to change to no religion over a lifetime.

Reconsidering Religious Assimilation

Our findings show that it is important to take the experience of nonreligious Latinos into account when examining the relationship between religion and assimilation. Such an idea sounds paradoxical at first. But if we limit ourselves to studying the effect that different religions have on the process of immigrant integration, we may lose sight of the fact that immigrants and their children have other options today. It is possible for people to assimilate without establishing ties to a community through a religious organization or even professing a religious lifestyle; indeed, in some cases it is more likely.

It is true that were we to limit our sample to religious Latinos in Richmond, we would have found the usual patterns for the effect of religion on assimilation. We would find religion aiding assimilation either as a connection to the homeland (for those who remain in their religion of origin), or as a bridge to the cultural space of the host country (for those who choose Protestantism). In each case, religion still provides a means to increase familiarity with the cultural dimensions of the new country, while encouraging social assimilation, socioeconomic attainment, and political participation. There are some notable differences between Catholics, mainline Protestants, and evangelical Latinos, but religion is still functioning in Richmond as previous scholars have hypothesized it does.

What the inclusion of nonreligious Latinos brings to the picture is the awareness that there are other pathways to assimilation, some that do not require religion at all. Even in a city such as Richmond, where religion plays an important role, nonreligious Latinos can be involved and integrated into the community even if they do not belong to a religious organization. The nonreligious Latinos surveyed do not report any greater stress or hardship than the rest of the sample in becoming acculturated to the Richmond area.

Furthermore, not only is the nonreligious process of assimilation as functional as the religious ones, nonreligious Latinos are the most integrated in the entire sample! The group that consistently and significantly shows the highest levels of adaptation, especially economic adaptation, for the measures employed by our study is precisely the one with no religious affiliation. By every measure (with the exception of education)—their use of the language, work orientation, occupational attainment, and levels of political participation—they are the most adapted to the dominant culture and institutions of their host society. Despite our reputation as a religious nation, "becoming American," for these respondents, involves becoming nonreligious.

Some of these patterns hold true even when we examine conversion patterns specifically rather than merely religious preference. Though the numbers of Latinos in our sample who changed from some religious preference to none is small, they can be compared to those who remained Catholic or Protestant or who converted to Protestantism. The nonreligious changers are less likely to be immigrants, indicating the likelihood that such a change happens between generations. As further evidence of their integration into the dominant society, those who change from Catholicism or Protestantism to no religion are more likely to use English, have a higher occupational status, and be involved in the Richmond political landscape. Nonreligious Latinos tend to have higher levels of integration in Richmond despite their nonparticipation in the local religious networks. Perhaps it is these very connections to work and political institutions that provide acculturation mechanisms that differ from those of religious organizations.

To be sure, "no religion" here may simply mean "no organized religion," and it does not mean that spirituality is unimportant. We have no measures to study whether nonreligious Latinos have beliefs in God or partake in forms of spirituality that extend beyond church boundaries. Moreover, some of them do occasionally attend religious services—about 20 percent attend church "several times a year" or more. Richmond Latino Catholics, it should be noted, also vary considerably in their church attendance; almost 40 percent say they attend church only "several times a year" or less frequently, and 70 percent are not involved in church activities other than attendance at mass. However, we suspect that the behavioral choice of Latinos to lead a nonreligious life indicates an important level of secularity that may be related to ethnic adaptation for certain populations. We leave it to other researchers to more thoroughly examine increasing secularity among Latinos, using variables such as intention, the importance of religious practices, and other questions related to a decidedly secular disposition.

When it comes to religion, the Latino experience in Richmond is marked both by religious switching and by secularization. Religion remains a persistent force in the immigrant experience. But life in Richmond, as segmented assimilation theory would indicate, has led to a widening of the options. While a large majority of Hispanics grew up Catholic and a good number remain so, another group among them converted to different Protestant denominations as a process of adaptation. Working-class Latinos still find a haven in religion as they maintain cultural and religious heritage by remaining Catholic or by becoming Evangelical Protestant. They may especially perceive the increasing secularization of the United States as a process to be avoided. More striking is the fact that educated and wealthier Latinos have experienced assimilation as freedom *from* religion. For these respondents, becoming American provides the space to lead a nonreligious lifestyle.

Chapter 8

Public Life, Political Participation, and Community Presence

It is very important that there are people like us in the government, so
that we have more strength or force in political things and that they
listen to us. The Latinos are very important for the political parties.
—Twenty-six-year-old Salvadoran

In addition to everyday concerns, such as work or family life, moving into a
new area also involves negotiating other aspects of local life, such as access
to political institutions. Political participation marks an important transition
as newcomers establish themselves. Individually, for an immigrant, political
action means moving from the status of outsider to becoming a fully active U.S.
citizen. Collectively, the transition can transform an anonymous fringe group
into a vocal political segment of the U.S. population (Jones-Correa 1998). The
integration of Latinos into the political arena is currently reshaping regional
and national political dynamics in the United States (see, e.g., Campo-Flores
and Fineman 2005; DeSipio 1996).

Participation in political activities and organizations of the host society is
an important indicator of structural assimilation, signaling entry into primary
group relations. According to Portes and Rumbaut (1996), the longer an immigrant population lives in the United States, the more likely it is that political
concerns will shift from home country struggles. As the ethnic group becomes
more incorporated into various aspects of U.S. society, its interest gravitates
toward U.S.-based political matters.

Particularly for immigrants in the first large wave of the twentieth century,
political participation presented the means to become more accepted and also
to influence the policymaking of the host society (Yans-McLaughlin 1990).
Once assimilated, though, immigrants often continued to act as a political
bloc by nationality, even though the politics were local. The Irish provided
a classic example of that process, with the first generation remaining deeply
interested in the Irish struggles, only to become part of the local political scene
in New England by the second generation, and eventually an important part
of national politics. Portes and Rumbaut refer to this multigenerational trend

as "the fundamental matrix of American-based politics" (1996:102). Does the same pattern hold true for the second wave of migration, especially among immigrant groups such as Latinos, who are more likely to have lower citizen and voting rates nationally?

Politics and community involvement have the potential to unify the Latinos in Richmond. But just how developed a process is political incorporation in Richmond, especially given the segmented nature of the Latino population we have already explored? It is likely that groups will begin to split, perhaps based on class interests, perhaps along party lines. In this chapter we explore the degree to which political participation is also related to social class, especially as realized through length of residency and assimilation measures. We conclude with qualitative data on the degree to which Latinos in Richmond are involved in the political community. Despites the emergence of some in pan-ethnic Latino organizations and events, the segmented experiences of Richmond Latinos interfere with the creation of a unified Latino community.

The Importance of Latino Political Participation

Political participation is important for Latino newcomers as a means of further incorporation into a local community, but their expansion in political life is also relevant to the U.S. political landscape. Given the growth of the community, it is not surprising that interest in Latino political participation has risen steadily among political actors and groups in the United States. Efforts to recruit Latinos began as early as the 1950s, as evidenced by the *Viva Kennedy!* campaign. Latinos, particularly Mexican Americans organizing Kennedy clubs, became actively involved in President Kennedy's election (DeSipio et al. 1999). During the 1970s Latino support for Democrats exceeded 80 percent. In the 1976 presidential election, Jimmy Carter received 76 percent of the Latino vote (Garcia 1997).

For the next decade, Latino support remained steady: around 60 to 70 percent of the Latino vote went to Democratic presidential candidates (de la Garza and DeSipio 1992). More concerted attention to Latinos developed in the 1980s, when candidates, campaigns, and political parties intention-ally targeted Hispanics as an aggregate group as part of their outreach (de la Garza and DeSipio 1992, 1996). Reagan's opponents received plenty of Latino support—Carter had 61 percent of the Latino vote in 1980, and Mondale received 62 percent in 1984. Dukakis received 69 percent of the Latino vote in 1988 (Cain and Keiwiet 1987; Garcia 1997).

Despite some erosion of interest in the party during the 1990s, Latino support for Democratic presidential candidates remained high: 62 percent for Bill Clinton in 1992 and 72 percent in 1996 (DeSipio et al. 1999; Garcia 1997). In 1992, Bill Clinton and George Bush competed for Latino votes in six states with the largest Latino electorates (Texas, Florida, Arizona, New Mexico, Colorado, and New Jersey). Bush won the first two but Clinton carried the other four, the Latino vote making a difference in the margin of victory in all states. As DeSipio et al. report, "had no Latino voted for the winning candidate, the outcome would have changed in all six" (1999:11). Moreover, during the 1996 election, 94 percent of Latinos voted for Democratic Congressional candidates (DeSipio et al. 1999; Garcia 1997).

By 2000 Latinos represented 8 percent of the national electorate (a 60 percent increase from the previous presidential election). As the Latino franchise continues to grow, Latino participation becomes even more vital in close elections. In the words of two *Newsweek* political analysts, "with turnout increasing from about six million in 2000 to an estimated 8 million last year, the Hispanic vote has become the El Dorado of American elections" (Campo-Flores and Fineman 2005:26), especially as the likelihood of Democratic support has become less certain. While Gore carried 64 percent of the Latino vote in 2000, John Kerry received only 53 percent of the Latino vote in 2004 (Campo-Flores and Fineman 2005).

Fundamental to understanding the recent significance of Latino political involvement in the United States is an increasing ambiguity about their partisanship. While Latinos have traditionally sided with the Democratic Party, Latino support still varies widely by national origin. The political context of the sending countries significantly shapes the immigrants' politics in the United States, particularly among the first generation. Most notably here, Cuban Americans have historically been loyal to the Republican Party given the party's strong stance against Castro and policies that seek to limit Cuba's ability to be a player in the Caribbean basin (see Moreno and Warren 1992). Mexicans and Puerto Ricans, on the other hand, tend to be more liberal in orientation and to vote for Democrats (Kenski and Tisinger 2006).

As the Latino population grows, it becomes a deciding factor in various jurisdictions—much more so than other ethnic groups, as their political loyalties are less clear. Although Latinos are more likely to vote for Democratic presidential candidates, their political preferences and party affiliations are not always as predictable. In one study, party affiliations among Latinos broke down as follows: 63 percent Democrat, 16 percent independent, and 21 percent Republican (Leal et al. 2006). Only about 40 percent of Latinos registered to vote are Democrats, however, with about 20 percent Republican

(Campo-Flores and Fineman 2005). Moreover, according to data collected by Kenski and Tisinger in 2004, about 40 percent of Latinos use the label conservative or very conservative, 38 percent consider themselves moderate, and only 21 percent would say they are either liberal or very liberal (2006). Should the U.S. electorate continue to be divided into red and blue states, as it has been, partisan competition for Latino votes will only grow over time.

Rapid integration into the U.S. political system also means a rise in the number of Latino elected officials at the local, state, and federal levels. García notes that, "in California alone Latinos now hold 762 elective offices, twenty percent of assembly and senate positions, and six members of the state's congressional delegation" (2003:112). Research on Latinos in other parts of the country shows that Latinos tend to be more concerned with problems and policies at the state level than with national issues. Activism and political involvement among Latinos is stronger at the local and neighborhood levels as well (Cruz 1998; Hardy-Fanta 1993; Jennings 1994; Pardo 1998; Portes and Stepnick 1993; Saito 1998). It is often through local struggles against unfavorable governmental proposals and actions that Latinos develop their own leadership and become more politically mobilized (Falcón 1988; Grenier et al. 1994). As they reach a certain level of success in local struggles, they become more motivated to play an important role as political actors in a wider setting, "[pursuing] other issues of importance and interest with similar energy and commitment" (García 2003:87).

Signs of Latino importance were present during Virginia's gubernatorial election of 2001, which took place during our data collection. With a quarter of a million Latinos living in the state, both Mark Warner and Mark Earley organized concerted efforts into the Latino community (especially in central and northern Virginia). The candidates recruited Latinos to campaign, organized Latino fundraisers, and translated campaign materials into Spanish. Such targeted mobilization—that is, when groups identify and recruit Latinos who are likely to respond positively to involvement—significantly affects Latino political participation (García 2003; García and de la Garza 1985).

Latino votes translated into increased representation in Virginia. Right after the 2001 election a Latino was appointed to lead the Department of Motor Vehicles, and in 2004 another became the first Latino member of the Virginia Board of Education (Wermers 2004:B3). Governor Warner set up a Latino Advisory Commission to hold regular hearings on a number of issues related to Virginia Latinos. He also appointed the first Latino liaison in the state's history. Following the state example, in 2004 the city of Richmond established its own Hispanic Liaison office.

An example of local mobilization surfaced in a demonstration staged by the Latino community at Governor Mark Warner's Alexandria home in 2003. Along with dissatisfaction about a new Virginia bill that would refuse driver's licenses to undocumented immigrants, Latinos were also protesting against an earlier bill that would also deny in-state college tuition to their children (Cho 2002, 2003a, 2003b). The mobilization prompted a conciliatory meeting between Warner and local Latino leaders. While protests against the same driver's license and in-state college tuition policies took place in the Richmond area, they did not reach the level of organization found in Northern Virginia. Nevertheless, it is only a matter of time before that sort of political expression reaches the central Virginia area.

Latino votes also mattered in the governor's race of 2005, although to what extent is unclear. Leading up to the election, media commentators noted Tim Kaine's ability to speak Spanish as well as his outreach to the Latino community, but there were no exit polls of either the gubernatorial elections of 2001 or 2005 noting the breakdown in voting by Hispanic ethnicity. Given Virginia's population patterns and new prominence on the national political map, it will not be surprising if the question is finally asked in 2009.

Factors Affecting Latino Political Participation

Despite the fact that Latino participation in U.S. politics is on the rise, nationwide Latino levels of participation are still relatively low compared to those of the general population, including both whites and African Americans (Leal et al. 2006). This is certainly a function of both citizenship—obviously an immigrant must be naturalized to take advantage of the franchise—and the youth of the Latino population. Even with citizenship, voting and other forms of political participation continue to be correlated with factors that are specific to immigrant and/or ethnic status—for example, length of residence and English facility. It takes time for newcomers to achieve the political advantages of participation.

Historical and even current anecdotal evidence suggests that immigrant ethnic communities are likely to vote as a unified block, but the statistical evidence shows a more nuanced picture of the relationship between immigrant status, ethnic identity, demographic variables, and political behavior. In a landmark study of political participation among Latinos, Calvo and Rosenstone reviewed Latino turnout rates between 1974 and 1986. The authors found that age, gender, class, and education were all related to political participation. Older, male, middle- and upper-class, and highly educated Latinos were more likely to vote. National origin is also significant, with Puerto Ricans being the least politically involved, followed by Mexican Americans. Cubans have very high rates of voting even comparable to those of non-Latinos. However, when controlling for other effects in a multivariate analysis, age and class were the only variables that retained their effect on increased turnout, especially for Mexicans and Puerto Ricans (Calvo and Rosenstone 1989).

Other researchers have emphasized the effect of cultural factors on Latino political participation. Cultural measures include the use of Spanish language, culture of origin, and the importance placed on Latino cultural values (Hero 1991; McClain and García 1993; Verba et al. 1993). Culture of origin impacts the move from the politics of one cultural universe into the mainstream patterns of participation in the host culture. Some aspects of the original ethnic culture may enhance participation, while others might inhibit it.

More recent literature confirms the importance of socioeconomic status as a major determinant of Latino political participation (Brady et al. 1995). Income levels and education are a strong determinant of immigrant political involvement (Bueker 2006; Huckfeldt and Sprague 1992; Leighley 1990). A supposition about the general population—that those who have a direct economic stake in political outcomes are more likely to participate—holds true for Latinos.

Finally, and perhaps in conjunction with socioeconomic status, prior research also finds political determinants that influence Latino voting. Among the political variables that contribute to Latino involvement are political trust, a voter's sense of political efficacy, and the amount of political interest in a given campaign. Interaction with other politically active actors or groups is another important factor, along with one's level of political mobilization, which includes signing petitions, posting campaign signs, registering to vote, or attending rallies (García 1997). We use examples of several of these noted measures in our analysis of political participation among Richmond Latinos.

Political Preferences and Political Participation

A review of the political preferences of Richmond Latinos shows that they mirror fairly closely the overall predilections of Latinos across the United States: fewer than 30 percent would call themselves liberal or even somewhat liberal; a larger group would opt for label moderate (nearly 40 percent); while the remaining 32 percent chose somewhat conservative or very conservative. These differences in political preference in our sample do not vary significantly by country of origin or gender.

When asked about political party preference, a slightly but not altogether different pattern emerges. Slightly more Latinos would call themselves Democrats than would use the label liberal. Thirty-two percent are Democrats, while only 23 percent say Republican. Fourteen percent call themselves independents, while 28 percent remain undecided. Nor are official political affiliation and political philosophy necessarily aligned. Approximately 20 percent of those who self-identify as Democrats also label themselves as conservative (although the reverse is not true for Republicans).

Needless to say, both of these questions on our survey include Latinos who are ineligible to vote in the United States. But the numbers change hardly at all if we look only at those Latinos who are citizens (though citizens are slightly more likely to choose a party affiliation than noncitizens, increasing to 35 percent Democrat and 30 percent Republican). Given the high levels of independent and undecided Latinos in the community, there are considerable opportunities for new voters that could be mined by the traditional political parties, if they are willing to address the concerns of independent Latinos. "I care about the issues that politicians have opinions about, not the party," remarked one respondent, a Columbian-born woman who has lived in the United States almost twenty years.

Richmond Latinos are unusually active in politics, with high levels of participation compared to Latinos nationwide. That fact is extraordinary considering the lack of historical Latino presence in the Richmond area and the short period they have had in which to become politically active here.

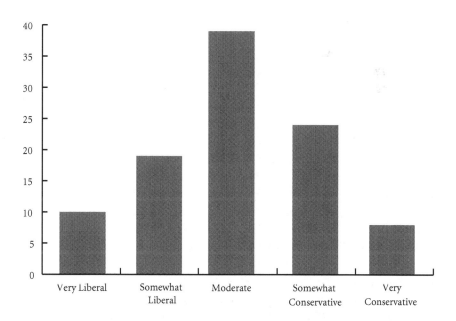

Figure 8.1. Political Preferences of Richmond Latino Respondents (in Percentages)

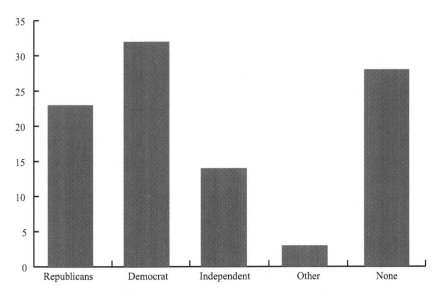

Figure 8.2. Party Affiliation of Richmond Latino Respondents (in Percentages)

Of course, high levels of citizenship facilitate this participation. Two-thirds of our sample are U.S. citizens, and of these, 26 percent by virtue of naturalization. For comparative purposes, 45 percent of the adult Latino population of the United States are noncitizens, with approximately 55 percent of these undocumented (Pew Hispanic Center 2007). Moreover, those who are not citizens show high levels of interest in becoming so. Of the 32 percent of our sample who are not citizens, approximately 80 percent state they will or would like to undergo the naturalization process. From all indications, Richmond Latinos set a premium on citizenship.

This is a community that also emphasizes voting. Among those respondents who are eligible to vote, 72 percent voted during the 2000 presidential election. This is considerably higher than the national turnout in presidential elections, even for whites, which is approximately sixty percent (Sierra 2000).[1] In local elections, voter turnout is not as strong even among the general population, and we expected much lower rates for local elections among our respondents. But 64 percent of Richmond Latinos say that they vote in local elections (a combination of the responses "always" and "sometimes miss one"). While we do not assume that self-reported voting automatically equals actual turnout (see Shaw et al. 2000), the numbers reported by our respondents strongly suggest that Richmond Latino citizens are much more politically involved than

Latinos in other parts of the country, although it is possible that this reflects higher political participation in Richmond overall.

Given these high rates of political involvement, we were curious about which variables might predict Richmond Latino participation in the political process. Immigrant status has no effect on voting patterns, but country of origin is a significant zero-order predictor of voting for both national and local elections (Table 8.1). As indicated by the literature, Cubans have the highest voting records in Richmond; Mexicans are slightly lower; and Puerto Ricans have among the lowest voting levels for presidential elections of the larger immigrant groups (which is unusual given their automatic U.S. citizenship, unlike the other migrant groups). Unexpectedly, ethnic groups that have little history of political participation even in their countries of origin—especially Salvadorans, but also other Central and South American groups—are highly active here. Furthermore, while Puerto Ricans have among the lowest voting rates in presidential elections, they have higher rates of participation in local elections.

We looked at the effects of other political measures on voting. The effect of political preference (a five-value measure from "very liberal" to "very conservative") on Latino voting is somewhat surprising—the more conservative Latinos are, the more likely they are to vote. Party preference is also a predictor of voting behavior. Republican Latinos are more likely to vote in presidential elections: 86 percent to 81 percent for Democrats. Seventy-four percent of independent

Table 8.1 Voting Patterns in Presidential and Local Elections, by Country of Origin (in Percentages)

	Presidential Elections*	Local Elections
Cubans	89	77
Colombians	54	46
Guatemalans	71	57
Mexicans	78	63
Other C. Americans	67	88
Other S. Americans	79	65
Puerto Ricans	58	69
Salvadorans	81	69
Overall Percentage	71	64
N	206	203*

*$\chi 2 = 13.6$, p < .1

Source: Latinos in Richmond Survey.

Latinos vote compared to 37 percent of undecided. More typically in other areas of the country, Democratic Latinos are more likely to turn out and vote than Republican Latinos (Segura, Falcon, and Pachon 1997).

From our two voting variables (presidential and local elections), we created a scaled variable to measure voting in a more continuous fashion (this is a different variable from the political index used in chapter 7). The new variable ranges from a high of seven, indicating those who voted in the presidential election and always vote in local elections, to a low of zero, or those who say they did not vote for president in 2000 and never vote in local elections. For this variable, we weighted participation in presidential elections higher than in local elections, such that someone who never votes in local elections but voted for president in 2000 would rate higher than someone who votes in local elections but did not vote for president. About one-third of Richmond Latinos eligible to vote fall into the highest voting category, meaning they vote consistently in both presidential and local elections.

Calvo and Rosenstone's predictions about the effect of demographic variables on voting hold for Richmond Latinos, as shown by correlations with the voting scale in Table 8.2. Older Richmond Latinos are more likely to vote than younger ones. Similarly, high-income, college-educated Latinos are more likely to vote than their less privileged counterparts. The only surprise in our study is related to gender. Whereas male Latinos are more politically active than females nationwide, in Richmond we find the opposite effect: Richmond *Latinas* are more likely to vote, showing levels of participation that are higher than those for the male Latino population. Women average almost a 5 on the seven-point scale, and men only a 4.4. Although the difference in mean voting behavior between genders is not great (and the t-test of the difference is not statistically significant at the .05 level), these values are in the opposite direction from what is predicted and thus remain compelling. Latinas are strong participants in local Richmond politics and are active in the community, spearheading many of the events Latino organizations put together.

Cultural factors affect Richmond Latino voting participation as well. Latinos who are more likely to vote in the Richmond area are also those who are most assimilated both culturally and socially, using the measures of language assimilation and social distance outlined in chapter 3.[2] Latinos whose cultural lives more closely reflect those of mainstream Anglos (in terms of using English or associating with Anglos over other Latinos) have the highest levels of political participation.

Of course, members of a community can participate politically in ways other than voting. Hero and Campbell (1996) argue that Latinos are just as

Table 8.2. Correlates of the Voting Index

Demographic Variables	
Age	r = .36**
Household Income	r = .35**
Education	r = .26**
Female	X = 4.95
Male	X = 4.41
Cultural Variables	
Language Use	r = .20**
Social Distance	r = −.24**
Political Variables	
Donated Money **	
Yes	X = 5.83
No	X = 4.27
Attended Rallies **	
Yes	X = 5.93
No	X = 4.23
Political Efficacy	r = −.26**
Political Preference	r = .14*
Total N	207

*p<.05,   **p<.01

Source: Latinos in Richmond Survey.

likely to participate in conventional nonvoting political activities (for example, signing petitions, attending rallies) as non-Latinos. We do find a relatively high participation in these other types of political pursuits: about 15 percent of our sample gave money in the last three or four years to a political party or candidate (this includes some immigrants who contribute money to political campaigns or issues in their countries of origin; a man who gave money to pave roads in Costa Rica is one example). Almost 17 percent have attended a political rally over the same period of time. The numbers are slightly higher when only citizens are examined. These participation variables can be important predictors of voting participation. Those Richmond Latinos who attend political rallies are significantly more likely to vote, and those who give money to political campaigns also participate more in elections more often than those who do not (Table 8.2).

The strongest predictor of voting is political efficacy. When asked to agree or disagree with the statement, "People like me do not have any say in what the government does," 69 percent disagree. Those who disagreed with the statement—that is, those who feel the most politically efficacious—are significantly more likely to vote (the correlation between the two variables is –.26, meaning the more one disagrees, the more likely one is to vote; it is significant at .01).

In order to test the interconnected effects of these demographic, cultural, and political variables, we regressed them in three stages on our dependent variable, the voting scale (see Table 8.3). To examine the effects of demographic variables on voting behavior we included age, measures of social class (both education and household income), and a dummy variable for gender. To control for country of origin we included dummy variables for Mexicans, Puerto Ricans, and Salvadorans, our three largest sub-ethnic groups (Model 1). Of all these variables, age, household income, and level of education are significant predictors of voting (The r-squared value for model 1 is .26). Thus, even controlling for country of origin and demographic variables, social class indicators have a strong effect on voting patterns.

Table 8.3. Unstandardized Coefficients from OLS Regressions of Demographic, Cultural and Political Variables on the Voting Index (Standard Errors in Parentheses)

	Model 1		Model 2		Model 3	
Demographic Variables						
Age	0.7***	(.01)	0.8***	(.01)	.06***	(.02)
Household Income	.30**	(.12)	.18	(.12)	.03	(.13)
Education	.32**	(.15)	.29**	(.14)	.36**	(.15)
Gender (Male=1)	-.54	(.38)	-.61*	(.37)	-.39	(.38)
Mexican	.41	(.45)	.04	(.45)	.18	(.46)
Puerto Ricans	-.43	(.42)	-.56	(.40)	-.28	(.42)
Salvadorans	.59	(.69)	1.26*	(.69)	1.50**	(.69)
Cultural Variable						
Language Use			.83***	(.21)	.64***	(.22)
Political Variables						
Attended Rallies					.53	(.43)
Donated Money					.45	(.45)
Political Efficacy					-.52***	(.20)
Political Preference					.24	(.16)
Intercept	1.35	(1.05)	-3.87***	(1.19)	-2.23	(1.36)
R2	.26		.32		.32	

* p < .1, ** p < .05, *** p < .01

Source: Latinos in Richmond Survey.

We then added to the model one of the measures of cultural assimilation that had a high significant zero-order correlation to voting, extent of language assimilation. This variable is highly significant in this model and even more influential than education and income in predicting how people vote (the higher r-squared for Model 2, .316, indicates that more is explained by the addition of the new variables). Certainly, those who are more assimilated, and specifically those Latinos who use more English in their daily life, are far more likely to be more aware of political issues and thus more involved in U.S. politics. Moreover, when we added language assimilation, one of our ethnic group dummy variables, Salvadoran, becomes significant. Salvadorans have the largest variation in terms of the language assimilation index, so this significantly impacts the effect of language on voting for this group. Household income, on the other hand, is no longer significant, indicating that income by itself was masking an effect on voting that actually happens as a result of English language acquisition (especially for Salvadorans).

The addition of the political measures discussed in the literature has very little impact on the predictive power of the model (Model 3 r-squared = .323). Measures that we included for political preference and dummy variables for attending rallies and donating money are not significant. Only one variable, political efficacy ("People like me do not have any say in what the government does") is a clear predictor of Latino voting, even controlling for these other variables. Latinos who agree with the statement are much less likely to vote. Age, language assimilation, education, and being Salvadoran (in that order) remain significant in this model. Political efficacy may be a conduit through which social class impacts voting behavior (the two variables are significantly correlated, r = −.331, p < .001). People who feel empowered by their socioeconomic position are also more likely to feel that their voices are heard politically. Thus, we see the effects of social class on voting participation primarily through education and political efficacy.

Local Agencies, Local Acceptance

Political efficacy, of course, can be related to how, as well as how much, residents control what goes on around them, particularly whether Latinos feel accepted in a community and how responsive a community is to newcomers, both issues confronting Richmond in the last decade as Latinos have become more visible. Initially, the sudden growth of the Latino community in the Richmond area caught local organizations by surprise. Serving a growing immigrant community became an important part of the local agenda for businesses, schools, hospitals, human service agencies, fire stations, real estate offices, and legal services. The need for translators, along with Latino representation in organizations that dealt directly with the Latino community, became part and parcel of providing more efficient assistance to Latino migrants to the area. From local fast food restaurants and supermarkets, to police stations and motor vehicle bureau branches, the entities that make up the Richmond area had to scramble to respond to Latino requests.

As a result, in the early part of the decade, we still encounter complaints and frustration in respondent comments, especially in regard to dealings with local government agencies. Almost one-half of our respondents agreed or strongly agreed that "public agencies are more concerned about Anglos than Hispanics" in Richmond. "On one hand, everybody who asks for an appointment gets one, but on the other hand, this society is made for its own people, and so the benefits are designed to help Anglos," remarked a Salvadoran male who works installing pipes. Another respondent, a female immigrant from Colombia who worked as a machine operator in a local box factory, said, "Social services are not friendly to Hispanics. It makes you feel as though you don't have a right to get public benefits."

Our respondents were quick to point out the need for even more culturally adequate local programs and support for Spanish speakers in government agencies than already exists. "I believe that we need more representation and respect in hospitals," a legal secretary of Puerto Rican origin argued. "We need more programs and support for Spanish, especially in government agencies. More Spanish-speaking people [in those agencies]." Cultural differences can be intimidating or sometimes disorienting, so Latinos wish they could address one of their own, in their own language, when they need those services.

In health care especially, Latinos note a high demand for the availability of low-cost clinics. As a working-class Latina from Mexico told us, "We work in order to pay bills, rent, [and there is] nothing left over for health care. Clinics are sometimes slow to attend to Hispanics because they might not have Medicaid or insurance. There is a need for low-cost clinics." Lack of Medicaid, Medicare, or insurance also creates difficulties. As a result many Latinos shy away from seeking out the health services they need.

At the same time, respondents would like to see more opportunities for learning English. "I would like to see a program started that would aid the Hispanics that come here already with some type of education, in learning English faster so instead of having to start from the bottom, say first grade, they can use the education they have received, plus this help, and get a quicker at getting an education here," suggested an immigrant from Guatemala who has worked fourteen years in Richmond as a roofer. Respondents asked for a community-based means to disseminate information, along with the translation of educational materials.

By the time we finished our research, local agencies and businesses were adapting to the Latino presence. Hospitals hired Latinos to work as liaisons with the community. Chesterfield County began offering health care services in Spanish and even has a Spanish Web site. Hanover County, too, is offering literature on health and social services in Spanish. Police stations in the nine counties incorporated Latinos into their workforce. The Richmond Police Department hired bilingual police officers and set up a Latino tip line. During our data collection, the police department also graduated its first class of Latinos trained as community liaisons. The Henrico county fire department printed fire prevention materials in Spanish. County schools attracted Latino teachers to meet the needs of the school-age Latino population, providing a limited number of translated documents (Lizama 2004:H8). Businesses responded quickly: lawyers expanded their services to include Spanish-speaking assistance to the community, and banks hired qualified Latinos to help tailor their services to the banking needs of the population. Growing ESL services prepare Latinos for an English-speaking workplace.

Compared to other areas of the South, Latinos in Richmond have probably experienced more receptivity from the general population because the increase of the population happened at a much slower pace. They have found local businesses, government agencies, and other organizations more willing to reach out to the Latino population, especially the middle class. In some cases organizations even anticipated ways in which they can connect: through job opportunities, services, and enterprising policies that attempt to make the most of the Latino newcomers. But adjusting to a different clientele means also dealing with misperceptions from both ends: professionals who provide services not understanding those being served, and Latinos, especially more recent arrivals, who face the challenge of dealing with impersonal, bureaucratic systems, which are still struggling to become more user-friendly for the community. All in all, dealing with local agencies reflects the growing pains of an ethnic community in an area with no previous history of Latinos.

Latino Community Presence and Activism

Latinos in Richmond are aware that local politics and community resources can be tapped as a means for solving some of these problems. For example, we talked to a highly educated Puerto Rican engineer, who though a conservative voter, strongly supports "the promotion of Hispanic culture and language by the government, [as well as] more assistance from the government for Hispanics." In another case, we asked a forty-year-old Colombian who has been in the United States. for seventeen years about Latino dealings with local agencies. His comments indicate the efficacy he feels—his vote and opinion do mean something: "Public opinion in politics does matter," he said, especially when compared with his native country. Still, he feels that local politicians could be more responsive to needs of Latinos. Finally, a fifty-year-old respondent in the United States for seven years described how despite having his own business in Colombia, he was unable to get a credit card loan once he arrived, not knowing the proper channels to access for support. He feels very strongly that Latinos in Richmond could use more help from community leaders and organizations. But the idea is to use these resources to empower their own community organizing. "The community is growing, so there are many disadvantages. We need more leaders here to create more and better jobs for Hispanics."

Latinos in Richmond exhibit a degree of community organization congruent with their political participation, which is especially outstanding given the short period in which they have been in the area. While still expanding leadership, they have reached high visibility through the development of local associations. During the course of our research, for instance, Richmond Latinos created not one but two Hispanic chambers of commerce catering to distinct strata of the Latino business community. The Virginia Hispanic Chamber of Commerce, headquartered in Richmond, is led by a "1.5" generation Mexican business owner who grew up in Richmond and is a graduate of local schools. The organization bridges the world of the Richmond business elite and Latinos by promoting contacts between the Richmond Chamber of Commerce and Latino-owned large and midsized businesses. It has offered workshops on how to bid for local and state government services, how to start a business in central Virginia, tax preparation, accounting, and other business-related activities. Another function of the Chamber is to organize networking receptions, where Richmond executives and Latinos meet.

An Argentinean small business owner who arrived in Richmond in 1982 leads the second organization, the Hispanic Chamber of Commerce of Central Virginia. This Chamber caters to smaller Latino businesses, and has developed ties with the Minority Business Enterprise of the City of Richmond. It offers seminars and workshops related to doing business in the area, but it also serves as a clearing house for information on health care and community services for Latinos. This Chamber publishes the first high-quality local magazine focused on the Richmond Latino community, *La Voz Hispana*. Both organizations, of course, contain and serve largely middle-class Latinos.

Similarly, Richmond Latinos also count on the presence of two cultural associations, both organized by middle-class Latinos but with decidedly different memberships, goals, and outreach. The American Hispanics of Richmond Association (AHORA) is a group that reached high visibility during our data collection. AHORA is the brainchild of two Puerto Rican transplants to Richmond. Both grew up in New York, went to selective U.S. colleges, and found job opportunities in Richmond, one as a community manager for a large media organization, the other as a local anchorman. The group's membership is drawn mostly from the professional Latino community, and its goals are to push for Latino recognition from Richmond's movers and shakers. Its members organize highbrow (performances of the Latino ballet company and visiting professional folk troupes) and popular events (the Cinco de Mayo celebration as part of Richmond's summer cultural schedule). In addition, AHORA organizes cultural seminars in high schools, supports school policies that celebrate Latino culture, and provides scholarships for local Latino youth.

The other example, La Asociación de Hispano-Americanos de Richmond (AHAR) is the oldest cultural association for Latinos in Richmond. AHAR's leadership comes from college-educated immigrants and U.S.-born Latinos. AHAR directs relief and immigrant services, reaching a large segment of the Latino population—primarily working-class Mexicans and Central Americans—in the Chesterfield area south of Richmond city. The association is also responsible for an annual Latino Day, well attended by the larger community, at one of Richmond's largest state parks. It sponsors soccer tournaments, teams, and workshops, along with promoting folk dances and exhibits in local hospitals and schools.

Latino visibility in the area has even prompted local non-Latino organizations to become more active in the development of policies and services that increase Latino quality of life in Richmond. The Richmond Chapter of the Red Cross, for instance, has a multicultural committee that coordinates efforts among local Latino organizations to avoid duplication in the provision of services to the Latino community. The Red Cross also offers children and adult first aid courses in Spanish. Telamon Corporation in Hopewell offers educational and job training to migrant workers (Lizama 2004:H8). Restaurants in the area also began offering Latino nights with local bands and salsa lessons. Local community colleges have added courses to interest the Latino community. The city itself takes great pains to provide events for its Latino citizens. In 2004 a Hispanic Market was created in the downtown area with good attendance by the Latino community. Along the way, news and print media have profiled local Latino artists, musicians, and writers.

Bringing the Latino Community Together

This level of community organization, attention, and activity is not necessarily enough to provide Richmond Latinos with a sense of belonging to a single, integrated group. While Latinos sense that their numbers in Richmond are increasing, they still grapple with the means to re-create in Richmond the communities they left behind, or at least to reconnect, in the case of native-born Latinos, with a group of people who share their culture of origin. Many of the organizations we describe are most heavily populated by a single ethnicity, sometimes Mexican, sometimes Puerto Rican, but the numbers of Latinos that hail from one country of origin are not great enough to create solidarity by themselves. Or the groups represent Latinos from a given area of the region, like Chesterfield or Ashland. Several groups have tried to stand for the entire community, but have so far failed in their efforts to generate a pan-ethnic group.

Latinos do have a desire to come together. Respondents made a number of comments about the need to develop mechanisms for making Latinos more aware of each other, for bringing them together more often, and for developing a deeper sense of community through cultural activities, Spanish concerts, movies, and so on as part of the process of educating Richmond about their presence here. Latinos in Richmond still feel quite atomized in relation to other members of their community. As one man, a Puerto Rican whose parents were born on the island, put it,

> Radio, TV cable connections to Spanish language would be nice, for example. Are they listed in Yellow Pages? If there is a Hispanic society in Richmond, it's not made known to the Hispanic community! Mexico restaurants should get their flyers out, maybe the Hispanic Chamber of Commerce. Try the *Richmond-Times Dispatch*. For the Richmond area, people need to realize there are different Hispanic ethnic groups—not all are Mexican.

It is not surprising to find our respondents wishing for even more venues that would bring them together, making them feel included and represented. The activities are there, and ofttimes diverse groups of Latinos are making connections, but not in a fashion conducive to the creation of a single community, speaking with a one voice.

In this sense, the Latino experience is very different from the Asian experience in Richmond. While there are eleven different Asian ethnic associations in town—including Japanese, Chinese, Thai, and Filipino groups—Asians in Richmond are unified by an overall association (the Asian American Society of Central Virginia) that provides its members with the idea of belonging to something greater than a collection of nationality groups. The umbrella Asian organization sponsors events in town, scholarships, and meetings with local authorities. There is a strong sense that when one deals with the Asian community in Richmond, one is dealing with a well-established and cohesive body of people. Tseng (2006) discusses the ways in which the resources of ethnic-specific organizations can be pooled in order to form forceful coalitions among different ancestry groups.

While some Latinos are quick to label themselves as Latino and/or Hispanic, and often have a strong individual desire for unity, this does not automatically translate into a larger pan-ethnic sense of a Latino *community*. In fact, as noted in chapter 4, the pan-ethnic concept of Latino is artificial to some. The segmented experiences of Latinos in the Richmond area make the emergence of ethnic solidarity even more problematic. With the community divided into groups for college-educated, professional/business owner families and for low-educated, working-class later arrivals, it becomes harder to create a common sense of identity.

The search for a shared identity is, ironically, more difficult because of their perception of other groups' overemphasis on identity politics and difference. A second-generation college-educated Mexican argued that some groups create their own social distance: "This whole racial thing is blown out of proportion. I don't like segregation. Sometimes I think certain groups, be it black, white, Mexican, and Hispanics, create those groups and distance themselves. They carry the culture of difference through." Another respondent, a Colombian immigrant who worked in finance, volunteered that this philosophy actually discouraged him from joining any Latino organization. "I'm going to be an exception—I don't play victim. I expect others [in your study] may play victims. I was thinking of joining the Hispanic Chamber of Commerce, but after contacting them, I don't think I will." Many middle-class Latinos would like to carry some identity as Latino, but not to the exclusion of other things.

As we explained in chapter 3 to some extent, these divisions are based on perceptions that other groups, including other Latin American groups, hold different values. Those who take the selective acculturation path often relate these differences as a way of avoiding identification with groups that might be associated with an ethnic minority. "Some Latinos need to get away from a transfixing focus on homeland," said a college-educated, U.S.-born respondent of Cuban descent. He argued that they run the risk of "ghettoization into an underclass." To him, Latinos are "a loyal people that could help a lot in the U.S., but there is discrimination" against those who do not assimilate.

These attitudes reflect the segmentation of the Latino community by social class, but even among the middle class, divisions are not unified. Arguments about how to help or how to relate to working-class Latinos actually reflect specific middle-class ideologies about identity, politics, and assimilation. The concern for some in the middle class is that immigration (and working-class status) is related to a lack of aspiration to assimilate, although theirs is an individual argument rather than a structural one. The middle-class groups are also divided along political lines—for example, during the Warner election in 2001 the middle-class cultural associations split, each sponsoring their own rallies for the two political candidates. The result is that groups who might have common community and political concerns are not integrated into a powerful whole.

In this chapter, we have noted a number of factors that make Richmond Latinos different politically from Latinos in other parts of the country. Richmond Latinos are unusually active voters. They have similar political preferences to Latinos nationally, although even some self-identified conservatives sometimes vote the Democratic ticket. While country of origin is a predictor of this level of political participation, is it not as strong as education, efficacy, and our assimilation measures. Indeed, what we see is that political participation is largely a factor of socioeconomic status. Latino efforts to be politically active, first as citizens and also as voters, show their interest in the political issues that are relevant to life in Richmond and in Virginia, such as tougher policies on illegal immigrants (Southall 2007).

Despite the level of political activity of Richmond Latinos, a unified Latino community in Richmond has yet to be realized. The different political and community organizations that try to capture the allegiance of Richmond Latinos have so far met with only with partial success. By creating their own organizations to promote business or cultural interests related to the life of the Latino community, Richmond Latinos increase the visibility of the Latino community in the area, but it is a visibility that focuses on middle-class Latinos rather than the entire group. Class, in conjunction with immigrant status and country of origin, fragments Latino efforts to develop a pan-ethnic sense of solidarity. The next step for Richmond Latinos will be to figure out how to increase participation for all—how to take efforts directed at individual social mobility and turn them into political organizing toward group empowerment.

Chapter 9

What Does It Mean to Be Latino in Dixie?

> I love being Hispanic, especially in Richmond, because I get to shock people. I am very animated and outgoing and most people in my industry are boring. It's fun teaching people how to live life. Our liveliness is something we add to the American culture. Even when taking on American traditions and customs, I hope we never lose our spice.
>
> —Forty-nine-year-old Cuban professional woman

In our review of what it means to be Latino in a Southern city, we have looked at different aspects of Latino life in Richmond and used diverse measures of assimilation to map out the experiences. From language use, the preservation of ethnic customs, and family life, to the dynamics of the workplace, and finally to political and religious participation, we have examined both what Richmond Latinos experience in moving to the South and what they bring to a city previously marked by only a black/white ethnic divide. The intersection of geographic mobility, isolation, and segmented assimilation processes in the Richmond metropolitan area actually intensifies class differences and thereby hinders the development of a community in Richmond.

An examination of migration to Richmond demonstrates how segmented assimilation and selective acculturation play out with the two very distinctly classed communities. Elite, well-educated Latino professionals dominate the cultural and political landscape. The newer, less-well-off immigrants remain marginal, sometimes lacking essential experience and facing discrimination based on ethnicity, language, and social status. Although Waldinger and Lee, among other scholars, have examined the notion of Latinos living in two worlds, the focus of such an assumption has typically been on the contrasts between two ancestry groups or the differences between Latinos in different cities (2001:75). In our case, we have explored the communities side by side and shown how their interactions have fashioned the Latino community of Richmond thus far.

In the beginning of this book, we questioned whether the census evidence that Richmond Latinos overall were better off economically meant that primarily middle-class, well-educated Latinos were moving to Richmond, or whether Latinos were faring better once they came to Richmond. What this book provides is evidence for both possibilities. However, as we have shown in the preceding chapters, the situation for Latinos is even more complicated than it seems at first glance, as we find a much more diverse community than we expected, in terms of economic opportunities and cultural identity. We have highlighted both the advantages and disadvantages of moving to an area with no history of Latino migration. Specifically, invisibility means that Latinos, especially those in the middle class, can blend in, if that is what is desired. At the same time, such adaptation has costs, including loss of ethnic solidarity and a decline in family connections. And of course, as the community grows and becomes more diverse, the challenge is to create a positive representation of the new visibility for those with no familiarity with (and indeed, often vast misconceptions of) Latinos.

The key finding, nonetheless, is the deeper understanding our analysis provides of the magnified role that class plays in ethnic integration. Latinos at different levels of the social strata may experience Richmond either with an eventual sense of familiarity or as an increased cultural burden. For those well educated and well placed occupationally, the transition to Richmond is one of relative ease. They find themselves remarkably similar to other Richmonders in the way they are immersed in American ways in their family life, work activities, levels of political participation or a secular response to faith. They are Latinos for whom Latino heritage is merely a symbolic identity, similar to that experienced by the third- and fourth-generation white Europeans studied by Mary Waters (1990). They can choose to celebrate this "symbolic ethnicity" by observing customs, eating ethnic foods, and celebrating their heritage, while doing little damage to social position. Symbolic ethnicity is, furthermore, tied to geographic mobility (just as it once was for white ethnics). Geographic mobility, even to an area with few Latinos, has only increased the ability to choose one's ethnicity.

However, we extend the concept of Mary Waters one step farther. Symbolic ethnicity is theoretically costless to those who enjoy it, but in this case, the promotion of middle-class symbolic ethnicity can in fact be detrimental to the working-class Latinos in the area because an emphasis on middle-class cultural events removes resources and public attention from the working class, and renders their concerns less visible. Political organizing, too, is a white-collar phenomenon with a middle-class agenda, even when issues under consideration are predominantly the concerns of new, less-well-off arrivals.

Selective acculturation is another option for Richmond migrants, particularly those in the middle class. These respondents have successfully integrated into Anglo economic life while retaining a significant Latino identity and cultural elements. Though few are transmigratory, in addition to learning English they continue to use Spanish quite frequently. They retain a preference for Hispanic or Latino labels or may prefer to refer to themselves by country of origin. They want their children to learn Spanish as well as English, and to protect their families from aspects of Anglo culture. Here we have provided ample evidence that economic advancement, even upward mobility, can be accomplished without abandoning a strong preservation of cultural ties and values.

A third option presented by segmented assimilation theorists, the minority-identified subculture, is present in Richmond most notably by its absence. There are respondents to whom this label could be applied, to be sure, but for most respondents, particularly immigrant parents, both middle- and working-class, Richmond provides the physical space to avoid the fate of life in the urban underclass. Their actions demonstrate fear of this outcome. Many respondents moved to Richmond as a means of protecting their families from the dirt, danger, and discrimination of life in large metropolitan areas. Likewise, the preservation of culture that is so highly touted by many Richmond Latinos reflects that the alternatives, not merely of a potentially bland existence of a fully assimilated Anglo life but also the perilous journey involved in adapting to the ways of inner-city Latinos or African Americans (for those Latinos with darker skin), are not desirable.

For the very newest immigrants to the United States living in Richmond, their story remains to be fleshed out. Certainly, many of these respondents are poor, in need of services such as English as a Second Language classes, health, housing, and legal services, and naturalization assistance. Although Richmond agencies and organizations have been relatively quick to respond in most cases, working-class Latinos experience drawbacks and difficulties given their recent arrival in the United States, including low pay in ethnically concentrated occupations. More than one-quarter of our respondents have lived in Richmond for five years or less, and of these almost half have lived fewer than five years in the United States. For these new immigrant Latinos, Richmond is still experienced as a very foreign culture, one that must be decoded if they are to be successful in their newly adopted home. That level of strangeness does not keep them from hoping or pursuing their own dreams, but it may delay the process of their fulfillment.

Unlike earlier immigrant waves, neither middle-class nor working-class Latinos always settle now in geographic propinquity to their country of origin. Both groups are venturing forth from ports of entry. Although it is more likely

that better-off Latinos move first into areas with little previous Latino presence—in the Richmond case the first wave of Latinos consisted primarily of
college-educated professionals—these Latinos are not the only ones who are
leaving large cities and ethnic enclaves. Eventually, working-class counterparts
arrive, and now even come directly from their countries of origin to southern
cities such as Richmond (or Atlanta, Raleigh, or Nashville), in some cases
bypassing the cities with traditional Latino populations altogether. These new
migration trends indicate classed and raced aspects of the global marketplace
writ small in cities such as Richmond: highly technological professional occupations seeking a more diversified workforce, a flexible service sector economy
that is both eager for and attractive to Latinos (despite vulnerable working
conditions), and employers who recruit factory workers directly from Latin
America.

Moreover, both middle- and working-class Latinos are making *permanent*
moves to areas like Richmond; virtually none of the Latinos we interviewed
were transmigratory. Although professional and working-class Latinos are
primarily motivated by the economic opportunities of local job markets rather
than by family ties, specific occupational reasons for moving vary by social
class. Working-class Latinos are attracted by the higher wages in central Virginia
or are pushed out by poor economic situations elsewhere. Latinos who are
professionals and managers come because of job transfers or entrepreneurial
prospects. These moves, although they represent greater opportunities for both
groups, do not lead to greater economic success for all, but the reestablishment
of class differences once in Richmond. Geographic and social mobility are thus
tied to different assimilation experiences via these internal migration waves.

As a result of this geographic and social mobility, there is no one narrative of
assimilation illustrated by Latinos, especially given the complicated relationships
between Richmond Latinos and whites, African Americans, and other Latinos.
Relations with whites show that social assimilation is not as important as it once
was. Latinos are structurally assimilated in some ways—they work and live near
whites—but their social interactions remain predominantly a mixture of Latinos
and whites. Respondents' feelings about African Americans, although sympathetic, indicate Latino concerns about urban underclass life. Our respondents
have few interactions with African Americans in Richmond, and few identify
as black. Relationships with other Hispanics, too, reflect concerns about the
too-careless adaptation into certain Latino or other minority subcultures in the
United States predicted by segmented assimilation.

Factors including language and cultural acquisition predict whether or
not the outcomes for Richmond Latinos will be traditional assimilation,

assimilation to a culture outside of the dominant one, or selective accultura-tion. We uncover considerable use of both English and Spanish, of continued Latino contact, and the observance and importance of Latino customs. Use of English and Spanish, cultural integration, and adoption of Anglo customs all vary significantly by country of origin and time in the United States. Although class is connected to acculturation, we do not find a clear pattern wherein a higher economic status always translates into more traditional acculturation.

The ethnic labels our respondents prefer show tensions surrounding ethnic identity. Respondents identify strongly as "Hispanic" or even by country of origin, even after living in the United States a long time. Although it is the dominant response, our respondents also have a lower preference for "white" when describing their race than census data indicates, while the biggest second option for race, and it is a growing one, is Hispanic. These choices of ethnic and racial markers reflect a lack of consensus about U.S. racial and ethnic terminology. Despite the predominance of the term *Hispanic* among Richmond Latinos, however, little sense of shared identity emerges from it. Respondents desire the individual identity, but unity is not forthcoming. The concept of pan-ethnicity, rather than being or becoming a more inclusive view for Latinos, does not manage here to cover completely the heterogeneity of the community (see also Suárez-Orozco and Páez 2002). Indeed, the idea of a shared, more pan-ethnic concept is antithetical to some.

Some variables remain impervious to social class effects, suggesting that to some extent Latinos do share in these areas a common identity. For instance, ethnic identity as Hispanic is strong for both middle-class and working-class groups. Different identities do not develop at different strata of society (see Suro and Singer 2002), although other variables distinguish the social class groups. Despite varying levels of assimilation, preserving Latino culture and resisting the pressures of the larger society are important to Latino families regardless of their social station. In part, this may be due to the fact that Latinos in the South often have fewer relatives nearby on whom they can depend. Families must demonstrate greater self-sufficiency, although this also means that they do not have heavy obligations to extended family, which has both positive and negative repercussions. Families are unified around the preservation of family and culture and the importance placed on education, but differ on what this actually means and how it should be manifested in the community. For parents who emphasize the importance of speaking both English and Spanish, bilin-gualism is not merely a way of adapting, but a means of keeping one's cultural ties intact. Finally, although some Latinos prefer Spanish classes in the public schools and others do not, these differences are due to individual beliefs about Spanish use and are not class-based.

Latinos of both classes are successfully adapting to occupational demands, and have found the situation in Richmond an improvement over their previous locations. However, working-class Latinos are more likely to experience occupational discrimination than middle-class professionals, especially in terms of job retention and promotional opportunities. Blue-collar workers proclaim, "Who knows?" if they have experienced discrimination, but do say that there is little (or less) of it in Richmond. There is evidence for traditional occupational integration ("Hire me because I'm good"), especially for white-collar workers. Many white-collar respondents see little discrimination, and argue for the likelihood of success based solely on one's merits. At the same time, we find many middle-class Latinos who see a professional benefit to being *Latino*—using Spanish to their advantage, using ethnic networks for clients, creating a niche for Spanish products, and participating in the Richmond Hispanic Chambers of Commerce. But middle-class workers adopt prejudices similar to those in the dominant culture about other Latinos, especially immigrants, those with accented English, and Mexicans.

Segmented assimilation suggests a variety of ways of adapting to life in the United States. We expand on previous literature on religion and assimilation by looking also at the nonreligious. Latino religious life in Richmond is marked both by religious switching and by secularization. Class, assimilation, and religious practices are all intertwined. For many, religion is still a haven during the process of assimilation. Some remain steadfast in the faith of their childhood, while others become Evangelical Protestants. A large majority grew up Catholic and a good number remain so, but a sizable group has converted to different Protestant denominations as a result of living in the United States.

What our data on religious switching show is that it is no longer clear what is meant by "traditional" religious assimilation. It used to be that converting to Protestantism would be a reliable sign of adopting Anglo values, but now assimilation may be signified by actually leaving religion behind. The more educated Richmond Latinos are, the higher their occupational prestige, and the more comfortable they are with U.S. ways of life (whether in terms of language use or familiarity with the dominant culture), the more likely they are to claim no religious affiliation or practice. The rise of the appeal of Protestant Fundamentalism among Latinos, moreover, suggests that working-class immigrants are using religion to avoid aspects of "amoral" U.S. society, perhaps even some of those associated with rising secularization. Religious conversion and abandonment both illustrate an even greater variety of paths to becoming American.

Political participation encompasses another area of the Latino experience in Richmond that is influenced by social class elements of assimilation. Political participation among ethnic groups, scholars hypothesize, leads to integration and unity. In Richmond, the majority of non-citizens seek citizenship as a first priority; those who are already citizens are unusually politically active and civically engaged. Richmond Latinos have high participation in national and local elections especially compared to countrywide trends. But participation breaks down along social class lines, although class is not as much a predictor of voting as is political efficacy and language acquisition. The strong presence of business and cultural Latino organizations in Richmond are a function of middle-class Latinos' interests in representation. Because the political organization of Latinos in Richmond remains a professional class phenomenon, an important task ahead is to figure out how to enfranchise working-class Latinos.

Throughout this book we have talked about how living in the South alters what it means to be Latino in the United States. When Latinos live in a region where the numbers of other Latinos are low, being Latino becomes much more intentional. Unlike Los Angeles or Dallas, in the Old South the social boundaries between the Anglo and Latino worlds are drawn more sharply—especially those lines related to race and ethnicity—even though there is no physical segregation. The idea that where one is from or how one looks might be a matter of central importance is something that many of our respondents are still getting accustomed to. What develops is the importance of showing "who we are" (which suggests an embrace of pan-ethnicity) but also of emphasizing individual ability and strength, which sometimes requires distancing oneself from the concept of Hispanic or Latino, thus preventing unity.

Southerners have difficulties accepting outsiders; the superficial friendliness of Southern hospitality creates even more misunderstanding. Richmond residents are not familiar with Latino culture. Even when Latinos speak the language, have become familiar with local customs, and can interact easily, there is still a sense of feeling and experiencing life as the other. This feeling is reflected in Latino efforts to educate locals about their unique identity, even as Richmond Latinos strive to become to be accepted as contributing members of the community.

Class is related to the development of different segments—it provides the options, especially for the upwardly mobile, for either complete acculturation or selective acculturation, wherein full integration with the dominant society is not necessarily a goal. What do these segments mean for Richmond? Traditionally, assimilated Latinos continue to celebrate their symbolic ethnicity, with some community costs. Other Latinos rally around fleeing the potential downward mobility of a minority subculture, but at the expense of some of the newest, most vulnerable members of the population. Finally, although Hernandez and Glenn (2003) theorize that the "third way" of selective acculturation has the potential to confront dominant American values, at this point, challenging values such as individualism has not been a part of the experiences of Richmond Latinos. Moreover, the social mobility experienced by many Richmond Latinos has not yet meant greater empowerment for all. Segmented assimilation in the South means more options for being "American"—some to be embraced, some not—but it has also meant greater fragmentation.

Appendix A

Incorporating Feminist Reflexivity into Survey Methodology,

Or What Are a German Woman and an Italian Man Doing Studying Latinos?

Early in this project, a reporter for the *Richmond-Times Dispatch* interviewed us for an article about our research. At that point we had compiled a census profile of greater Richmond and were writing our survey based on preliminary forays in the community. We did not yet have a lot to say about Latinos in Richmond, but reporters called us constantly, and community groups wanted us to speak to them about our project. When one of our colleagues saw our picture in the paper—a somewhat "staged" photo in which our heads were together, diligently studying a pile of yet-to-be administered surveys—he asked, "Here we have what appears to be a blond German-looking woman and an Italian man. What are they doing studying Latinos?"

He did well to ask this question about representation. How did our backgrounds and identities influence our choice of project and what we were doing? Both of us were concerned about what we brought to the table on this project. One author is a Portuguese-speaking Brazilian immigrant (although he does bear an Italian surname), who has struggled with identity during his twenty-year sojourn in the United States ("Am I Brazilian? Hispanic? Latino? American?") The other author had to consider the perspective (and privilege) she brings to the research project, as a white middle-class professional and fifth-generation German American woman.

We were keen to have the motivation and design of this project reflect our personal and epistemological concerns. Both of us had long been interested in race and gender issues, having taught and written in these areas for several years before undertaking this project. We wanted to design a survey research project that incorporated feminist epistemology and an emphasis on the intersection of race, gender, and social class. But where to begin?

The Literature on Feminist Methodology and Intersectionality

Feminist Reflexivity

Scholarship on feminist sociology and using feminist reflexivity in research focuses almost exclusively on qualitative, interview-based or ethnographic methodology. Like most feminist scholars, we are seeking to move beyond research that merely adds women to the population under study. Rather, we recognize that a feminist sociology emphasizes research that seeks to uncover power relationships, expose the inadequacies of dichotomies (black/white, male/female, objective/subjective, nature/nurture, even quantitative/qualitative), and question the fundamental ordering of our social worlds.

Often this scholarship questions the "traditional" sociology framework, and (usually implicitly rather than explicitly) the positivist, survey research methodology. For example, when Dorothy Smith writes of a feminist sociology that "preserves the presence of subjects as knowers and actors. It does not transform subjects into the objects of study or make use of conceptual devices for the eliminating the active presence of subjects (1987:105)," she is critiquing a process that does not ask the research subjects for their interpretation of social reality, merely for "data."

It is not surprising that much feminist scholarship tends to be qualitative, rather than quantitative, in nature—survey research tends to create more distance between observer and observed, to objectify the respondent, and to turn her nuanced perspectives into data points that can be plotted along a regression line. Ethnography, participant observation, and semi-structured interviews, on the other hand, allow far more room for the contextual exploration desired of feminist methodology. It empowers the respondent to play a greater role in the research process by defining some of the terms of inquiry and shaping the meaning of her or his own observations and interpretations.

The differences between the two are far less vast than it would ordinarily seem, but the archetypes can adequately summed up as follows: quantitative utilizes numbers, tables, statistics to predict or explain; qualitative research analyzes text, narrative, language as a way of interpreting or understanding social reality, answering the question of how, not if or why as in quantitative research. Quantitative researchers ordinarily search for one permanent cause for a social behavior; efforts to isolate one variable—to control for all other explanatory variables—require a causal homogeneity in all units (see Ragin 1994).

Qualitative researchers, on the other hand, can revel in the complexity of their data—there can be causal heterogeneity, for example; the more context and textuality the better. The parsimony required in much quantitative research (the expectation that there be as few variables in explanation as possible) suggests it would be much more difficult to think about the multiplicative and complex nature of race, gender, and class. One would always be trying to control for the other two while seeking the one true explanatory cause for a dependent variable (variation in income, for instance).

Qualitative research can be the very best (indeed, sometimes the only) method for certain topics and theoretical assumptions (especially exploratory research). It is a technique often used to explore concepts related to culture, meaning, ideology, relationships, behavior, and socialization that provides an intimate, in-depth, insider perspective so important to feminist epistemology. As a result, ethnography often provides for greater validity and flexibility (although less reliability and generalizability).

And yet, we were committed to a large-scale survey. We thought that in order to reach the audience we wanted (both sociological and public policy–oriented) we needed to generate a random sample of the Richmond Latino population. However, the typical survey research project, which places respondents into neat categories based on their responses to rigidly structured, close-ended survey questions, was something that we were trying to avoid. Although we wanted to systematize our results, we also wanted to make sure that our research instrument, and our method of analysis, was flexible enough that we could incorporate as many as we could of our respondents' statements that stood "outside the box" of chosen responses. We did not want our respondents to be our puppets, manipulated by us to say and believe the things that we expected of them. For this reason, although we did have some basic premises, we did not structure our survey around specific testable hypotheses.

Multivocal Perspectives

The second objective we were committed to was incorporating race, class, and gender perspectives into our research approach. For us, it is impossible to examine social reality without acknowledging that race, class, and gender are central categories of description and analysis as well as multiple (and multiplicative, rather than additive), interlocking forms of oppression (King 1988). The relationship between the three is varied and complex.

Like many, however, it is not always clear to us how one goes about incorporating these concepts into our theoretical or analytical approaches. As Paula Rothenberg states in the introduction to her anthology on race, class, and gender, "Now the challenge is to find a model or theory broad enough, flexible enough, and complex enough to capture and reflect the way these elements function together; to determine how we see ourselves and each other; and to

circumscribe the opportunities and privileges to which each of us has access"
(2003:1). Indeed, we have found no useful primer for using race, class, and
gender in survey research methodology. Survey research that incorporates
measures of race, class, and gender in a self-conscious, explicitly multicultural
way still does not problematize the relationships between epistemology and
methodology (see, e.g., Hill and Sprague 1999). The idea that race, class, and
gender are not merely additive, but potentially multiplicative, complex, interlocking, dynamic, and difficult to interpret, is not easily uncovered by statistical
techniques.[1] A few researchers use interaction terms to capture this multiplicative nature (Fazio and Mattingly 2002; McCall 2001), but most continue to
focus on one variable (e.g., gender) and control for the other two. Just how
successful we were at this is also unclear, but it does indicate the extent of the
difficulties involved.

Although seldom explicitly stated, it appears that survey research methodology is often anathema to epistemological writings about both feminist
sociology and sociology incorporating a race/class/gender perspective. While
writing this appendix, the second author received a research methods textbook
designed to be used for teaching quantitative, qualitative, and mixed methods
approaches. The section on qualitative research design, in a section titled
"Characteristics of Qualitative Research," suggests many qualities that overlap
with feminist epistemology. Qualitative research "takes place in the natural
setting," involves active participation, is "emergent rather than tightly prefig-
ured," and is interpretive, holistic, and reflexive. The quantitative section, on
the other hand, begins with "Components of a Survey Method Plan," in which
the authors describe the steps of survey design, with nothing on the unique
features of quantitative research (Creswell 2003:154, 181–83).

Similarly, in an otherwise stellar volume on feminist research practices,
Hesse-Biber and Yaiser (2004) devote very little space to quantitative methods.
Next to chapters on focus groups, interviews, oral history, and ethnography,
there is but one article on survey research (by the aforementioned Hill and
Sprague) and another titled "Some Thoughts by an Unrepentant 'Positivist'"
by Janet Chafetz which, although arguing for hypothesis testing, is otherwise
silent on the issue of method.

Cannot survey research, we wondered, involve active participation on the
part of the researchers? Could not we, too, be reflexive about our role in this
inquiry and be sensitive to how our personal biographies shaped our research?
Could we not create a more interpretive and holistic approach, even when
analyzing survey data? Indeed, our own research proclivities are geared toward
qualitative, rather than quantitative, sociology, so we sought ways to bring

some of the benefits of qualitative sociology to our survey. Our work should be interpreted as a cautionary tale for those attempting this task; as we discuss below, we were successful in some ways, and less so in others.

Problems in the Case Study

Sampling Frame Issues

As we mention in chapter 1, we ended up purchasing a sample: a list of members of the greater Richmond metropolitan area who had Hispanic surnames. The procedure provided the possibility of a random probability sample for the subset of the Richmond Latino population with Hispanic surnames. However, the drawbacks, especially from the perspective of our commitment to race/class/gender issues, proved to be considerable.

The sample uses existing lists and databases such as such as telephone directories, lists from the Department of Motor Vehicles, and other public agencies. Such sources of information tend to be heavily male-dominated, and indeed our original sampling frame contained only 28 percent women. In retrospect, this male bias could have been mitigated somewhat by randomly asking for a male or female respondent when dialing the number provided, rather than asking for the exact person whose name was listed in our sampling frame, though that also would reduce the likelihood of finding Latinos.

Using a sampling frame of this nature also disproportionately and unintentionally excludes Latinas specifically, thus adding another wrinkle in our desire have a representative sample. We ended up creating a second, nonprobability sample. This second sample provided additional data on individuals difficult to locate. Approximately 50 percent of this sample was female. Almost half of these women did not have typical Hispanic surnames (as did some of the men), so we feel assured that we captured a large number of women who fall into this category.

However, we encountered a typical drawback of this type of qualitative sample, one that often develops as a result of using lists of community leaders. Although the first sample has a distribution of income and occupational status that reflected the 2000 Census, the qualitative sample does not. Because a number of the organizations we contacted (Hispanic Chamber of Commerce, American Hispanics of Richmond Association, AHAR) were dedicated to the growth of Latino businesses and/or Latino culture in the region, the individuals we made contact with through the second sample technique were disproportionately middle-class professionals, with higher levels of income and employment. So although we increased the gender diversity in this part of the sample, we ran the risk of sampling largely a Latino elite. Actually, we ended up with a fairly bifurcated second sample, as some of the other modes of acquiring respondents (discussed below) meant that some respondents were disproportionately low-income immigrants working in service-sector occupations.

This latter group brought to the fore another issue we encountered in sampling, which was finding and persuading out-of-status individuals to participate in our study. We wished to have a representative sample of those individuals in Richmond who were illegal immigrants. Several of our contacts within the Catholic Church and the legal community had indicated that the size of the illegal population in Richmond was larger than projected by official sources, and rapidly growing, particularly among Central American refugees.

However, early on in our study design we resolved an ethical dilemma about collecting data on illegal immigrants by not including a question in our survey specifically about the respondent's legal status. We promised complete confidentiality from the outset, but we did not want to discourage respondents (even legal immigrants) from answering our survey if they felt there were problematic questions on legal status or questions that could in any way be used against them. Second, we did not want to be responsible for maintaining files that could potentially be seized by official authorities for information, however remote that possibility.

We decided that whatever information we could gain would not outweigh the ethical risks to our respondents, so although we asked questions about migration and citizenship status, we did not ask about legal resident status, although some respondents volunteered that they *were* legal residents. Consequently, we do not know how many of our respondents are illegal immigrants, although we do know that 31 percent of the purchased sample were not U. S. citizens. Slightly less of the qualitative sample, 22 percent, were not citizens, and although the first group of individuals in the qualitative sample were either long-term immigrants or U.S.-born respondents, the second group were found in Latino groceries, restaurants, and connected to Spanish-speaking Catholic parishes, where illegal immigrants were more likely to be located. So, although we do not know the exact number, we are confident that our survey captures some of Richmond's illegal resident population.

In order to fully represent the "race" portion of a race/class/gender perspective, we felt it important to find as much diversity across the sub-ethnicities within Richmond as we could. Although 60 percent of Latinos in the United States are of Mexican origin (U.S. Bureau of the Census 2000), this distribution is less true in Richmond. According to the 2000 Census, one-third of the Richmond metropolitan area was Mexican, 20 percent were Puerto Rican, with the rest of the population made up of smaller amounts of various countries of origin. Our sample matches those proportions.

In sum, we would argue for a careful consideration as to whether the use of random sampling will actually culminate in a useful and representative race, class, and gender distribution. Many Latino researchers use quota samples, rather than random samples. Portes and Bach (1985), for example, used community centers to distribute surveys in cities with large Latino populations. While we are in no way dismissing the importance of random probability samples, we also find that other methods of sampling, carefully conducted, can also be attempts at finding balance in methodological goals without compromising other epistemological concerns.

Designing Research Questions

Both principal investigators are trained in qualitative research, and although we had participated in survey research projects before, designing and administering a large-scale survey was a first for us. Ideally, we would have designed and tested our own questions with our epistemological concerns foregrounded, but in actuality, given our lack of experience, we turned to survey sources with already established levels of reliability. The survey contains mostly close-ended questions modeled after the U.S. Census, the General Social Survey, and other empirical questionnaire instruments focusing on Latinos. These questions were not necessarily questions sensitive to the intersection of race, class, and gender or preserving the complex experiences and subjective selves of the respondents. Questions in the instrument are organized into six major clusters: immigration; cultural integration; family and community life; and workplace experience, political participation, and religious practice. Of the nearly one hundred questions, approximately 10 percent are open-ended or provide an "other" category with an open-ended response. Creating (and analyzing fully) a large number of open-ended questions was one method we used to expand the opportunities for more contextual, feminist interpretations of the data.

One example of a particularly useful "other" categorization had to do with race. We wanted to keep our question on racial identity basically open-ended, rather than impose racial categories on our respondents. Avoiding the standard census or official categories, we worked for a long time on the wording of the question to make it as subjective and meaningful as possible. Finally, we decided to ask, "Do you think of yourself as you white, black, or some other race?" with a blank after other, and instructions to interviewers to write in whatever label the respondent provided. Of course, we received about forty different variations of racial and ethnic descriptors, some of them in English, and some in

Spanish (including "color" terms such as *moreno, morena clara*, café, yellow, brown, *morocha*, and *luza*; "mixed" submissions such as *mestizo, criollo, trigena*, and person of color; and even the playful ("human," "Atlantis") rendering the data more difficult, although not impossible, to analyze, and providing us with a wealth of information far beyond the traditional categories.

There were other limitations of surveys and survey administration that we found difficult to avoid. Surveys, because they maximize the reliability of the data, cannot easily be tailored to individuals, but have to be given in the same fashion to each respondent. Interviewers must read the questions as written in exactly the order in which they are written. There is very little leeway for the interviewer to probe too deeply for answers that change the nature of the question or lead the respondent in any way. Nor can the respondent alter the survey questions, or add much to the survey as written to put his/her answers into a context more relevant to that experience. All of these things make survey administration a more removed experience for the respondent, turn the respondent into an object rather than a subject, exactly what we wished to avoid.

One thing that we did insist on was that the interviews be conducted face-to-face, and as much as possible in the respondent's own home, a setting in which they would feel most comfortable. Usually the interviews were conducted in private, but in a few cases there were children, other family members, or friends present or nearby, some of who also interacted with the researchers during and after the formal interviews. Interviewers were sometimes invited to share meals with respondents, look at family pictures, and the like. Indeed, many respondents told their interviewers at the end of the session that they had so much more to tell, information that was not covered in the questions we had asked. For example, it was very difficult to capture the rich texture of migration experiences through quantitative data alone, and so during this period respondents related more lengthy stories about their experiences. All additional statements of this type were all recorded in the researcher's notes.

Recruiting, Training, Retaining, and Supervising Student Volunteers

From the time we did the pretest of the Latino sample, in the fall of 2000, until we exhausted our data collection, in April 2002, fifty-two University of Richmond students volunteered for the project, and an additional twenty-nine students signed up for a research practicum class in sociology. Students at Mary Washington College were involved on a more limited basis as part of a research methods class. All of them received training in interviewing and survey techniques. The whole project was student-driven—students called the individuals listed in our sample, scheduled and conducted interviews, and helped to build the codebook and organize administrative forms.

Many of the calls were done in Spanish, so the schedulers were all bilingual (about one-third of the students each semester). Contacting all of the potential respondents was a difficult task. Schedulers often called the same potential respondent twenty times, and connecting with each was a function of the persistence of the schedulers, and the flexibility of the time they had to call the individuals in the sample. Students coded the interviews, but all coding was reviewed by one of the principal investigators to ensure accuracy and consistency. Coders remained in constant contact with us to keep up updated of changes to the codebook. Students who completed data entry were also closely monitored by the principal investigators.

During the spring semester of 2002, we were able to begin paying students from a research grant that we got from the University of Richmond. Interestingly, being paid to schedule and conduct interviews did not seem to affect students' work output in any way. They did not schedule or conduct more interviews than when they were merely volunteering or getting course credit, which suggests that time is the main barrier to undergraduate student participation in research projects. In fact, it is likely that the volunteer students were more dedicated, since they tended to support the research agenda and were more likely to persuade respondents to complete surveys.

Matching Interviewers and Respondents

Ideally, we had hoped to recruit largely volunteers who were bilingual and bicultural, and to match interviewees by gender, race, and ethnicity. Numerous studies have indicated that the context of an interview can matter: the gender, race, and ethnicity of the interviewer can affect the way a respondent answers questions, particularly for race and ethnic issues in Latino interviews (Rodriguez 2000). In reality, although we followed this practice as best we could, it often turned out to be impractical. We were fairly successful at matching respondents by gender, even though our respondents were overwhelmingly male and interviewers overwhelmingly female.

Although we recruited students from a number of departments on campus, including Spanish and International Studies, most of them were not fluent in Spanish, and few were native speakers of Spanish, so we could rely on few connections to respondents through common cultural backgrounds. As a practical matter we did not know the skin color of the respondents we were interviewing ahead of time, so we were not able to match respondents to interviewers in this way. Even if we had had the luxury of a variety of hues and nationalities of interviewers, assumptions made about the potential rapport between interviewers and respondents might have proved less than fruitful, as some respondents identified as white ("I'm not your typical Hispanic") regardless of the shade of their skin. They may have resented our attempts to match them with a "similar" Latino, and therefore our largely white, middle-class student interviewer population actually worked to our advantage.

Overall, we learned to recognize the limitations posed by using student researchers to implement many aspects of the research methodology. We suggest the following: Train your students in the intersection of race, class, and gender and in feminist reflexivity in addition to the usual survey training. During training, remind them that an interview is a particular type of social interaction, and though they have to be professional and objective, they also must establish relationships of understanding, negotiation, and mutual trust. Interviewers should be careful listeners and be able to make the respondents feel that the interaction will be pleasant and rewarding. Assume that it is going to take twice as much time to complete your data collection as you think it will. Above all, be flexible.

Feminist Analysis of Quantitative Data

We utilized techniques that all survey researchers use—rigorous inter-rater reliability, for example. At each stage of the data analysis—coding, data entry, cleaning—the data were checked and rechecked for accuracy. Of course, virtually all but the most inexperienced researchers use these techniques. At the same time, we are sure that we have spent far more time going over the survey responses with a fine tooth comb than any of the other survey research projects we have participated in during our careers, because we wanted to analyze the data in a more thorough, holistic, feminist manner.

All interviewers were expected to complete a "researcher's notes" section at the end of the survey, where they could jot down any additional comments made by the respondent, either in response to particular questions or about issues not fully covered on the survey. These sections provided us with some of the richest data we acquired, and especially allowed us to consider issues we had not fully thought about (a more grounded theory approach). Rather than a supplement to the quantitative data, however, the findings were often central to how questions were interpreted and provided us with a few of our basic results.

We also did things that are *not* typical of survey analysis. We read through each interview/survey individually several times, not as an aggregate of different variables to be analyzed separately but as a complete entity. Did each interview hang together as a *narrative* of this individual's experience? Did it tell the whole story? Did the interview notes reveal something the responses to close-ended questions did not? What we wanted to do was to analyze the surveys in context: What could respondents have meant?

An extensive quote from one of our more detailed entries will serve to illustrate both the types of things included in the notes and also how these notes led us to think differently about the questions that we had asked:

> The interview took place in an Arby's that is near to the apartment where the respondent lives. We spoke while making the appointment, over the phone in both English and Spanish. When we met for the interview, we introduced each other in English, and chatted in English. When it came time to begin the interview, I asked R. if he'd prefer the interview in English or Spanish, he said Spanish. About halfway through the interview he switched to telling me his comments in English. The interview, overall, was mixture of English and Spanish. At times it was noisy in the restaurant, I positioned the questionnaire such that he could read the questions and what I wrote in the survey. He sometimes responded in a combo of English and Spanish, for example, he might say "I choose two, nunca."
>
> Respondent was very confused by the word "Anglo" [authors' note: this was a series of questions, D16–18, related to dealings with Anglos]. He said that he did not understand or know that word. I explained to him that I needed him to answer the question as best he could, but I would not interpret that word for him. I told him that if he liked, he could tell me how he understood the word and that I would make a note of that in the survey. He understood Anglo as American. He arrived at this conclusion by looking at the survey in English. He originally asked me to see the English version so he could see from what English word Anglo was being translated. When he saw that for questions D16–D18 it uses the same word in English, he asked what word Anglo translates to in Spanish. I said he needed to do the best he could, and he continued to look at the English survey and saw questions D5 and E1, where the English version lists, "Anglo/American" and that was how he decided to interpret "Anglo" as American. At this same point he switched from making his comments in Spanish to making them in English.
>
> As we were leaving and walking towards our cars, respondent began telling me about how he learned English. He learned English purely by ear—he can't write it or read it very well (his observation), but he can converse with ease (my observation). He said he has been thinking

about taking English classes—he mentioned something about going for further education and the necessity of reading and writing English well to do that. He stressed how important it is to be surrounded by a language to learn it.

In the end, we decided to refer to the data about the Anglos questions only once in this book. In other situations, we used to the notes to help us think about how to *interpret* the data rather than just statistically analyzing the numbers we had at face value.

We kept a data file for each question, and used it to capture the comments that respondents made while answering questions that contextualized their responses. Usually these responses were innocuous, but not always. We found out that our question about listening to the radio in Spanish (Question D9) was problematic from these comments, because respondents were not aware of the stations. However, respondents could still answer, "If I had a Spanish station, I would listen." Occasionally, however, they even prompted us to reconsider our fundamental constructions of the variables under study. For example, we asked respondents questions that were designed to capture income discrimination: "Do you think that your present income is comparable to that of your fellow workers?" and "Do you think your present income reflects your educational level?" Respondents who answered "probably no" or "definitely no" would sometimes insist that they knew this had nothing to do with their ethnicity or surname, even when they would tell us elsewhere in the survey that they had moved down the occupational ladder when coming to the United States, or that their educational credentials had not transferred from their home country. Although it is possible that these respondents were unaware of discrimination, we also had to consider that our definition of income discrimination could vary from theirs, and to take seriously their interpretation that no discrimination had occurred (see chapter 6).

We were also forced to think about the difficulty of answering questions about being treated unfairly in applying for jobs or promotions. Rather than responding, "No," many respondents choose to leave the question blank, telling the interviewer "Who knows?" They were hesitant to equate their personal lack of evidence with discrimination with the actual likelihood that it had never occurred, and we ultimately included this equivocation in the data analysis about occupational discrimination as well.

Our advice, then, is as much as possible to treat each survey as an individual narrative. Do not feel as if a completed survey is the end of the relationship with that respondent. We were able to call respondents back on the telephone to confirm responses or to ask for an expansion on responses that were incomplete or that we were still not clear about. Needless to say, following up with a respondent is a technique that is not ordinarily used in survey research, but is much more common in qualitative research. All of these methods are ways of dealing with the canned nature of quantitative questions, although if we had a chance to do it differently, we would design our own questions with our epistemological goals foregrounded.

Appendix B

Survey Questionnaire

ID Number: _____   Date: _____ /_____/_____

Researcher Name: _____   Time began: _____

Researcher ID #: _____   Time ended: _____

A. Demographic Questions

A1. *(Record the respondent's sex)*
   1. Female
   2. Male

A2. What year were you born? *(If R doesn't know date of birth, ask how old s/he is)*
   98. No date of birth given

A3. What is the highest degree or level of school you have **completed**?
   1. No schooling
   2. Grade school
   3. High School (incomplete)
   4. High School (complete)
   5. College (incomplete)
   6. College (complete)
   7. Master's degree
   8. Professional degree
   9. Doctorate degree

A4. What is your marital status?
   1. Now married
   2. Widowed
   3. Divorced
   4. Separated
   5. Never married

A5. How many children do you have?

    0. No children

    _____ children

A6. Is the place where you live:

    1. Owned by you or someone in your household

    2. Rented for cash rent

    3. Occupied without payment of cash rent

A7. What was your personal income from all sources, before taxes, last year?

    0. No personal income

    1. Less than 14,999

    2. 15,000–24,999

    3. 25,000–34,999

    4. 35,000–49,999

    5. 50,000–74,999

    6. 75,000–99,999

    7. 100,000–and up

A8. What was your household income from all sources, before taxes, last year? *(Use list from A7)*

B. Religiosity Questions

B1. In what religion were you raised? Was it Protestant, Catholic, Jewish, some other religion, or no religion?

    1. Protestant _____

       (If so ask specific church and/or denomination)

    2. Catholic

    3. Jewish

    4. Other _____

       (If so ask specific religion and/or denomination)

    5. No religion

B2. What is your current religious preference? Is it Protestant, Catholic, Jewish, some other religion, or no religion? *(Use list from B1)*

B3. How important do you think it is to raise your child/ren in your own beliefs? *(Read options)*
1. Not important at all
2. Somewhat important
3. Very important

B4. How often do you attend religious services?
1. Never (Skip to C1)
2. Less than once a year (Skip to C1)
3. About once or twice a year (Skip to C1)
4. Several times a year
5. About once a month
6. Two to three times a month
7. Nearly every week
8. Every week
9. Several times a week

B5. In addition to attending religious services, do you regularly participate in other church/synagogue activities?
0. No
Yes (List up to three activities)

_____

_____

_____

C. Migration Questions

C1. In what country were you born? (If U.S., skip to C6) _____

C2. At what age did you move to the U.S.? _____ (If "Don't know," was it)
97. as a small child
98. as a teen
99. as an adult

C3. Are you a U.S. citizen? *(Read options)*
1. Yes, born in U.S. territories
2. Yes, born abroad of American parents
3. Yes, U.S. citizen by naturalization
4. No, not a citizen of the U.S.

C4. Do you intend to become a U.S. citizen? *(If "No" to C3)*, ask:
   0. No
   1. Yes
   2. Don't know

C5. What is the <u>main</u> reason that you came to the U.S.?
   (If hesitant, probe w/ list)
   1. Came with parents
   2. Came with spouse
   3. Reunite with family
   4. Better job opportunities
   5. Better educational opportunities
   6. To escape war or persecution in homeland
   7. Other _____

C6. How satisfied would you say you are with life in the U.S.?
   (Read options)
   1. Very unsatisfied
   2. Unsatisfied
   3. So-so
   4. Satisfied
   5. Very satisfied

C7. In what country was your mother born? _____

C8. In what country was your father born?_____

C9. In what country were your mother's parents born? _____

C10. In what country were your father's parents born? _____

C11. What was your mother's occupation as you were growing up?
   (Employed if working for pay or profit)

   _____

   (If more than 1 job, use the 1 person worked most hours)
   0. Unemployed *(Include homemaker)*
   88. Don't know.

C12. What was your father's occupation as you were growing up?
(See C11 instructions)

_____

0. Unemployed
88. Don't know

C13. What is the highest degree or level of school your mother **completed**?
1. No schooling
2. Grade school
3. High School (incomplete)
4. High School (complete)
5. College (incomplete)
6. College (complete)
7. Master's degree
8. Professional degree
9. Doctorate degree
88. Don't know

C14. What is the highest degree or level of school your father **completed**?
(Use C13 list)

D. Cultural Integration Questions

(If native language is not Spanish or English, use language for questions D1—D10)

D1. What language is spoken in your home?
1. Only Spanish
2. Mostly Spanish, some English
3. Spanish and English equally
4. Mostly English, some Spanish
5. Only English

D2. What language is spoken at family gatherings? *(Christmas, Thanksgiving)*
1. Only Spanish
2. Mostly Spanish, some English
3. Spanish and English equally
4. Mostly English, some Spanish
5. Only English

D3. What language do you speak with most of your friends?
   1. Only Spanish
   2. Mostly Spanish, some English
   3. Spanish and English equally
   4. Mostly English, some Spanish
   5. Only English

D4. Would you say that you speak Spanish . . .
   1. Not at all
   2. Very little or not very often
   3. Moderately
   4. Much or very often
   5. Extremely often or almost always

D5. Would you say that you speak English . . .
   1. Not at all
   2. Very little or not very often
   3. Moderately
   4. Much or very often
   5. Extremely often or almost always

D6. Would you say that you enjoy listening to music in . . .
   1. Only Spanish
   2. Mostly Spanish, some English
   3. Spanish and English equally
   4. Mostly English, some Spanish
   5. Only English

D7. Would you say that you enjoy reading newspapers and magazines in . . .
   1. Only Spanish
   2. Mostly Spanish, some English
   3. Spanish and English equally
   4. Mostly English, some Spanish
   5. Only English

D8. Would you say that you enjoy watching television in . . .
   1. Only Spanish
   2. Mostly Spanish, some English
   3. Spanish and English equally
   4. Mostly English, some Spanish
   5. Only English

D9. Would you say that you enjoy listening to the radio in . . .
1. Only Spanish
2. Mostly Spanish, some English
3. Spanish and English equally
4. Mostly English, some Spanish
5. Only English

D10. Would you say that you enjoy watching movies in . . .
1. Only Spanish
2. Mostly Spanish, some English
3. Spanish and English equally
4. Mostly English, some Spanish
5. Only English

D11. What ethnicity do you think of yourself as?
_____

D12. Do you think of yourself as?
1. White
2. Black
3. Other _____

(Insert ethnicity given in D11 on questions D13 and D14)

D13. How important is being _____ to you?
1. Not important at all
2. Somewhat important
3. Very important

D14. Would you say that your family cooks _____ foods
1. Not at all
2. Very little or not very often
3. Moderately
4. Much or very often
5. Extremely often or almost always

D15. What are the dominant customs in your home?
1. Anglo/American
2. Latino/a or Hispanic
3. Black, African-American
4. Mixed
5. Other _____

How much would you say that you agree with the following statements . . .
(Use for questions D16-D18)

D16. I have difficulty accepting some behaviors exhibited by Anglos
    1. Not at all
    2. Very little or not very often
    3. Moderately
    4. Much or very often
    5. Extremely often or almost always

D17. I have difficulty accepting certain customs of Anglos
    1. Not at all
    2. Very little or not very often
    3. Moderately
    4. Much or very often
    5. Extremely often or almost always

D18. I have or I think I would have difficulty accepting Anglos
    as close personal friends
    1. Not at all
    2. Very little or not very often
    3. Moderately
    4. Much or very often
    5. Extremely often or almost always

E. Social Integration Questions

E1. At the present time, are your friends mostly
    1. Anglo/American
    2. Latino/a or Hispanic
    3. Black, African-American
    4. Mixed
    5. Other _____

E2. Are the people that you work with mostly
    1. Anglo/American
    2. Latino/a or Hispanic
    3. Black, African-American
    4. Mixed
    5. Other _____
    9. Not working

E3. Are the people in your church mostly
    1. Anglo/American
    2. Latino/a or Hispanic
    3. Black, African-American
    4. Mixed
    5. Other _____
    9. Not religious

E4. Are your neighbors mostly
    1. Anglo/American
    2. Latino/a or Hispanic
    3. Black, African-American
    4. Mixed
    5. Other _____

E5. Are the people at the places where you go to have fun and to relax (at parties, dances, picnics) mostly
    1. Anglo/American
    2. Latino/a or Hispanic
    3. Black, African-American
    4. Mixed
    5. Other _____

(If R has young children ask:)

E6. Are the children that your child/ren play with mostly . . .
    1. Anglo/American
    2. Latino/a or Hispanic
    3. Black, African-American
    4. Mixed
    5. Other _____

E7. How difficult is it for a Hispanic to get a job or a promotion?
    1. Not difficult at all
    2. Somewhat difficult
    3. Difficult
    4. Very difficult
    5. No opinion

E8. How difficult is it for a Hispanic to rent or buy a home?
   1. Not difficult at all
   2. Somewhat difficult
   3. Difficult
   4. Very difficult
   5. No opinion

E9. How difficult is it for a Hispanic to get a loan from a bank?
   1. Not difficult at all
   2. Somewhat difficult
   3. Difficult
   4. Very difficult
   5. No opinion

E10. How likely is it that a Hispanic will be treated rudely or given poor service in a store or restaurant?
   1. Not likely at all
   2. Somewhat likely
   3. Likely
   4. Very likely
   5. No opinion

Do you agree or disagree with the following statements: (Use for E11 and E12)

E11. People who work for public agencies *(like welfare, social security and health clinics)* are more concerned about Anglos than Hispanics
   1. Strongly disagree
   2. Disagree
   3. Agree
   4. Strongly agree
   5. No opinion
   6. Don't know

E12. In this geographic area, Hispanics have to work a lot harder to get ahead than Anglos
   1. Strongly disagree
   2. Disagree
   3. Agree
   4. Strongly agree
   5. No opinion
   6. Don't know

E13. Do you feel most Anglos accept you as their equal? *(Read options)*
1. Definitely yes
2. Probably yes
3. Undecided
4. Probably no
5. Definitely no
6. No opinion

F. Family Life Questions

F1. Please list the members of your household by their ages and relationship to you:
0. No one else lives here

Age   Relationship

———   ————————————
———   ————————————
———   ————————————
———   ————————————
———   ————————————
———   ————————————

Now, is there anyone else who lives in your household? Relatives or friends?

———   ————————————
———   ————————————
———   ————————————

F2. How many of your children can talk in Spanish?
0. None

——————————

F3. Do you think the U.S. way of life . . . *(Read options)*
1. Weakens the family
2. Does not weaken the family
3. Neither
4. Undecided

F4. How important is it to raise children in one's own culture?
(Read options)
1. Not important at all
2. Somewhat important
3. Very important

G. Education Questions

G1. Do you have children in school? *(Report yes if children in K-12)*
    0. No *(If "No," skip to G4)*
    1. Yes

G2. How involved are you in your child/ren's school? *(Read options)*
    1. Not involved at all
    2. Somewhat involved
    3. Involved
    4. Very involved

G3. Are you a member of the Parent-Teacher Association?
    0. No
    1. Yes
    2. No PTA

G4. How important is having a good education for getting ahead in life? *(Read options)*
    1. Not important at all
    2. Somewhat important
    3. Very important

G5. How important is it that Spanish-speaking children be taught Spanish in American schools? *(Read options)*
    1. Not important at all
    2. Somewhat important
    3. Very important

G6. How should children who don't speak English when they enter school be taught? *(Read options)*
    1. Classes only in English
    2. Classes in their native language for a year or two
    3. Classes in their native language through High School
    4. Other _____
    5. Don't know

H. Work-Related Questions

H1. Are you now employed at a paying job? *(If R answers 2–6, skip to H13)*
   1. Yes
   2. Not employed
   3. Homemaker
   4. Student
   5. Retired
   6. Disabled

H2. What is your occupation? *(Employed if working last week for pay or profit)*
   _____

   (Ask specific occupation. If more than 1 job, describe the 1 person worked the most hours at last week)

H3. What kind of business or industry do you work for? _____

H4. How many paying jobs do you now have, including night jobs, and any part time work in addition to your main job? _____

H5. How many hours did you work for pay last week? _____

H6. In your main job, how are you paid? *(Read options)*
   1. Salaried
   2. Paid by the hour
   3. Other _____

H7. Are you a member of a union?
   0. No
   1. Yes _____
   2. No union

H8. How satisfied are you with your current job? *(Read options)*
   1. Very unsatisfied
   2. Unsatisfied
   3. So–so
   4. Satisfied
   5. Very satisfied

H9. Do you think your present income is comparable to that of your fellow workers? *(Read options)*
   1. Definitely yes
   2. Probably yes
   3. Undecided
   4. Probably no
   5. Definitely no

H10. Do you think your present **income** reflects your educational level?
   (Read options)
   1. Definitely yes
   2. Probably yes
   3. Undecided
   4. Probably no
   5. Definitely no

H11. Do you think your present **occupation** reflects your educational level?
   (Read options)
   1. Definitely yes
   2. Probably yes
   3. Undecided
   4. Probably no
   5. Definitely no

H12. Do your chances for promotion reflect your talent and ability?
   (Read options)
   1. Definitely yes
   2. Probably yes
   3. Undecided
   4. Probably no
   5. Definitely no

H13. Have you been treated unfairly in applying for jobs because of being Hispanic? *(Read options)*
   1. No, never
   2. Rarely
   3. Occasionally
   4. Frequently

H14. Have you been treated unfairly in seeking promotions because of being Hispanic? *(Read options)*
1. No, never
2. Rarely
3. Occasionally
4. Frequently
9. Not applicable

Thinking of work in general, how much do you agree or disagree with each of the following statements: *(Use for H15–H17)*

H15. A job is just a way of earning money, no more *(Read options)*
1. Strongly disagree
2. Disagree
3. Agree
4. Strongly agree
5. No opinion

H16. I would enjoy having a paying job even if I did not need that money *(Read options)*
1. Strongly disagree
2. Disagree
3. Agree
4. Strongly agree
5. No opinion

H17. Work is a person's most important activity *(Read options)*
1. Strongly disagree
2. Disagree
3. Agree
4. Strongly agree
5. No opinion

H18. Which of the following statements best describes your feelings about work? *(Read options)*
1. I work only as hard as I have to
2. I work hard but not so as to interfere with the rest of my life
3. I make a point of doing the best work I can even if it sometimes does interfere with the rest of my life

I. Political Participation Questions

I1. Generally speaking do you usually think of yourself as a Republican, Democrat, Independent or what?
1. Republican
2. Democrat
3. Independent
4. Other _____
5. None or undecided

I2. Would you place yourself politically on a scale of liberal to conservative: *(Read options)*
1. Very liberal
2. Somewhat liberal
3. Moderate
4. Somewhat conservative
5. Very conservative

I3. Did you vote in the 2000 presidential election?
0. No
1. Yes
9. Not applicable/Not a citizen

I4. What about local elections? Do you: *(Read options)*
1. Always vote in those
2. Sometimes miss one
3. Rarely vote
4. Never vote
9. Not applicable

I5. In the past three or four years, have you contributed money to a political party, or candidate, or to any other political cause?
0. No
1. Yes

I6. In the past three or four years, have you attended any political meetings or rallies?
0. No
1. Yes

I7. Do you agree or disagree with this statement: "people like me do not have any say in what the government does?" *(Read options)*
   1. Strongly disagree
   2. Disagree
   3. Agree
   4. Strongly agree
   5. No opinion

J. Richmond Migration Questions

J1. At what age did you move to Richmond? _____
   (If "Don't know," Probe: Was it)
   97. as a small child
   98. as a teen
   99. as an adult
   0. Born in Richmond (SKIP TO J4)

J2. What were the last 3 cities you lived in before you moved to Richmond?
   _____
   _____
   _____

J3. Why did you move to Richmond?
   _____
   _____
   _____ _____

J4. Not counting your immediate family, how many of your relatives live in the Richmond area?
   0. No relatives
   _____ relatives
   (Fill in the number of relatives)

J5. How often do you receive help from your relatives in the area?
   (Read options)
   0. No relatives in the area
   1. Not at all
   2. Very little or not very often
   3. Moderately
   4. Much or very often
   5. Extremely often or almost always

J6. How satisfied are you with life in Richmond? *(Read options)*
1. Very unsatisfied
2. Unsatisfied
3. So-so
4. Satisfied
5. Very satisfied

J7. Do you wish or do you have plans to move to another city?
0. No
1. Yes
2. Don't know

Appendix C

Comparisons of Latinos in Richmond Data with 2000 Census

Table C1. Ages for Survey Respondents (Counts and Percentages)

Age	N	%
18–19	2	1
20–29	54	18
30–39	80	27
40–49	92	31
50–59	50	17
60+	23	6
Total	301	100

Source: Latinos in Richmond Survey.

Table C2. Education of Survey Respondents Compared to 2000 Census Data
(Counts and Percentages)

Education	LIR Survey		Census 2000
	N	%	%
Less than 9th Grade	28	9	17
9th Grade to 12th Grade, No dipl.	20	7	15
High School Graduate	49	16	21
Some College, No degree	89	29	27
Bachelor's Degree	72	24	13
Graduate/Professional	45	15	13
Total	303	100	100

Source: Latinos in Richmond Survey, Bureau of the Census 2000.

Table C3. Household Income for Survey Respondents
Compared to 2000 Census Data (Counts and Percentages)

Income	LIR Survey		Census 2000
	N	%	%
0 to 14,999	17	6	12
15,000–24,999	23	8	17
25,000–34,999	35	13	15
35,000–49,999	63	22	19
50,000– 74,999	62	22	19
75,000–99,999	35	12	10
100,000 and up	48	17	9
Total	283	100	100

Source: Latinos in Richmond Survey, Bureau of the Census, 2000.

Table C4. Employment Status by Gender for Survey Respondents Compared
to 2000 Census Data (Counts and Percentages)

Employment Status	Census 2000		LIR Survey
	N	%	%
Male			
In Labor Force	2,506	80	77
In Armed Forces	3	8	5
Civilian	2,245	72	72
Unemployed	58	2	4
Not in Labor Force	612	20	23
Total	3,118	100	100
Female			
In Labor Force	2,101	65	62
In Armed Forces	0	0	3
Employed	1,925	60	55
Unemployed	102	3	4
Not in Labor Force	1,085	35	38
Total	3,186	100	100

Source: Latinos in Richmond Survey, Bureau of the Census 2000 Survey.

Table C5. Household Type for Survey Respondents Compared
to 2000 Census Data (Counts and Percentages)

Household Type	LIR Survey		Latinos 2000	
	N	%	N	%
Married Couple				
With children under 18	138	57	2,125	47
No children under 18	62	26	1,067	22
Male head, no wife				
With children under 18	9	4	232	4
No children under 18	13	5	447	9
Female head, no wife				
With children under 18	8	3	669	14
No children under 18	11	5	206	4
Total	241	100	4,746	100

Source: Latinos in Richmond Survey, Bureau of the Census 2000.

Table C6. Housing Tenure for Survey Respondents Compared
to 2000 Census Data (Counts and Percentages)

Tenure Status	LIR Survey		Census 2000
	N	%	%
Owner	187	62	40
Renter	106	35	60
Other	8	3	
Total	301	100	100

Source: Latinos in Richmond Survey, Bureau of the Census 2000.

Notes

Chapter 1. Why Study Latinos in Richmond?

1. Whether the second wave immigrants and their children retain language and culture longer in ethnic enclaves than their earlier counterparts has been debated. Certainly the willingness and speed with which European immigrants adapted a century ago has been exaggerated, while contemporary research about the reluctance to learn English among recent immigrants has been overstated. Current studies of ethnic communities suggest that the "traditional pattern of intergenerational shift to English remains unchanged," even among Latinos in the Southwest. Retention of native language lasts no longer than two or three generations, with most in the second generation highly proficient in English (Bayley 2005:276).

2. Reviewing some eighty years of planning and city development in Richmond, Silver concludes, "As the preceding analysis suggests, Richmond's approach to planning was not apolitical. The planners' definition of the 'public good' often lacked broad appeal and reflected the predilections of one key political constituency—the city's growth-minded business and civic elite. One of the major characteristics of the city's planning and political legacy is the persistence and influence of a homegrown variety of 'progressivism,' premised largely upon the urban imperialistic impulses of Richmond's ruling social and economic elite" (1984:325). He further argues that "when compared to experiences of Atlanta and Norfolk during this period, what stands out in Richmond is how much of the traditional social fabric of the center city persisted" (327).

3. Although Richmond's small Latino population experienced a steady increase over the past four decades (for instance, in 1970 the Census recorded a population of 2,951 "Persons of Spanish Language" for the Richmond metropolitan area), it is not until the late 1990s that the population reached both a significant size and a perception in the media and the popular imagination as a visible constituency.

4. We acquired our sample from GeneSys Sampling Systems, a Philadelphia-based company. GeneSys maintains that it covers 94 percent of residential households in the United States. The company determines its list of seventeen thousand "high incidence Hispanic surnames" based on Latino data from the Census Bureau. The company finds the sources for Hispanic surnames in telephone directories, automobile and motorcycle registrations, real estate listings, and driver's license data; their records are updated quarterly.

Chapter 2. Segmented Paths to Richmond

1. All names used are pseudonyms.

Chapter 3. Many Roads to Richmond

1. About 22 percent of Latinos in the Richmond Standard Metropolitan Statistical Area are categorized by the census as "other Hispanic" because they do not include a country of origin, writing instead answers such as "Hispanic" or "Latino." About 17 percent of the overall U.S. population is thus categorized, making them the next largest Latino group after Mexicans (Guzman 2001:2). Since we ask about the place of birth of our respondents' parents and grandparents, and cross-reference these with respondents' self-identification, we avoided this problem.

2. Researchers of the Puerto Rican exodus from the island to the mainland often use many of the same terms and research conventions used for Latin American transnational migrants (see Aranda 2006:21–23). On the one hand, it is certainly strange to think of Puerto Ricans as immigrants migrating to a country they already live in and of which they are already citizens. On the other hand, the transition from island to mainland has always borne many of the markers of other transnational migrants—differences in language, adaptation to a sometimes strange and unwelcoming culture, journeys to and from each location affected by global capitalism—making their immigration vastly different from a mere internal migration. These fundamental tensions in identity follow all researchers of Puerto Ricans. For this reason, we will typically treat Puerto Ricans in the U.S. South much in the same way we treat other Latin American immigrants.

3. The reasons Richmond Latinos came to the United States also vary significantly by gender. Women were far more likely to say that the main reason they came was to be with their spouse or reunite with family (27 percent versus 9 percent for men); whereas men were more likely to say that they came for better wages (32 percent versus 27 percent for women).

4. A Pearson's Chi square for the relationship between ancestry and reasons for coming to the United States equals 42.2, which is significant at the .001 level; only one time out of one thousand would such a distribution of choices be seen if the results happen merely by chance.

5. We feel that our model differs from the ethnic enclave model for two reasons. First, the relative size of the Latino population that resettles in areas without a traditional Hispanic presence will likely remain smaller than that of the larger settlements in the traditional Latino areas of the United States. Second, unlike their counterparts in traditional areas, these Latinos do not concentrate in "ethnic neighborhoods." In Richmond Latinos are spread throughout all nine counties and four cities that comprise the larger statistical metropolitan area of the city.

Chapter 4. Living in Multiple Worlds

1. Women were somewhat significantly more likely then men to say that the dominant customs were Latino rather than Anglo or mixed (Chi-square is 6.98, with a significance level of 0.1, meaning that such a distribution of choices is likely to happen by chance only once in ten times).

2. Strangely enough, ethnic cooking was the one assimilation variable in which there were no gender differences. In all other cases, women were less assimilated then men. In terms of language assimilation women were significantly more likely to use Spanish than men (female mean is 2.96, male mean is 3.24; t-test for the significance of the differences of means is 2.2, with a significance level of less than .05). For cultural integration, women were more likely than men to use Spanish in their cultural activities (female mean is 3.51, male mean is 3.88; t-test for difference of means is 3.2, p is .005). When it comes to social distance, women are more likely to associate with other Latinos/as than men are (female mean = 1.84, male mean = 1.73; t-test is 1.9, although only significant at the .1 level).

3. Ancestry is also significantly related to household customs, but the presence of one set of customs does not necessarily rule out the others. Cubans, for instance, are the most assimilated group, with 41 percent of respondents choosing the Anglo household customs. Nevertheless, one-third of them choose to identify their household customs as Latino. Thirty-three percent of Mexicans indicate they have adopted Anglo customs in their households, but another 43 percent choose the Latino category. Central Americans are heavily inclined to report Latino customs. Salvadorans are predominantly Latino, followed by other Central Americans and Guatemalans. Puerto Ricans, Mexicans, Colombians, and other South Americans are more evenly divided among all three types.

4. *Language use:* Those who have been in this country less than twenty years still predominantly use Spanish in all of these settings. Those who have been here twenty or more years mix Spanish and English equally, while those who are born in the United States speak English almost exclusively. We also find significant variation in language use in terms of country of origin. Cubans and Puerto Ricans typically lean toward using slightly more English than Spanish. Mexicans and South Americans, on average, use English and Spanish equally, slightly behind the first two groups but averaging about the same as the sample overall. Of all Latinos in Richmond, Central Americans are more likely to use Spanish than English, especially Salvadorans and Guatemalans. Scores that vary by country are the result of the proportion from each country who are immigrants. Groups with more individuals born in the United States are more likely to use English more than Spanish.

   Media use: The longer one is here, the more likely that person is to favor the use of English when participating in cultural activities. Nevertheless, even those who have lived in the United States between zero and twenty years tend to use both English and Spanish when using media, while those here more than twenty years use English much more than Spanish. Those born in the United States use English almost exclusively in their cultural activities. Central Americans, especially Salvadorans and Guatemalans, are the least culturally integrated of the groups (although they still employ English as well as Spanish in their media use). Mexicans and South Americans are in the middle, while Cubans and Puerto Ricans have the highest levels of cultural integration, using considerably more English than Spanish when reading, listening to music, or watching films and television.

Social Distance: Similar to the other assimilation variables, there are important differences in social distance based on country of origin. Mexicans, Salvadorans, Guatemalans are more likely to associate with other Latinos. Cubans are least likely to do so, with Puerto Rican and other Central Americans falling somewhere in the middle. Time in the United States also counts: recent immigrants are more likely to associate with other Latinos; those born in the United States are least likely to do so.

Ethnic cooking: Recent arrivals are more likely to cook ethnic dishes at home. Salvadorans, Guatemalans, and other Central Americans are more likely to retain their ethnic tables, while Colombians and other South Americans are less likely to cook ethnic foods. The largest groups in Richmond—Mexicans, Puerto Ricans, and Cubans—fall somewhere in the middle.

5. The remaining 14 percent choose "American" as their ethnicity.

6. One example may suffice to illustrate the complexity for Latinos of describing race in the context of a brief questionnaire, especially when not interviewed in English. An interviewer's notes for the race question read, "He first said 'Blanco,' but as I moved to circle that, he said, 'no.' He pointed to his skin and asked me to tell him which color. I explained that was not something I could decide, that I was interested in what he said. I then mentioned to him that if he was unsure, that 'I don't know' was an option. He was comfortable with that response. He added that his wife is 'morena,' and that people do not believe him when he says he is Mexican." His reaction indicates not a mere misunderstanding of U.S. color labels, but of a fundamental contradiction in reconciling the concepts of race and ethnicity in U.S. and Latin American cultures. We discuss how we handled some of the difficulties of representing complexity holistically while doing large-scale survey research in the appendix to this book; see also Rodriguez, 2000.

Chapter 5. Richmond Latino Families

1. For Table 5.1, given the small Ns in the male and female heads-of-household cells, we combined those with children under eighteen with those without children prior to running the statistical tests.

2. On the other hand, other economic and cultural elements seem to have no predictive value when it comes to family type. The education and occupational prestige of respondents are unrelated to family type, as is country of origin.

3. Other studies have found, however, that true bilingualism—fluency in both English and Spanish, not merely English usage per se—can be associated with higher school achievement, (Portes and Rumbaut 2001b).

4. Latinas in our sample have a greater proportion of children who speak Spanish (.75 vs. .59 for men, t = 2.34; the differences of means is significant at the .05 level), and also place more importance on speaking Spanish, with a mean of 2.36 (3 being very important) to a male mean of 2.16 (t = 1.99, significant at .05).

Chapter 6. Blue Collar Latinos, White Collar Latinos

1. In terms of personal income, Latinas average an entire income bracket below males.

2. Women are significantly more likely to be employed in service industries and less likely to be employed in construction ($\chi2 = 33.0$, significant at .005).

3. Gender is not significantly related to any of the discrimination variables.

4. On the other hand, at least one respondent felt it was important to explain the kindness of Anglos. Now a manufacturing manager in a local chemical plant, he said that he could never have gotten the position he has now if it had not been for an Anglo's help approximately thirty years ago entering the industry. He said he needed that door opened by a white person because Richmond does discriminate (against all "outsiders," he said) although he does think nowadays things are a lot less openly discriminatory.

5. The white collar mean is 4.2, while the blue collar mean is 3.8 (a 4 denotes "somewhat satisfied"). The difference of means test is significant at .01.

Chapter 7. Religion and Secular Assimilation in Richmond

1. To be sure, the early wave also included some pockets of secular immigrants (including freethinking liberals, socialists, and communists, especially among Jewish and Finnish migrants). Nevertheless, our claim holds true for the vast majority of immigrants who reached the United States by the end of the nineteenth century.

2. We recognize that secularity has multiple dimensions not captured in a mere measure of nonreligion. Because we happened upon the prevalence of the nonreligious during data collection, our measures of secularity were necessarily limited to religious preference and church attendance.

3. There are potentially problems of collinearity between variables such as political participation, socioeconomic status, and attitudes toward work. We acknowledge that our simple analyses skim over important differences, and that a multivariate study should be done. However, our sample size prevents us from employing more sophisticated tests.

4. For both indices, analyses of variance for the differences in language use among the religious groups are significant at .05.

5. The analysis of variance is significant at the .05 level.

6. The analysis of variance for the different means is significant at .05.

7. These patterns of religious conversion hold true for both men and women.

Chapter 8. Public Life, Political Participation, and Community Presence

1. There are typically large gaps between whites and Latinos in voter turnout, even for presidential elections. Sierra reports a 64 percent turnout for the 1992 election and 56 percent in 1996 for whites, with only 29 percent and 27 percent for Latinos, respectively. When controlling for citizenship and socioeconomic characteristics, however, Latino rates do not differ significantly from non-Latino rates (Sierra 2000:328; see also Hero and Campbell 1996).

2. Another measure of assimilation, the language of one's media use discussed in chapter 4, failed to achieve a significant zero-order correlation with the voting scale, so we do not include it here.

Appendix A

1. On the other hand, sometimes evidence that the multiple discrimination of race, gender, and class is varied and complex can be shown quite readily with quantitative data, such as evidenced by government labor statistics on race, gender, education, and income (King 1988:49).

References

Alba, Richard, John Logan, Brian Stutts, Gilbert Marzan, and Wenquan Zhang. 1999. "Immigrant Groups in the Suburbs: A Reexamination of Suburbanization and Spatial Assimilation." *American Sociological Review* 64:446–460.

Alba, Richard, and Victor Nee. 1997. "Rethinking Assimilation Theory for a New Era of Immigration." *International Migration Review* 31:826–874.

———. 2003. *Remaking the American Mainstream: Assimilation and Contemporary Immigration.* Cambridge, MA: Harvard University Press.

Alexander, June G. 1987. *The Immigrant Church and Community: Pittsburgh's Slovak Catholics and Lutherans, 1880–1915.* Pittsburgh, PA: University of Pittsburgh Press.

Aranda, Elizabeth. 2006. *Emotional Bridges to Puerto Rico: Migration, Return Migration, and the Struggles of Incorporation.* Lanham, MD: Rowman and Littlefield.

Atiles, Jorge H., and Stephanie Bohon. 2002. "The Needs of Georgia's New Latinos: A Policy for the Decades Ahead." *Public Policy Research* 3:1–51.

Baca Zinn, Maxine. 1978. "Chicano Family Research: Conceptual Distortions and Alternative Directions." *The Journal of Ethnic Studies* 7: 59–71.

Bailey, Ronald, and Guillermo Flores. 1973. "Internal Colonialism and Racial Minorities in the U.S.: An Overview." Pp. 151–153 in *Structures of Dependency*, edited by Frank Bonilla and Robert H. Girling. Nairobi (E. Palo Alto), CA: Nairobi Bookstore.

Bankston, Carl L. and Min Zhou. 1997. "The Social Adjustment of Vietnamese American Adolescents: Evidence for a Segmented-Assimilation Approach." *Social Science Quarterly* 78:509–523.

Bartel, Ann P. 1989. "Where Do The New U.S. Immigrants Live?" *Journal of Labor Economics* 7:371–391.

Bayley, Robert. 2005. "Linguistic Diversity and English Language Acquisition." Pp. 268–286 in *Language in the USA: Themes for the Twenty-first Century*, edited by Finegan and Rickford. Cambridge: Cambridge University Press.

Becker, Gary S. 1971. *The Economics of Discrimination.* Chicago, IL: University of Chicago Press.

Bendick Jr., Marc, Charles W. Jackson, Victor A. Reinoso and Laura E. Hodges. 1992. *Discrimination Against Latino Job Applicants: A Controlled Experiment.* Washington, DC: Fair Employment Council of Greater Washington.

Bernal, Martha E., and George P. Knight (eds). 1993. *Ethnic Identity: Formation and Transformation among Hispanics and Other Minorities.* Albany, NY: State University of New York.

Birman, Dina. 1994. "Bi-Culturalism and Ethnic Identity: An Integrated Model." *Focus* 8:9–11.

Blank, Susan, and Ramon S. Torrecilha. 1998. "Understanding the Living Arrangements of Latino Immigrants: A Life Course Approach." *International Migration Review* 32:320.

Blau, Peter, and Otis Dudley Duncan. 1967. *The American Occupational Structure.* New York: John Wiley and Sons.

Blauner, Robert. 1972. *Racial Oppression in America.* New York: Harper and Row.

Bobo, Lawrence, Melvin Oliver, James Johnson, and Abel Valenzuela Jr. 2000. *Prismatic Metropolis: Inequality in Los Angeles.* New York: Russell Sage Foundation.

Bobo, Lawrence, and Susan A. Suh. 2000. "Surveying Racial Discrimination: Analyses from a Multiethnic Labor Market." Pp. 523–560 in *Prismatic Metropolis: Inequality in Los Angeles.* New York: Russell Sage Foundation.

Bonacich, Edna. 1972. "A Theory of Ethnic Antagonism: The Split Labor Market." *American Sociological Review* 37: 547–559.

———. 1973. "A Theory of Middleman Minorities." *American Sociological Review* 38: 583–594.

———. 1984. "Asian Labor in the Development of California and Hawaii." Pp. 130–185 in *Labor Immigration Under Capitalism,* edited by Lucie Cheng and Edna Bonacich. Berkeley, CA: University of California Press.

———, and J. Modell. 1980. *The Economic Basis of Ethnic Solidarity: Small Business of a Japanese-American Community.* Berkeley, CA: University of California Press.

Bond, Lynne A., and James C. Rosen (eds.). 1980. *Competence and Coping During Adulthood.* New Haven, CT: University Press of New England.

Borjas, George J. 1985. "Assimilation, Changes in Cohort Quality, and the Earnings of Immigrants." *Journal of Labor Economics* 3: 463–489.

———. *Friends or Strangers: The Impact of Immigrants on the U.S. Economy.* New York, NY: Basic Books.

Bowes, Mark. 2008. "Thirty-three Workers Arrested in Immigration Raid." *Richmond Times-Dispatch,* May 7.

Bowles, Samuel, and Herbert Gintis. 2002. "Schooling in Capitalist America Revisited." *Sociology of Education* 75:1–18.

Bradley, Paul. 1999. "Northern Virginia Has Become a Magnet for Immigrants." *Richmond Times-Dispatch,* May 9, A8.

Brady, Henry, Sidney Verba, and Kay Schlozman. 1995. "Beyond SES: A Resource Model of Political Participation." *American Political Science Review* 89:271–294.

Brodie, Mollyann, Roberto Suro, Annie Steffenson, Jaime Valdez, and Rebecca Levin. 2002. 2002 National Survey of Latinos. Washington, DC.: PEW Hispanic Center/Kaiser Family Foundation.

Bueker, Catherine. 2006. *From Immigrant to Naturalized Citizen: Political Incorporation in the United States.* New York: LFB Scholarly Publishing.

Burr, Jeffrey, Omer R. Galle, and Mark A. Fosset. 1991. "Racial Occupational Inequality in Southern Metropolitan Areas, 1940–1980: Revisiting the Visibility-Discrimination Hypothesis." *Social Forces* 69:831–850.

Cabezas, Amado, and Gary Kawaguchi. 1990. "Industrial Sectorization in California in 1980: The Continuing Significance of Race/Ethnicity, Gender, and Nativity." Pp.

57–99 in *Income and Status Differences Between White and Minority Americans: A Persistent Inequality,* edited by Sucheny Chan. New York: Edwin Mellen Press.

Cafferty, Pastora San Juan. 2000. "The Language Question." Pp. 69–96 in *Hispanics in the United States,* edited by Pastora San Juan Cafferty and David W. Engstrom. New Brunswick, NJ: Transaction Publishers.

Cain, Bruce, and D. Roderick Keiwiet. 1987. "Latinos and the 1984 Election: A Comparative Perspective." Pp. 47–62 in *Ignored Voices: Public Opinion Polls and the Latino Community,* edited by Rodolfo O. de la Garza. Austin, TX: Center for Mexican American Studies.

Calvo, Maria A., and Steven J. Rosenstone. 1989. "Hispanic Political Participation." *Latino Electorate Series.* San Antonio, TX: Southwest Voter Research Institute.

Campo-Flores, Arian, and Howard Fineman. 1995. "Latino Power Surge." *Newsweek.* May 30, 25–31.

Carmichael, Stokely, and Charles Hamilton. 1967. *Black Power.* New York: Vintage Books.

Carter, Rochelle. 2003. "Schools Adjust to Rise in Spanish Speakers." *The Atlanta Journal-Constitution,* September 18, 10A.

Catanzarite, Lisa. 1998. "Immigrant Latino Representation and Earning Penalties in Occupations." *Research on Social Stratification and Mobility* 16:147–179.

Cavalcanti, H. B., and Debra Schleef. 2001. "The Melting Pot Revisited: Hispanic Density and Economic Achievement in American Metropolitan Regions." *Hispanic Journal of Behavioral Sciences* 23:115–135.

Chapman, Dan. 2004. "Politics Vs. Trade Bid; Stand Against Driver's Licenses Sparks Concern." *The Atlanta Journal-Constitution,* November 10, 1F.

Chavez, Leo R. 1996. "Borders and Bridges: Undocumented Immigrants from Mexico and Central America." Pp. 250–262 in *Origins and Destinies: Immigration, Race, and Ethnicity in America,* edited by Silvia Pedraza and Rubén G. Rumbaut. Belmont, CA: Wadsworth.

Chen, Carolyn. 2002. "The Religious Varieties of Ethnic Presence: A Comparison between a Taiwanese Immigrant Buddhist Temple and an Evangelical Christian Church." *Sociology of Religion* 63:215–238.

Cho, David. 2002. "Warner Meets With Latino Leaders; Governor Plans Study on Whether Colleges Should Bar Illegal Immigrants." *The Washington Post,* Nov 20, B4.

———. 2003a. "Va. Immigrants Urge Veto Of Driver's License Bill." *The Washington Post,* Mar 19, B4.

———. 2003b. "Driver's License Legislation Pushes Hispanics into Va. Politics." *The Washington Post,* Mar 23, C4.

Chong, Kelly H. 1998. "What It Means to Be Christian: The Role of Religion in the Construction of Ethnic Identity and Boundary Among Second-Generation Korean Americans." *Sociology of Religion* 59:259–286.

Ciscel, David H., Barbara Ellen Smith, and Marcela Mendoza. 2003. "Ghosts in the Global Machine: New Immigrants and the Redefinition of Work." *Journal of Economic Issues* 37:333–341.

Clock, Michele. 2004. "Manassas Aims to Curb Crowding in Homes." *The Washington Post,* May 13, T1.

Cobas, José. 1984. "Participation in the Ethnic Community, Ethnic Solidarity, and Ambivalence toward the Host Society." Presented at the American Sociological Association Meeting, San Antonio, Texas (August).

Cohn, D'Vera. 2005. "Hispanic Growth Surge Fueled by Births in the U.S." *The Washington Post*, June 9, A1, A7.

Creswell, John W. 2003. *Research Design: Qualitative, Quantitative, and Mixed Methods Approaches.* 2nd Ed. Thousand Oaks, CA: Sage Publications.

Cruz, Jose. 1998. *Identity and Power: Puerto Rican Politics and Challenges of Ethnicity.* Philadelphia, PA: Temple University Press.

Cruz, Wilfredo. 1995. "Police Brutality in African American and Latino Communities." *Latino Studies Journal* 6:30–47.

Cuellar, Israel, Bill Arnold, and Roberto Maldonado. 1995. "Acculturation Rating Scale for Mexican-Americans II: A Revision of the Original ARMSA Scale." *Hispanic Journal of Behavioral Sciences* 17:275–304.

Dabney, Virginius. 1990. *Richmond: The Story of a City.* Charlottesville, VA: University Press of Virginia.

Davis, Carla P. 2004. "Beyond Miami: The Ethnic Enclave and Personal Income in Various Communities in the United States." *International Migration Review* 38:450–469.

DeFreitas, Gregory. 1991. *Inequality at Work: Hispanics in the U.S. Labor Force.* New York: Oxford University Press.

de la Garza, Rodolfo O., and Louis DeSipio. 1992. *From Rhetoric to Reality: Latino Politics in 1988 Elections.* Boulder, CO: Westview Press.

———. 1996. *Ethnic Ironies: Latino Politics in the 1992 Elections.* Boulder, CO: Westview Press.

DeSipio, Louis. 1996. *Counting on the Latino Vote: Latinos as a New Electorate.* Charlottesville, VA: University of Virginia Press.

———, Rodolfo O. de la Garza, and Mark Setzler. 1999. "Awash in the Mainstream: Latinos and the 1996 Elections." Pp. 3–45 in *Awash in the Mainstream: Latino Politics in the 1996 Elections,* edited by Rodolfo O. de la Garza and Louis DeSipio. Boulder, CO: Westview Press.

Dolan, Jay P. 1975. *The Immigrant Church: New York's Irish and German Catholics, 1815–1865.* Baltimore, MD and London, England: Johns Hopkins University Press.

Durand, Jorge, Douglas S. Massey, and Fernando Charvet. 2000. "The Changing Geography of Mexican Immigration to the United States: 1910–1996." *Social Science Quarterly* 81:1–15.

Ebaugh, Helen R., and Janet S. Chafez. 2000. *Religion and the New Immigrants: Continuities and Adaptations in Immigrant Congregations.* Walnut Creek, CA: AltaMira.

Eck, Diana L. 2001. *A New Religious America.* New York: HarperSan Francisco.

Edwards, Jack E., Paul Rosenfeld, Patricia Thomas, and Marie Thomas. 1993. "Willingness to Relocate for Employment: A Survey of Hispanics, Non-Hispanic Whites, and Blacks." *Hispanic Journal of Behavioral Sciences* 15:121–133.

Enchautegui, Maria E. 1995. *Policy Implications of Latino Poverty.* Washington, DC: Urban Institute.

Falcón, Angelo. 1988. "Black and Latino Politics in New York City." In *Latinos and the Political System*, edited by F. Chris Garcia. Notre Dame, IN: University of Notre Dame Press.

Falk, Gerhard. 1995. *American Judaism in Transition: The Secularization of a Religious Community*. Lanham, MD: University Press of America.

Falicov, Celia. 2002. "Ambiguous Loss: Risk and Resilience in Latino Immigrant Families." Pp. 274–288 in *Latinos: Remaking America*, edited by Suárez-Orozco and Páez. Berkeley: University of California Press.

Farley, John. 1987. "Disproportionate Black and Hispanic Unemployment in the U.S. Metropolitan Areas." *American Journal of Economics and Sociology* 46:129–150.

Farley, Reynolds, and Richard Alba. 2002. "The New Second Generation in the United States." *International Migration Review* 36:669–701.

Fazio, Elena M., and Marybeth J. Mattingly. 2002. "Thinking about an Intersectional Approach to Examining Stress: How do Race, Class, and Gender Interact?" Paper presented at American Sociological Association annual meeting, August.

Feagin, Joe R. 1991. "The Continued Significance of Race: Anti-Black Discrimination in Public Places." *American Sociological Review* 56:101–117.

Fisher, Marc. 2003. "Still Binding up a Nation's Wounds." *The Washington Post*, February 11, B1.

Fosset, Mark A., and K. Jill Kiecolt. 1989. "The Relative Size of Minority Populations and White Racial Attitudes." *Social Science Quarterly* 70:820–835.

Fox, Geoffrey. 1996. *Hispanic Nation: Culture, Politics, and the Constructing of Identity*. New Jersey: Birch Lane Press.

Frisbie, W. Parker, and Lisa Niedert. 1977. "Inequality and the Relative Size of Minority Populations: A Comparative Analysis." *American Journal of Sociology* 82:1007–1030.

Gans, Herbert J. 1973. "Introduction." In *Ethnic Identity and Assimilation*, edited by N. Sandberg. New York: Praeger.

Garcia, Eugene. 2001. *Hispanic Education in the United States: Raices y Alas*. Lanham, MD: Rowman and Littlefield.

Garcia, F. Chris. 1997. "Input to the Political System: Participation." Pp. 31–43 in *Pursuing Power: Latinos and the Political System*, edited by F. Chris Garcia. Notre Dame, IN: University of Notre Dame Press.

García, John A. 1997. "Political Participation: Resources and Involvement among Latinos in the American Political System." Pp. 44–71 in *Pursuing Power: Latinos and the Political System*, edited by F. Chris Garcia. Notre Dame, IN: University of Notre Dame Press.

———. 2003. *Latino Politics in America: Community, Culture, and Interests*. Lanham, MD: Rowman and Littlefield.

———, and Rodolfo O. de la Garza. 1985. "Mobilizing the Mexican Immigrant: The Role of Mexican American Organizations." *Western Political Quarterly* 38:551–564.

Gil, Rosa Maria, and Carmen I. Vazquez. 1996. *The Maria Paradox: How Latinas Can Merge Old World Traditions with New World Self-Esteem*. New York: G. P. Putnam's Sons.

Glick, Jennifer. 1999. "Economic Support from and to Extended Kin: A Comparison of Mexican-American and Mexican Immigrants." *International Migration Review* 33:745–765.

Gordon, Milton. 1964. *Assimilation in American Life.* New York: Oxford University Press.

Greenwell, Lisa, Julie DaVanzo, and R. Burciage Valdez 1993. *Social Ties, Wages, and Gender among Salvadorean and Filipino Immigrants in Los Angeles.* Santa Monica, CA: RAND Program for Research on Immigration Policy DRU-213-PRIP.

Gregory, Steven. 1999. *Santeria in New York City: A Study in Cultural Resistance.* New York: Garland Publishers.

Grenier, Gilles. 1984. "The Effect of Language Characteristics on the Wages of Hispanic-American Males." *Journal of Human Resources* 19:35–52.

Grenier, Guillermo J., Fabiana Invernizzi, Linda Salup, and Jorge Schmidt. 1994. "Los Bravos de La Política: Politics and Cubans in Miami." Pp. 161–196 in *Barrio Ballots: Latino Politics in the 1990 Elections,* edited by Rodolfo de la Garza, Mertha Menchaca, and Louis DeSipio. Boulder, CO: Westview Press.

Guzman, Betsy. 2001. *The Hispanic Population: Census 2000 Brief.* Washington, DC: U.S. Census Bureau.

Haddad, Yvonne Y., and Adair T. Lummis. 1987. *Islamic Values in the United States.* New York: Oxford University Press.

Hardy-Fanta, Carol. 1993. Latina Politics and Latino Politics: Gender, Culture, and Political Participation. Philadelphia, PA: Temple University Press.

Herberg, Will. 1960. *Protestant-Catholic-Jew: An Essay in American Religious Sociology.* Garden City, NY: Doubleday.

Hernández, David Manuel, and Evelyn Nakao Glenn. 2003. "Ethnic Prophecies: A Review Essay." *Contemporary Sociology* 32:418–429.

Hernández-León, Rubén, and Víctor Zuñiga. 2000. "'Making Carpet By The Mile': the Emergence of a Mexican Immigrant Community in an Industrial Region of the U.S. Historic South." *Social Science Quarterly* 81:49–66.

———. 2003. "Mexican Immigrant Communities in the South and Social Capital: The Case of Dalton, Georgia." *Southern Rural Sociology* 19:20–45.

Hero, Rodney. 1991. *Latinos and the U.S. Political System.* Philadelphia, PA: Temple University Press.

———, and Anne Campbell. 1996. "Understanding Latino Political Participation: Exploring the Evidence from the Latino National Political Survey." *Hispanic Journal of Behavioral Sciences* 18:129–141.

Hesse-Biber, Sharlene Nagy, and Michelle L. Yaiser. 2004. *Feminist Perspectives on Social Research.* New York: Oxford University Press.

Hezberg, Frederick. 1959. *The Motivation to Work.* New York: John Wiley.

Hill, Shirley A., and Joey Sprague. 1999. "Parenting in Black and White Families: The Interaction of Gender with Race and Class." *Gender and Society* 13:480–502.

Hirschman, Charles. 2001. "The Educational Enrollment of Immigrant Youth: A Test of the Segmented Assimilation Hypothesis." *Demography* 38:317–336.

"Hispanic Immigrants and Citizens in Virginia." 2007. Weldon Cooper Center for Public Service, University of Virginia. Charlottesville, VA: December.

Hoffman, Eva. 1989. *Lost in Translation: A Life in a New Language.* New York: E. P. Dutton.

Hoffman, Steven J. 2004. *Race, Class, and Power in The Building of Richmond, 1870-1920*. Jefferson, NC: McFarland.

Hogan, Richard, Meesook Kim, and Carolyn C. Perrucci. 1997. "Racial Inequality in Men's Employment and Retirement Earnings," *Sociological Quarterly* 38:431–438.

Hollinger, David A. 1995. *Postethnic America: Beyond Multiculturalism*. New York: Basic Books.

Huckfeldt, Robert, and John Sprague. 1992. "Political Parties and Electoral Mobilization: Political Structure, Social Structure, and Party Canvasses." *American Political Science Review* 86:70–86.

Hull, Anne. 2000. "Ascent and Eclipse in a Small Town." *The Washington Post*, October 8, A1, A22–23.

Hunt, Larry L. 1998. "The Spirit of Hispanic Protestantism in the United States: National Survey Comparisons of Catholics and Non-Catholics." *Social Science Quarterly* 79:828–845.

Hurh, Woo Moo, Hei Chu Kim, and Kwang Chung Kim. 1978. *Assimilation Patterns of Immigrants in The United States: A Case Study of Korean Immigrants in the Chicago Area*. Washington, DC: University Press of America.

Hurh, Woo Moo, and Kwang Chung Kim. 1990. "Religious Participation of Korean Immigrants in the United States." *Journal for the Scientific Study of Religion* 29:19–34.

Jennings, James. 1994. *Blacks, Latinos, and Asians in Urban America*. Westport, CT: Greenwood.

Jones-Correa, Michael. 1998. *Between Two Nations: The Political Predicament of Latinos in New York City*. Ithaca, NY: Cornell University Press.

Kazal, Russell A. 1995. "Revisiting Assimilation: The Rise, Fall, and Reappraisal of a Concept in American Ethnic History." *American Historical Review* 100:437–471.

Keefe, Susan E., and Amado M. Padilla. 1987. *Chicano Ethnicity*. Albuquerque, NM: University of New Mexico Press.

Kenski, Kate, and Russell Tisinger. 2006. "Hispanic Voters in the 2000 and 2004 Presidential General Elections." *Presidential Studies Quarterly* 36:189–202.

Keysar, Ariela, Barry A. Kosmin, and Egon Mayer. 2001. *Religious Identification among Hispanics in the United States*. New York: The Graduate Center of the City University of New York and Brooklyn College.

Kim, Meesook, and Carolyn C. Perrucci. 1994. "Race and Income: A Comparison of Employment and Retirement Determination Processes." *International Journal of Contemporary Sociology* 31:235–252.

King, Deborah. 1988. "Multiple Jeopardies, Multiple Consciousness: The Context of Black Feminist Ideology." *Signs: Journal of Women in Culture and Society* 14:43–72.

Kivisto, Peter A. 1992. "Religion and the New Immigrants." Pp. 92–107 in *A Future for Religion? New Paradigms for Social Analysis*, edited by W. H. Swatos Jr.. Newbury Park, CA: Sage.

Klein, Gil. 1999. "Hispanics Fueling Boom in Old South." *Richmond Times-Dispatch*, May 9, A1, A9.

Kochhar, Rakesh, Roberto Singer, and Sonya Tafoya. 2005. "The New Latino South: The Context and Consequences of Rapid Population Growth." Washington, DC: Pew Hispanic Center Report. July 26.

Kurien, Prema. 1998. "Becoming American by Becoming Hindu." Pp. 37–70 in *Gatherings in Diaspora,* edited by R. S. Warner and J. Wittner. Philadelphia, PA: Temple University Press.

Landale, Nancy, and R. S. Oropesa. 2002. "White, Black, or Puerto Rican? Racial Self-Identification Among Mainland and Island Puerto Ricans." *Social Forces* 81:231–254.

Lawrence, Bruce L. 2002. *New Faiths, Old Fears: Muslims and Other Asian Immigrants in American Religious Life.* New York: Columbia University Press.

Leal, David, Stephen A. Nuño, Jongho Lee, and Rodolfo de la Garza. 2008. "Latinos, Immigration, and the 2006 Midterm Elections." *PSOnline* April, www.apsanet.org.

Lee, Yean-Ju, and Isik Aytac. 1998. "Intergenerational Financial Support among Whites, African Americans, and Latinos." *Journal of Marriage and the Family* 60:426–441.

Leighley, Janet. 1990. "Social Interaction and Contextual Influences on Political Participation." *American Politics Quarterly* 18:458–475.

Lewis Mumford Center for Comparative Urban and Regional Research. 2002. "Neighborhood Inequality, the Ratio of Minority to White Values, Richmond-Petersburg, VA MSA."

Lieberson, Stanley. 1981. *Language Diversity and Language Contact.* Stanford, CA: Stanford University Press.

———, and Mary C. Waters. 1987. "The Location of Ethnic and Racial Groups in the United States." *Sociological Forum* 2:780–810.

Lin, Irene. 1996. "Journey to the Far West: Chinese Buddhism in America." *Amerasia Journal* 22:106–132.

Livingston, Gretchen, and Joan Kahn. 2002. "An American Dream Unfulfilled: The Limited Mobility of Mexican-Americans." *Social Science Quarterly* 83:1003–1012.

Lizama, Juan A. 2004. "A Growing Need: Agencies are Making Extra Language Effort as the Area's Hispanic Population Increases." *The Richmond Times-Dispatch,* April 21, H8.

Logan, John R., Richard D. Alba, and Wenquan Zhang. 2002. "Immigrant Enclaves and Ethnic Communities in New York and Los Angeles." *American Sociological Review* 67:299–322.

López. David. 1982. *Language Maintenance and Shift in the United States Today.* Vols. 1–4. Los Alamitos, CA: National Center for Bilingual Research.

Mar, Don. 1991. "Another Look at the Ethnic Enclave Thesis: Chinese Immigrants in the Ethnic Labor Market." *Amerasia* 17:5–21.

Marin, Gerardo. 1993. "Influence of Acculturation on Familialism and Self-Identification Among Hispanics." Pp. 181–196 in *Ethnic Identity: Formation and Transmission Among Hispanics and Other Minorities,* edited by Martha E. Bernal and George Knight. Albany, NY: State University of New York Press.

———, and Raymond. J. Gamba. 1993. "The Role of Expectations in Religious

Conversions: The Case of Hispanic Catholics." *Review of Religious Research* 34:375–371.

Martin, Walter T., and Dudley L. Poston Jr. 1976. "Industrialization and Occupational Differentiation: An Ecological Analysis." *Pacific Sociological Review* 19:82–97.

Martinez, Oscar J. 1994. *Border People: Life and Society in the U.S.-Mexico Borderlands.* Tucson, AZ: University of Arizona Press.

McCall, Leslie. 2001. *Complex Inequality: Gender, Class, and Race in the New Economy.* New York: Routledge.

McClain, Paula, and John A. García. 1993. "Expanding Disciplinary Boundaries: Black, Latino, and Racial Minority Group Politics in Political Science." In *Political Science: The State of the Discipline II,* edited by A. Finidter. Washington, DC: American Political Science Association.

McDaniel, Josh, and Vanessa Casanova. 2003. "Pines in Lines: Tree Planting, H2B Guest Workers, and Rural Poverty in Alabama." *Southern Rural Sociology* 19:73–96.

McIlwee, Judith S., and J. Gregg Robinson. 1992. *Women in Engineering: Gender, Power, and Workplace Culture.* Albany, NY: State University of New York Press.

McKeever, Matthew, and Stephen Klineberg. 1999. "Generational Differences in Attitudes and Socioeconomic Status among Hispanics in Houston." *Sociological Inquiry* 69:33–50.

Min, Pyong G. 1992. "The Structure and Social Functions of Korean Immigrant Churches in the United States." *International Migration Review* 26:1370–1394.

Mindel, Charles H. 1980. "Extended Familism Among Urban Mexican Americans, Anglos, and Blacks." *Hispanic Journal of Behavioral Sciences* 2:21–34.

Mohl, Raymond A. 2000. "Latinization in the Heart of Dixie: Hispanics in Late-Twentieth-Century Alabama." Paper presented at the Race, Ethnicity, and Migration Conference, Minneapolis, November.

Moeser, John V., and Rutledge M. Dennis. 1982. *The Politics of Annexation: Oligarchic Power in a Southern City.* Cambridge, MA: Schenkman.

Mor, Menahem. 1992. *Jewish Assimilation, Acculturation, and Accommodation: Past Traditions, Current Issues, and Future Prospects.* Lanham, NE: University Press of America.

Moreno, Dario, and Christopher Warren. 1992. "The Conservative Enclave: Cubans in Florida." Pp. 127–146 in *From Rhetoric to Reality: Latino Politics in 1988 Elections,* edited by Rodolfo O. de la Garza and Louis DeSipio. Boulder, CO: Westview Press.

Moreno, Sylvia. 2000. "Hope and Hardship: Latino Newcomers Struggle to Adapt and Excel." *The Washington Post,* January 23, A.1, A.16–17.

Murphy, Arthur D., Colleen Blanchard, and Jennifer A Hill (eds.). 2001. *Latino Workers in the Contemporary South.* Athens, GA: University of Georgia Press.

Murphy, Joseph M. 1994. *Working the Spirit: Ceremonies of the African Diaspora.* Boston, MA: Beacon Press.

Nam, Y. 2004. "Is America Becoming More Equal for Children? Changes in the Intergenerational Transmission of Low- and High-Income Status." *Social Science Research* 33:187–205.

Neal, Micki, and Stephanie A. Bohon. 2002. "The Dixie Diaspora: Attitudes toward Immigrants in Georgia." *Sociology Spectrum* 23:181–212.

Nee, Victor, and Jimmy Sanders. 2001. "Understanding the Diversity of Immigrant Incorporation." *Ethnic and Immigration Studies* 24:386–411.

Nieves, Evelyn. 2002. "Survey: Hispanics See Themselves as Diverse." *Washington Post*, December 18, A5.

Negy, Charles, and D. J. Woods. 1992. "The Importance of Acculturation in Understanding Research with Hispanic Americans." *Hispanic Journal of Behavioral Sciences* 12:224–251.

Nelson, Daniel. 1996. *Managers and Workers*. Madison, WI: University of Wisconsin Press.

Ng, Kwai H. 2002. "Seeking Christian Tutelage: Agency and Culture in Chinese Immigrants' Conversion to Christianity." *Sociology of Religion* 63:195–214.

Ouellet, Lawrence J. 1994. *Pedal to the Metal: The Work Lives of Truckers*. Philadelphia, PA: Temple University Press.

Padilla, A. M. 1980. "The Role of Cultural Awareness and Ethnic Loyalty in Acculturation." Pp. 47–84 in *Acculturation: Theory, Models, and Some New Findings*, edited by A. M. Padilla. Boulder, CO: Westview Press.

Padilla, Yolanda C. 1997. "Determinants of Hispanic Poverty in the Course of the Transition to Adulthood." *Hispanic Journal of Behavioral Sciences* 19:416–432.

Pattillo-McCoy, Mary. 1999. *Black Picket Fences: Privilege and Peril Among the Black Middle Class*. Chicago, IL: University of Chicago Press.

Palm, Lisa. 1985. "Ethnic Segmentation of Real Estate Agent Practice in the Urban Housing Market." *Annals of the Association of American Geographers* 75:58–68.

Pardo, Mary. 1998 *Mexican American Women Activists: Identity and Resistance in Two Los Angeles Communities*. Philadelphia, PA: Temple University Press.

Park, Robert E. 1950. *Race and Culture*. Glencoe, IL: Free Press.

———, and Ernest W. Burgess. 1921. *Introduction to the Science of Sociology*. Chicago, IL: Chicago University Press.

Pantoja, Adrian, Ricardo Ramirez, and Gary Segura. 2001. "Citizens by Choice, Voters by Necessity: Patterns in Political Mobilization by Naturalized Latinos." *Political Research Quarterly* 54:729–750.

Perez, Lisandro. 1986. "Immigrant Economic Adjustment and Family Organization: The Cuban Success Story Re-Examined." *International Migration Review* 20:4–20.

Perlman, Joel, and Roger Waldinger. 1997. "Second Generation Decline? Children of Immigrants, Past and Present—A Reconsideration." *International Migration Review* 31:893–923.

Pessar, P. 1995. "The Elusive Enclave: Ethnicity, Class, and Nationality among Latino Entrepreneurs in Greater Washington, DC." *Human Organization* 54:383–392.

Pew Hispanic Center. 2007. "National Survey of Latinos: As Illegal Immigration Issue Heats up, Hispanics Feel a Chill." Washington, DC. December.

Poole, Shelia M. 2004. "Report Finds Language Not Only Barrier to Latino Health Care." *The Atlanta Journal-Constitution*, September 18, 3A.

Portes, Alejandro, and Robert L. Bach. 1985. *Latin Journey, Cuban and Mexican Immigrants in the United States*. Berkeley, CA: University of California Press.

Portes, Alejandro, Patricia Fernandez-Kelly, and William Haller. 2005. "Segmented Assimilation on the Ground: The New Second Generation Early Adulthood." *Ethnic and Racial Studies* 28:1000–1040.

Portes, Alejandro, and L. Jensen. 1989. "The Enclave and the Entrants: Patterns of Ethnic Enterprise in Miami Before and After Mariel." *American Sociological Review* 54:929–949.

Portes, Alejandro, and Robert D. Manning. 1986. "The Immigrant Enclave: Theory and Empirical Examples." Pp. 47–68 in *Competitive Ethnic Relations*, edited by Joane Nagel and Susan Olzak. Orlando, FL: Academic Press.

Portes, Alejandro, and Rubén G. Rumbaut. 1996. *Immigrant America: A Portrait*. Berkeley, CA: University of California Press.

———. 2006. *Immigrant America: A Portrait*. Third edition. Berkeley, CA: University of California Press.

———, eds. 2001a. *Ethnicities: Children of Immigrants in America*. Berkeley: University of California Press.

———. 2001b. *Legacies: The Story of the Immigrant Second Generation*. Berkeley, CA: University of California Press.

Portes, Alejandro, and A. Stepnick. 1993. *City on the Edge: The Transformation of Miami*. Berkeley, CA: University of California Press.

Portes, Alejandro, and Min Zhou. 1993. "The New Second Generation: Segmented Assimilation and its Variants." *Annals of the American Academy of Political and Social Sciences* 530:74–96.

Pressley, Sue Anne. 2000. "Hispanic Immigration Boom Rattles South: Rapid Influx to Some Areas Raises Tensions." *The Washington Post*, March 6, A.3.

Ragin, Charles. 1994. *Constructing Social Research: The Unity and Diversity of Method*. Thousand Forks, CA: Pine Forge Press.

Ramirez, Roberto R. 2004. "We the People: Hispanics in the United States." U.S. Census Bureau, U.S. Department of Commerce, Economics and Statistics Administration. December.

Randolph, Lewis A. 2003. *Rights for a Season: The Politics of Race, Class, and Gender in Richmond*, Virginia. Knoxville, TN: University of Tennessee Press.

Reisler, Mark. 1996. "Always the Laborer, Never the Citizen: Anglo Perceptions of the Mexican Immigrant During the 1920s." Pp. 23–43 in *In Between Two Worlds: Mexican Immigrants in the United States*, edited by David G. Gutierrez. Wilmington, DE: Scholarly Resources.

Riemer, Jeffrey W. 1979. *Hard Hats: The Work World of Construction Workers*. Beverly Hills, CA: Sage.

Rodriguez, Clara. 2000. *Changing Race: Latinos, the Census, and the History of Ethnicity in the United States*. New York: New York University Press.

Rodriguez, Havidan. 1992. "Population, Economic Mobility, and Income Inequality: A Portrait of Latinos in the United States, 1970–1991." *Latino Studies Journal* 3:55–86.

Rodriguez, Gregory. 2005. "Why We're the New Irish." *Newsweek*. May 30, 35.

Roof, Wade C. 1993. *A Generation of Seekers: The Spiritual Journey of the Baby Boom Generation.* San Francisco, CA: Harper.

———. 1999. *The Spiritual Marketplace: Baby Boomers and the Remaking of American Religion.* Princeton, NJ: Princeton University Press.

Rose, Coleman. 2002. "Home Ownership and Life Satisfaction: An Examination of What Contributes to Life Satisfaction among Latinos in Greater Richmond, Virginia." MA thesis, Virginia Commonwealth University.

Rothenberg, Paula. 2003. *Race, Class, and Gender in the United States: An Integrated Study.* 6th Ed. New York: Worth.

Rouse, Parke. 1996. *We Happy WASPs: Virginia in the Days of Jim Crow and Harry Byrd.* Richmond, VA: Dietz Press.

Rumbaut, Rubén G. 1989. "The Structure of Refuge: Southeast Asian Refugees in the United States." *International Review of Comparative Public Policy* 1:97–129.

———. 1997. "Ties that Bind: Immigration and Immigrant Families in the United States." Pp. 3–46 in *Immigration and the Family,* edited by A. Booth, A. C. Crouter, and N. S. Landale. Hillsdale, NJ: Lawrence Erlbaum.

Saenz, Rogelio, Katharine M. Donato, Lourdes Gouveia, and Cruz Torres. 2003. "Latinos in the South: A Glimpse of Ongong Trends and Research." *Southern Rural Sociology* 19:1–19.

Saito, Leonard. 1998. *Race and Politics: Asian Americans, Latinos, and Whites in a Los Angeles Suburb.* Urbana, IL: University of Illinois Press.

Sanders, Jimmy, and Victor Nee. 1996. "Immigrant Self-Employment: Family as Social Capital and the Value of Human Capital." *American Sociological Review* 61:231–249.

Schmid, Carol. 2002. "Immigration and Asian and Hispanic Minorities in the New South: An Exploration of History, Attitudes, and Demographic Trends." *Sociological Spectrum* 23.

Schmidley, A. Dianne. 2001. *Profile of the Foreign-Born Population in the United States.* Washington, DC: U.S. Government Printing Office.

Scott, Jerry. 2004. "Influx of Hispanics, Asians Marks Metro Area's Growth." *The Atlanta Journal-Constitution.* August 27, 1A.

Segura, Gary M., Denis Falcon, and Harry Pachon. 1997. "Dynamics of Latino Partisanship in California: Immigration, Issue Salience, and Their Implications." *Harvard Journal of Hispanic Policy* 10:62–80.

Shaw, Daron, Rodolfo O. de la Garza, and Jongho Lee. 2000. "Examining Latino Turnout in 1996: A Three-State, Validated Survey Approach." *American Journal of Political Science* 44:332–340.

Sheridan, Mary B. 2004. "Immigrants' Cash Floods Homelands." *The Washington Post,* May 17, B.1, B.4.

Shibutani, Tamotsu, and Kian M. Kwan. 1965. *Ethnic Stratification.* New York: MacMillan.

Sierra, Christine. 2000. "Hispanics and the Political Process." Pp. 317–348 in *Hispanics in the United States,* edited by Pastora San Juan Cafferty and David W. Engstrom. New Brunswick, NJ: Transaction Publishers.

Silver, Christopher. 1984. *Twentieth-Century Richmond: Planning, Politics, and Race.* Knoxville, TN: University of Tennessee Press.

Silver, Christopher, and John V. Moeser. 1995. *The Separate City: Black Communities in the Urban South, 1940-1968.* Lexington, KY: University Press of Kentucky.

Smith, Dorothy E. 1987. *The Everyday World as Problematic: A Feminist Sociology.* Boston, MA: Northeastern University Press.

Smith, Heather A., and Owen Furuseth. 2004. "Housing, Hispanics, and Transitioning Geographies in Charlotte, North Carolina." *Southeastern Geographer* 44:216–235.

———, eds. 2006. *Latinos in the New South: Transformations of Place.* Aldershot, UK: Ashgate.

Solon, Gary R. 1992. "Intergenerational Income Mobility in the United States." *American Economic Review* 82:393–408.

Southall, Amanda. 2007. "Immigration Laws Hit Home." *Midlothian Exchange.com.* January 16. http://www.midlothianexchange.com/newsarchives/archivedetails. cfm?ID+560.

Sowell, Thomas. 1981. *Ethnic America: A History.* New York: Basic Books.

Steinberg, Stephen. 1981. *The Ethnic Myth.* New York: Atheneum.

Stewart, Phyllis, and Muriel G. Cantor (eds.). 1982. *Varieties of Work.* Beverly Hills, CA: Sage.

Suro, Robert, and Audrey Singer. 2002. *Latino Growth in Metropolitan America: Changing Patterns, New Locations.* Washington, DC: Center on Urban and Metropolitan Policy, The Brookings Institution.

Suárez-Orozco, Marcelo, and Mariela Páez (eds.). 2002. *Latinos: Remaking America.* Berkeley: University of California Press.

Szapocznik, J., and W. Kurtines. 1980. "Acculturation, Biculturalism, and Adjustment among Cuban Americans." Pp. 139–159 in *Acculturation: Theory, Models and Some New Findings,* edited by A. M. Padilla. Boulder, CO: Westview Press.

Taylor, Marylee. 1998. "How White Attitudes Vary With Racial Composition of Local Populations: Numbers Count." *American Sociological Review* 63:512–535.

Tienda, Marta. 1991. *Hispanics in the United States.* Chicago, IL: University of Chicago Press.

———. 1995. "Latinos and the American Pie: Can Latinos Achieve Economic Parity?" *Hispanic Journal of Behavioral Sciences* 17:403–429.

———, and Faith Mitchell. 2006. *Multiple Origins, Uncertain Destinies: Hispanics and the American Future.* Washington, DC: The National Academies Press.

Tseng, Winston. 2006. *Immigrant Community Services in Chinese and Vietnamese Enclaves.* New York: LFB Scholarly Publishing.

Vazquez, Manuel A. 1999. "Pentecostalism, Collective Identity, and Transnationalism among Salvadorans and Peruvians in the U.S." *Journal of the American Academy of Religion* 67:617–636.

Vélez, William, and Rogelio Saenz. 2001. "Toward a Comprehensive Model of the School Leaving Process among Latinos." *School Psychology Quarterly* 16:445–467.

Veltman, Calvin. 1983. *Language Shift in the United States.* Berlin: Mouton.

Verba, Sidney, Kay Schlozman, and Henry Brady. 1993. "Citizen Activity: Who Participates? What Do They Say?" *American Political Science Review* 87:303–318.

Waldinger, Roger. 1993. "The Ethnic Enclave Debate Revisited." *International Journal of Urban & Regional Research* 17:444–452.

———. 2001. "Strangers at the Gates." Pp. 1–29 in *Strangers at the Gates: New Immigrants in Urban America,* edited by Roger Waldinger. Berkeley, CA: University of California Press.

———, and Jennifer Lee. 2001. "New Immigrants in Urban America." Pp. 30–79 in *Strangers at the Gates: New Immigrants in Urban America,* edited by Roger Waldinger. Berkeley, CA: University of California Press.

Warner, R. Stephen. 1998. "Approaching Religious Diversity: Barriers, Byways, and Beginnings." *Sociology of Religion* 59:193–215.

———. 1990. "The Korean Immigrant Church in Comparative Perspective." Paper presented at the colloquium on the Koran Immigrant Church, Princeton Theological Seminary, February 16–18, Princeton, NJ.

Warner, W. Lloyd. 1953. *American Life.* Chicago, IL: University of Chicago Press.

———, and Leo Srole. 1945. *The Social Systems of American Ethnic Groups.* New Haven, CT: Yale University Press.

Waters, Mary C. 1990. *Ethnic Options: Choosing Identities in America.* Berkeley, CA: University of California Press.

———. *Black Identities: West Indian Immigrant Dreams and American Realities.* New York: Russell Sage Foundation; Cambridge, MA: Harvard University Press.

Welch, Susan, and Lee Sigelman. 2000. "Getting to Know You? Latino-Anglo Social Contact." *Social Science Quarterly* 81:67–83.

Wermers, Jason. 2004. 'First Hispanic Named to Board of Education." *The Richmond Times-Dispatch,* Mar 4, B3.

Whyte, William F. 1943. *Street Corner Society.* Chicago, IL: University of Chicago Press.

Wilcox, Jerry, and Wade Clark Roof. 1978. "Percent Black and Black-White Status Inequality: Southern Versus Non-Southern Patterns." *Social Science Quarterly* 59:421–434.

Wilson, William J. 1978. *The Declining Significance of Race: Blacks and Changing American Institutions.* Chicago, IL: University of Chicago Press.

Yang, Fenggang. 1999. *Chinese Christians in America: Conversion, Assimilation, and Adhesive Identities.* University Park, PA: Pennsylvania State University Press.

———, and Helen R. Ebaugh. 2001. "Religion and Ethnicity among New Immigrants: The Impact of Majority/Minority Status in Home and Host Countries." *Journal for the Scientific Study of Religion* 40:367–378.

Yang, Philip. 2000. *Ethnic Studies.* Albany, NY: State University of New York Press.

Yans-McLauglin, Virginia. 1990. *Immigration Reconsidered: History, Sociology, and Politics.* New York: Oxford University Press.

Yinger, Milton. 1994. *Ethnicity.* Albany, NY: State University of New York Press.

Index

Made in the USA
Lexington, KY
31 August 2015